I0815388

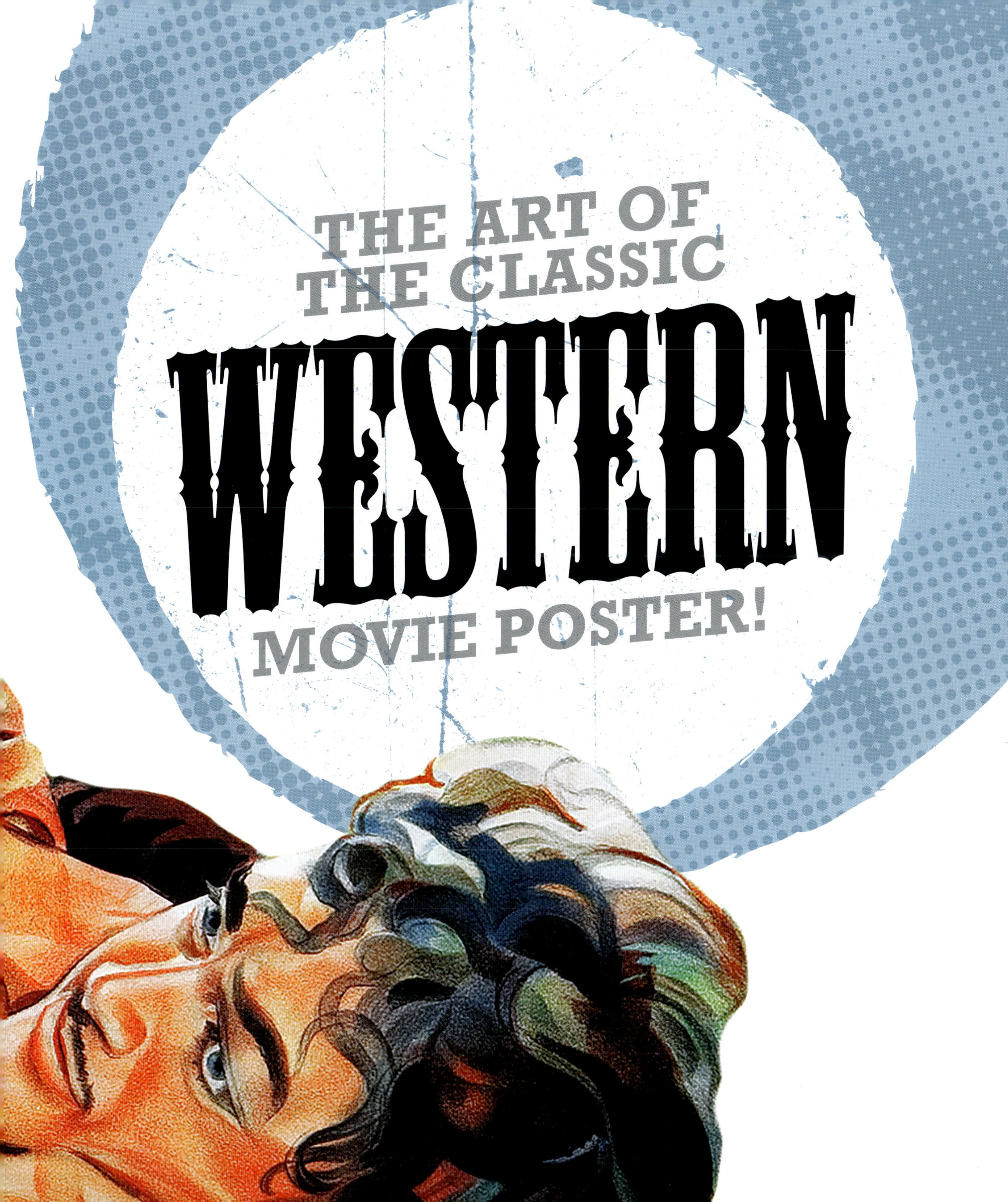
THE ART OF
THE CLASSIC
WESTERN
MOVIE POSTER!

Elephant Book Company Limited
Purcell, St. Mary's Hall
Rawstorn Road
Colchester
Essex, CO3 3JH
United Kingdom
www.elephantbookcompany.com

Editorial director: Will Steeds
Project manager: Tom Seabrook
Book design and cover artwork: Amazing 15

ISBN: 978-0-7643-6796-0
Printed in China

Published by Schiffer Publishing, Ltd.
4880 Lower Valley Road
Atglen, PA 19310
Phone: (610) 593-1777; Fax: (610) 593-2002
Email: Info@schifferbooks.com
Web: www.schifferbooks.com

For our complete selection of fine books on this and related subjects, please visit our website at www.schifferbooks.com. You may also write for a free catalog.

Schiffer Publishing's titles are available at special discounts for bulk purchases for sales promotions or premiums. Special editions, including personalized covers, corporate imprints, and excerpts, can be created in large quantities for special needs. For more information, contact the publisher.

We are always looking for people to write books on new and related subjects. If you have an idea for a book, please contact us at proposals@schifferbooks.com.

PAGE 1: Although it could be almost any cowboy from the 1920s or early '30s, this is a representation of Jack Perrin in *Silent Sheldon* (1925).

PAGES 2–3: Buck Jones throttles Wallace MacDonald in a detail from a poster for *The Texas Ranger* (1931).

PAGE 4: Poster art showing Jeff Chandler, James Stewart, and Debra Paget in *Broken Arrow* (1950)

PAGE 5: A hand-colored photo of Dana Andrews, as used on the poster for *Town Tamer* (1965).

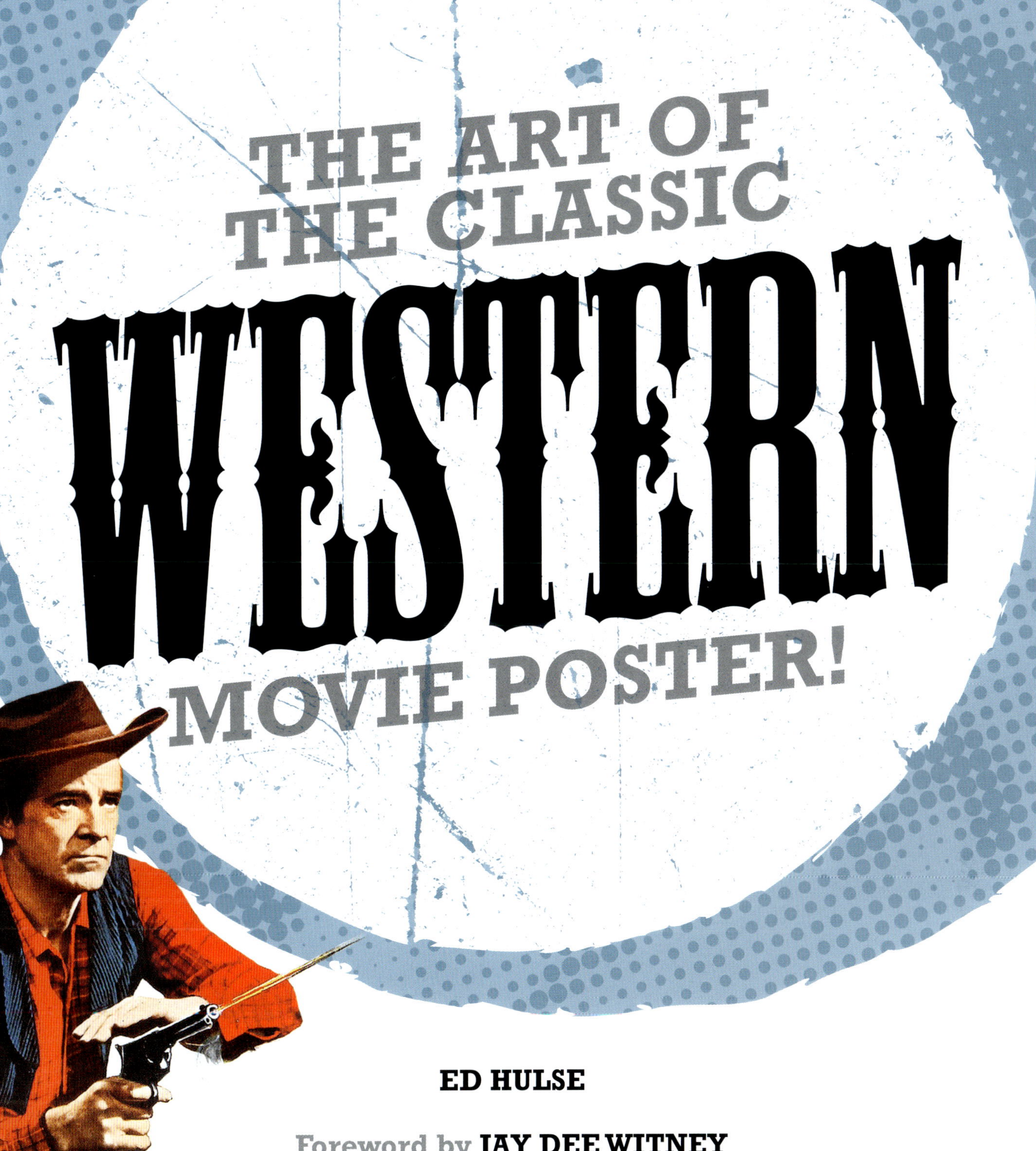

THE ART OF THE CLASSIC WESTERN MOVIE POSTER!

ED HULSE

Foreword by **JAY DEE WITNEY**

SCHIFFER PUBLISHING

4880 Lower Valley Road • Atglen, PA 19310

CONTENTS

FOREWORD BY JAY DEE WITNEY

My father, William Witney, entered the motion-picture business in 1933, not by chance but by luck. Upon graduating from Coronado High School in California, he spent the summer with his sister and brother-in-law in the San Fernando Valley. My uncle Bert Clark worked for a small independent studio there called Mascot Pictures and was then co-directing a Western serial titled *Fighting with Kit Carson*. Since Dad was a pretty fair rider, Bert got him a couple days' work as an extra, participating in outdoor action sequences. The job paid five dollars a day, with a box lunch thrown in. Dad played both an Indian and a Cavalry trooper, which meant he literally chased himself on film. It was hot, dusty, exhausting work—and Dad liked it so much he decided to stay in the picture business.

BELOW: Director William Witney (*left*) consults with Roy Rogers while on the Republic back lot, preparing to take a scene for *North of the Great Divide* (1950). Witney was at the helm of twenty-seven Rogers Westerns made between 1946 and 1951.

With Bert vouching for him, Dad wangled a job at Mascot for twenty-five dollars a week. He started out mimeographing scripts but soon left clerical duties behind to work as a second assistant director. Dad was a quick study and picked up a lot about filmmaking by observing directors and their crews in action. Nat Levine's scrappy independent studio was a low-budget operation that demanded ingenuity in problem-solving.

In 1935, Mascot was absorbed into the newly formed Republic Pictures. Levine and most of his people, including my father, continued as before. Dad was promoted to film editor and cut two early Republic "chapter plays," getting his first experience as a director by taking a camera crew to San Francisco and filming scenes of the just-opened Oakland Bay Bridge for *Dick Tracy*, Republic's biggest serial to date.

Dad earned his spurs during production of a 1937 Western serial titled *The Painted Stallion* when co-director Ray Taylor went on a bender and was relieved of his duties. Producer Larry Wickland asked Dad to take over until another experienced director arrived from Hollywood. My father, working with Alan James, shot quickly and effortlessly, and he was so good at it that Larry canceled his request to Republic's front office for another director.

Thrilled with the results of Dad's salvage job, Larry invited him to remain with the serial unit as full director. His next was *S.O.S. Coast Guard*, which means a lot to me because its leading lady, Maxine Doyle, married Dad and eventually became my mom. After that came another Western serial, *Zorro Rides Again*. And then a biggie, *The Lone Ranger* (1938), based on the popular radio show. Produced for a mere $168,000, it earned more than $1.1 million, making it the most profitable serial in Republic's history. Dad and his partner, John English (my godfather), continued directing Western serials, including Zorro and Lone Ranger sequels. He also directed B-Western features with the Three Mesquiteers and Don "Red" Barry.

My father enjoyed making Westerns, even though they entailed hard work and occasional privation, especially on faraway locations when bad weather interfered. He loved animals, he loved the outdoors, and he enjoyed the camaraderie of Western stuntmen like Yakima Canutt, Davy Sharpe, and Ken Cooper. Working on low budgets and short schedules, Dad learned the hard way how to keep a shoot going despite inevitable obstacles and productional shortcomings. Republic made the industry's best Western movies, primarily because the studio's crew members and department heads—many left over from Nat Levine's Mascot—had worked on a shoestring for so long that they could squeeze a nickel 'til the buffalo hollered.

Dad served in the Marine Corps during World War II and returned to Republic afterward, taking over the direction of Roy Rogers' Westerns. He made twenty-seven of them between 1946 and 1951, then was reassigned to the unit making Westerns starring another musical cowboy, Rex Allen.

Republic ceased film production in 1958 and, like many other B-Western directors, Dad moved into episodic television. He worked on *Zorro*, *Bonanza*, *Laramie*, *Laredo*, *Hondo*, *Wagon Train*, *The Virginian*, and *Tales of Wells Fargo*, among others. He also continued directing feature films now and then, and his very last was a Western, 1982's *Showdown at Eagle Gap*, in which he also had a cameo. Nearly fifty years had elapsed since he climbed on a horse to work two days on *Fighting with Kit Carson*.

In his later years, Dad learned that an entire subculture of serial and Western fans not only remembered but also revered and collected his work. He began attending film festivals in 1973 and guested at many over the next two decades. Among his most vocal boosters was Quentin Tarantino.

Ed Hulse was one of the young fans who met Dad at that first film-fest appearance. They spoke several times thereafter, and Ed has recalled those conversations as "a crash course in Western and serial production." In the following pages, he's assembled hundreds of posters from classic Western movies and written fact-filled essays to contextualize them. I've known Ed for many years, and I can honestly say that very few film historians love Westerns as much as he does. That's why I'm sure you'll enjoy this book. ✸

ABOVE: Bill Witney's early films with Roy Rogers, such as *Springtime in the Sierras* (1947), cost far more than the average B Western and boasted top-notch production values, including photography in Republic's Trucolor process. They also sported elaborately staged action sequences—a Witney trademark.

INTRODUCTION BY ED HULSE

BELOW: A popular series of paperbound books — the forerunners of today's mass-market paperbacks — Beadle's Dime Novels offered many lurid tales of the Old West, most of which had only a glancing relationship with actual facts. *Malaeska* (1860) was the first.

OPPOSITE: Although it does not rely on primary colors (as was the fashion in most posters of the late nineteenth and early twentieth centuries), this sheet promoting one of Buffalo Bill's Wild West shows is a striking one, with excellent renditions of the two subjects.

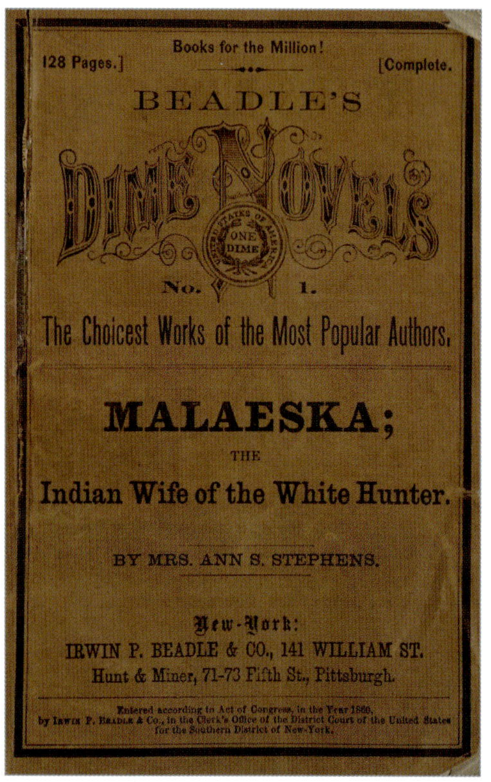

128 Pages.] Books for the Million! [Complete.

BEADLE'S

DIME NOVELS

ONE DIME

No. 1.

The Choicest Works of the Most Popular Authors.

MALAESKA;

THE

Indian Wife of the White Hunter.

BY MRS. ANN S. STEPHENS.

New-York:

IRWIN P. BEADLE & CO., 141 WILLIAM ST.

Hunt & Miner, 71-73 Fifth St., Pittsburgh.

Entered according to Act of Congress, in the Year 1860, by Irwin P. Beadle & Co., in the Clerk's Office of the District Court of the United States for the Southern District of New-York.

The American West became fertile ground for storytellers and dramatists when it was still wild, lawless, and unsettled. The earliest "dime novels" (forerunners of mass-market paperbacks) included such lurid yarns as 1860's *Malaeska: The Indian Wife of the White Hunter* and *Seth Jones, or, The Captives of the Frontier*.

The man who can reasonably be called the father of Western fiction was a rather questionable character named Edward Zane Carroll Judson, who wrote under the pseudonym Ned Buntline. Once credibly accused of murder, Buntline was hanged by a lynch mob and very nearly died. He served as an infantryman during the Civil War, but he was dishonorably discharged for drunkenness. A writer and occasional publisher, he met William F. "Buffalo Bill" Cody during a trip to Nebraska in 1869. Their conversations became the source for his fanciful yarn *Buffalo Bill, the King of the Border Men*, which was serialized in the story paper *New York Weekly* later that year before seeing publication as a dime novel. Buntline also authored the 1872 stage drama *Scouts of the Prairie*, in which Cody himself starred. Panned by critics upon opening in Chicago, the show nonetheless enjoyed tremendous success for years, playing at legitimate theaters across the country.

The American public's insatiable appetite for melodramatic adventure stories set in the Wild West continued to grow during the rest of the nineteenth and the early twentieth centuries. The tales appearing in story papers, dime novels, and "nickel weeklies" (forerunners of pulp-fiction magazines) were trash: marginally literate, wildly exaggerated, and scandalously violent.

The first Western novel with literary pretensions was published in hard covers by Macmillan and Co., a reputable New York firm, in 1902. The title character of Owen Wister's *The Virginian* is the archetypal cowboy hero. The foreman of the Sunk Creek Ranch outside Medicine Bow, Wyoming, he is tall, handsome, and laconic; a tough but fair boss and a perfect gentleman to women. The Virginian (who is given no other name) adheres to a rigid moral code forced onto most frontiersmen by the lack of reliable law enforcement. So committed is he to this code that, in the book's most poignant sequence, he allows his best friend to

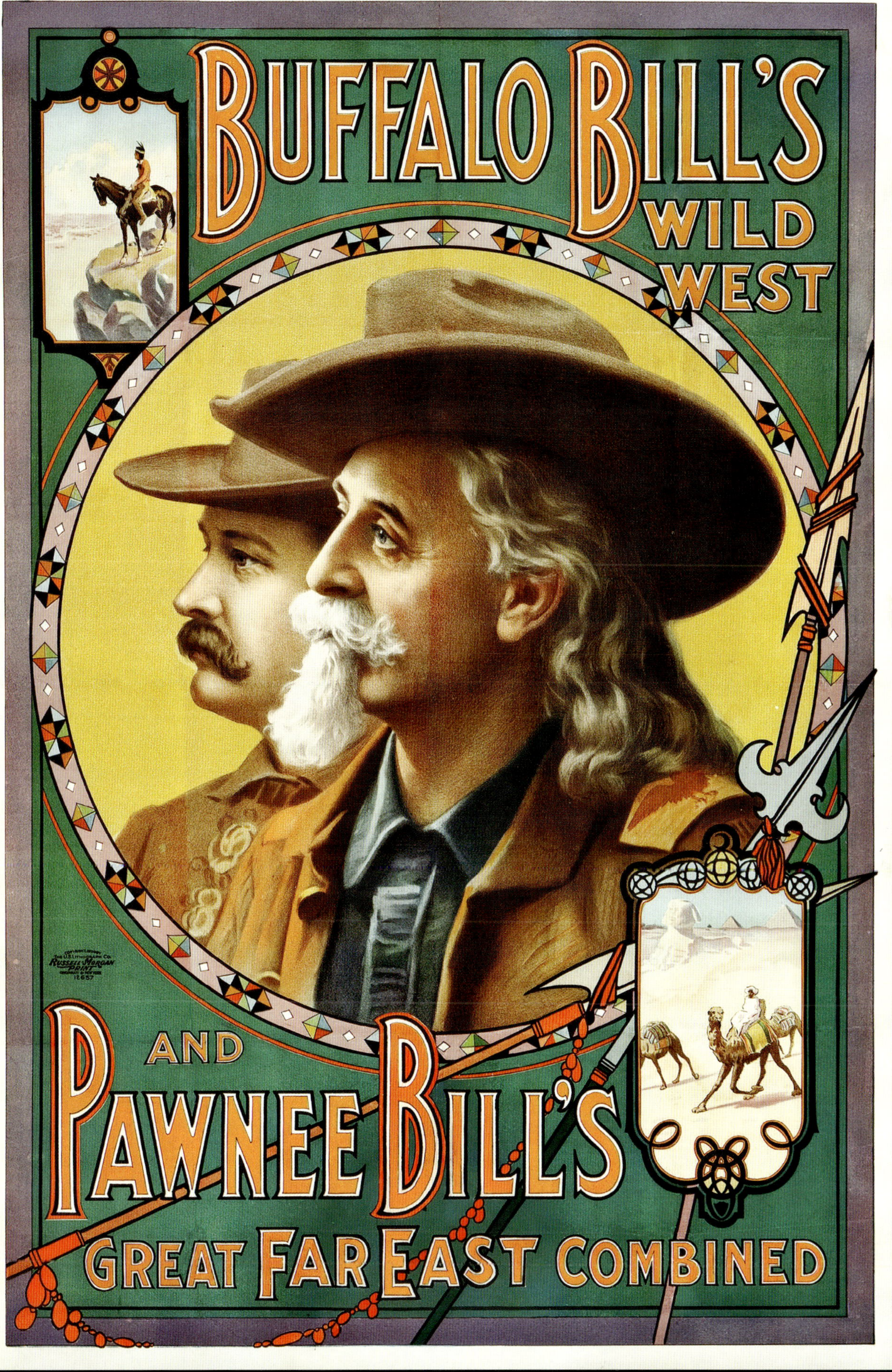
BUFFALO BILL'S
WILD WEST
THE U.S. LITHOGRAPH CO.
RUSSELL-MORGAN PRINT
12657
AND
PAWNEE BILL'S
GREAT FAR EAST COMBINED

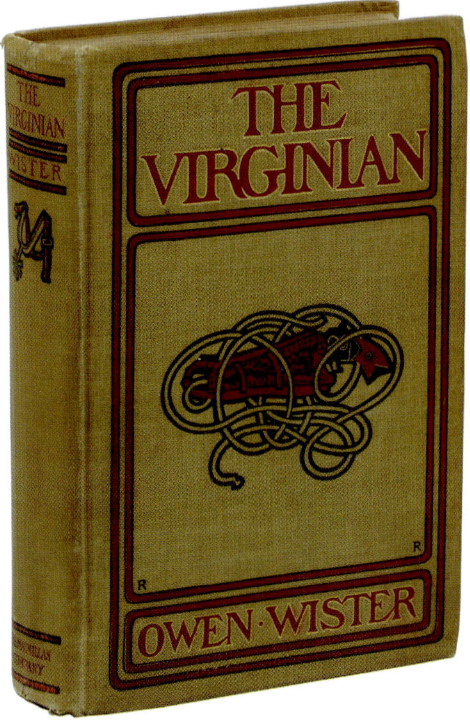

ABOVE: A staged photograph of three more-or-less-authentic frontiersmen: William F. "Buffalo Bill" Cody (*on the ground*); the chronicler of his larger-than-life exploits, Ned Buntline (*center*); and Texas Jack Omohundro, a frontier scout who also worked as a cowboy before becoming a performer.

BELOW: Owen Wister's 1902 novel *The Virginian* was the first Western yarn with literary pretensions and a mainstream publisher. The original Macmillan edition was reprinted fourteen times in eight months. Wister's tale is one of the fifty bestselling novels of all time.

be hanged after being caught rustling cattle. The novel ends with the Virginian being challenged to a gun duel on his wedding day by his implacable enemy, Trampas. Begged by his fiancée to run away, the foreman refuses to compromise his honor; the inevitable showdown follows, and, after giving Trampas the opportunity to draw his gun first, the Virginian fatally shoots his foe of many years' standing.

We've described *The Virginian*'s plot at length because it provided the wellspring for literally thousands of Western stories, plays, and, eventually, motion pictures. Such classic Wister lines as "When you call me that, smile!" and "This town isn't big enough for the both of us!" were paraphrased or used verbatim in countless Westerns written for all mediums. In fact, Wister and playwright Kirke La Shelle adapted *The Virginian* for the stage in 1904, and it enjoyed remarkable success in such cosmopolitan cities as New York and Chicago.

With interest in the genre flourishing, it was to be expected that producers of that early-twentieth-century novelty, the moving picture, would latch on to the American cowboy as a colorful subject for primitively staged Westerns shot in the wilds of New Jersey or upstate New York. These early efforts are discussed in chapter 1. (*The Virginian* itself came to the screen in 1914, directed by Cecil B. DeMille and starring Dustin Farnum, who had originated the role onstage. Wister's novel was so influential that it was remade four times, most recently in 2014, exactly one hundred years after the first version.)

Cowboy lore would soon insinuate itself into other aspects of mass-market entertainment. Rodeos had been popular for years in the western states, but they spread east in the early twentieth century. Buffalo Bill himself toured with a "Wild West Show" in which actual cowboys and Indians staged phony bank robberies, holdups, and Indian raids in outdoor arenas from one end of the country to another. Practically every circus had at least one "authentic Westerner" who enthralled audiences under the big top with exhibitions of riding, roping, and shooting.

It didn't take long for Westerns to become widely accepted by fans of moving pictures. Even in major metropolitan areas, these simple outdoor action films were much in demand, but exhibitors at first were hard pressed to tell the good from the bad. Critics for the show-business trade papers—most of which were headquartered in New York—were forced to review them. Cynical and streetwise, they generally lacked appreciation for any dramatic works taking place west of the Hudson River or in wide-open spaces larger than Central Park, and their notices reflected that urban bias.

Those "hard-boiled babies" writing for Sime Silverman's *Variety*, the most influential showbiz sheet, recognized the popularity of moving-picture Westerns but refused to take them seriously. Silverman's purveyors of what newspaper cartoonist Will Gould dubbed "slanguage" concocted several derisive terms to describe cowboy movies: "horse operas," "oats operas" (later shortened to "oaters"), and "gallopers." Once filmmakers began migrating to California and Westerns became more polished in their storytelling and more authentic in appearance, *Variety*'s scribes grudgingly accorded genre offerings a modicum of respect but still referred to them by the old slang terms. "Oaters" and "horse operas" continued popping up in reviews for decades, not just in Sime Silverman's sheet but in other trade papers as well.

Even back then, there was nothing new about employing brightly colored, eye-catching posters to draw attention to special events or theatrical performances. They could be seen everywhere, advertising rodeos, circuses, and state fairs. The first poster designed to promote a specific film—*L'Arroseur Arrosé*, a short by the Lumière brothers—used an illustration by French artist Marcellin Auzolle to draw patrons to a screening at the Grand Café in Paris on December 26, 1895.

American moving-picture exhibitors were not as quick to grasp the poster's utility in attracting patrons to their venue, but eventually they caught on. The twentieth century was just a few years old when practically every "nickelodeon" in the country began promoting its celluloid attractions with colorful paper sheets emblazoned with vividly illustrated scenes from those primitive one- and two-reelers. They were printed by lithography, a process that uses flat surfaces—smooth-ground limestone and, after 1920, zinc plates—specially treated with oil-based inks to transfer images to thin paper sheets.

Stone-litho posters had a unique textured look due to grain that remained on the sanded-down limestone slab. The printing process was relatively simple. Artists created images on tracing paper and transferred them to the stone with soft, waxy crayons and greasy paints. Carefully applied acid etched the artwork onto the slab, which was moistened with water in preparation for printing. Surface areas not protected by the greasy paints soaked up the water. Next, oil-based inks were rolled onto the stone. The greasy surfaces absorbed the inks while the water-moistened sections did not. Sheets of poster stock were then laid on the stone, and simple compression transferred ink to the paper.

The film-manufacturing companies made posters available in several configurations. The most versatile and therefore most frequently requested was the "one-sheet," which measured 27 × 41 inches. These were commonly displayed in front of theaters on large easels flanking the ticket booth, but also inside the lobby in glass frames along the walls. A "three-sheet" was just what the name suggested: three panels that, when properly aligned, formed one large poster of about 41 × 81 inches.

Three-sheets primarily adorned the outside of bigger venues with wider sidewalks but could also be pasted to the sides of nearby buildings or wooden fences in the neighborhood. The same was true of a "six-sheet" (81 × 81 inches). Too large for easels, they were invariably pasted onto walls or fences with wallpaper glue, which made them impossible to remove without shredding them, which therefore rendered them unusable for additional displays. The "twenty-four-sheet" (246 × 108) was printed in twelve sections and designed for use solely on outdoor billboards. They were printed on heavier, more durable stock in anticipation of exposure to the elements for weeks (or, when advertising serials, months).

ABOVE: Born in 1864 near what became the city of Butte, "Montana Frank" McCray claimed to be many things: army scout, Pony Express rider, and rustler-chasing rancher. But he was best known as a roper and trick rider with various Wild West shows, including his own.

Smaller posters were printed on card stock. "Lobby cards" (11 × 14) came in sets of eight and pictured various scenes from each film. As the name indicates, they typically were displayed in theater lobbies, generally arrayed on the wall around a one-sheet. "Window cards" (14 × 22) carried designs similar to a film's one-sheet but had a blank strip at top or bottom in which could be hand-lettered the local theater's name and the date of the film's engagement. They were intended for placement in the front windows of local retail establishments. "Inserts" (14 × 36, vertical) and "half-sheets" (22 × 28, horizontal) often combined painted images with photographs and were almost always part of extensive lobby displays.

Various printing firms scattered across the country produced posters for film production companies. Most were already involved in manufacturing posters for rodeos, circuses, state fairs, vaudeville houses, and legitimate theater venues. Cincinnati-based Hennegan Show Print began supplying movie posters for Thomas A. Edison films shortly after the turn of the century. New York's United States Printing and Lithograph Company serviced early studios. Other New York firms specializing in posters included Acme Litho, Greenwich Litho, and the Joseph H. Tooker Litho Company of New York.

By the 1920s, three printing firms accounted for most of the major studios' posters: the aforementioned Tooker Litho Company and two Cleveland-based outfits, the Morgan Litho Company and Continental Litho. The latter was started in 1928 by a Morgan employee who not only left to start his own company but also managed to poach the Warner Bros. account on his way out.

Printers were forbidden from tampering with original poster artwork supplied to them by film companies, except in extraordinary circumstances. The major studios all had fully staffed departments that turned out advertising and promotion materials. Several artists might be employed to produce a single Western poster. One might be assigned to paint the central image, whether the portrait of a star or the rendition of a scene, another might contribute background art, and a third would hand-letter titles and credits. These salaried employees worked anonymously; to this day, it's virtually impossible to identify movie-poster artists. Some, such as Columbia's Glenn Cravath, occasionally signed their work, but for the most part they labored without recognition.

The "Poverty Row" (B movie) companies couldn't afford to maintain art departments and therefore farmed out poster design to small Hollywood ad agencies that specialized in such work. These artists too went uncredited, even though their efforts often compared favorably with those of the major studios. You'll see that some of the most handsome posters of the twenties and thirties emanated from these shoestring producers.

In many cases, it was enough for a poster to feature a striking portrait of the star. Many Westerns—especially the B-series oaters intended for Saturday-afternoon consumption in small-town theaters—were star driven. Kids didn't say to their pals, "Let's go see *Three on the Trail*!" They said, "Let's go see the new Hopalong Cassidy picture!" Most of the time, they didn't remember titles at all. So, a poster

ABOVE: After his poorly managed Wild West show went bankrupt in 1913, Buffalo Bill was induced to join the popular Sells Floto Circus and partially recreate his act under the big top. He toured with the circus during the 1914–15 season.

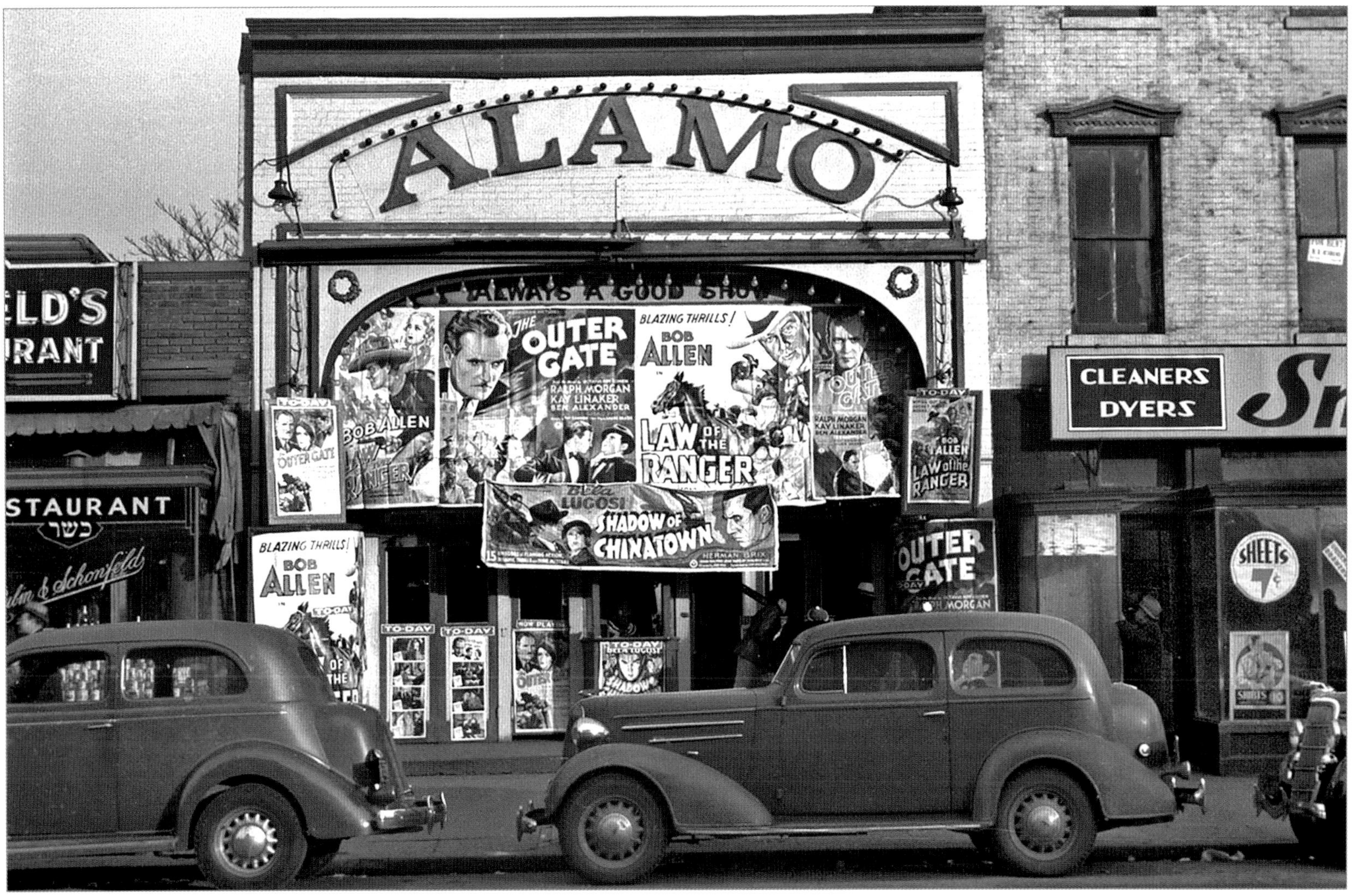

utilizing an image of Hoppy they hadn't seen on previous posters was enough to stimulate their interest.

For nearly three-quarters of the twentieth century, moviegoers enjoyed Hollywood horse operas. The old-fashioned morality plays—all influenced to one extent or another by *The Virginian*, whether filmmakers wanted to admit it or not—eventually yielded to a more realistic type of story that allowed for well-delineated characters and plots with situations more complex than searches for cattle rustlers, pursuits of train robbers, or squabbling over water rights. Perhaps inevitably, oaters made after World War II increasingly reflected the manners and mores of their time. Ultimately, it became fashionable to mock the genre's tropes and conventions, and Hollywood elitists felt emboldened to suffuse newly produced Westerns with subversive themes and attitudes, not least of which was the Vietnam-era disdain for institutions and law-enforcement agencies.

Poster reproductions in the following chapters tell a pictorial history of Western movies from *The Great Train Robbery* (1903) to *The Shootist* (1976). Both the biggest stars and the smallest are represented. By the time you've finished scanning the illustrations and reading the accompanying text, we expect you'll have a much better understanding of this genre's importance in cinema history. And now—ride 'em, cowboy! ✸

ABOVE: The Alamo Theatre in Pine Bluff, Arkansas, seen here in a 1937 photo, is a perfect example of a storefront nickelodeon that grew with the motion-picture industry and became a "subsequent-run" house catering to undiscriminating, action-hungry audiences.

1 THE EARLY YEARS

THE BIRTH OF THE WESTERN

Moving pictures are still novelty items when *The Great Train Robbery* stimulates demand for Western tales brimming with action. The nascent film industry responds quickly and decisively, first producing horse operas in the East but eventually moving west as audiences insist on a modicum of authenticity. The genre's explosive growth in popularity soon makes big stars of a number of minor or inexperienced performers.

BELOW: Edison Company motion-picture director Edwin S. Porter was more technician than artist, but in making the one-reel *Great Train Robbery* he unconsciously established several of the movie Western's fundamental narrative devices, especially the climactic chase and shootout. The film's closing shot features the mustached gent pictured in this poster. When he fired his revolver at the camera, it startled nickelodeon patrons not yet accustomed to action that threatened to burst from theater screens.

Although *The Great Train Robbery* (1903) is no longer considered the first Western or the first narrative motion picture, it remains a seminal work. After all, this simple morality tale—crime is punished and order restored, but only after a thrilling chase and climactic shootout—provided the thematic underpinning for thousands of horse operas to come.

The demand for Westerns predictably soared, and pioneering filmmakers labored to oblige an insatiable public. During the twentieth century's first decade, nickelodeon bills changed daily, and most exhibitors offered nightly programs of between three and five short subjects. Savvy theater owners included a Western in every show. The broadly drawn heroes and villains were easy to identify, and the surfeit of riding, fighting, and shooting enabled immigrant patrons to follow each story without needing to read explanatory title cards written in an unfamiliar language.

Before long, other types of outdoor films with period settings were marketed as Westerns. As early as 1909, a vogue existed for movies featuring American Indians, most of them sympathetically portrayed as stoic and honorable. Civil War films also enjoyed considerable popularity in the pre–World War I years, though they often relied on the same plot device: a Union or Confederate soldier, drafted to spy on the other side, is captured and faced with execution, evading a firing squad after the girl he loves begs an enemy officer to spare his life.

Yet, it was the traditional Western that really fired the imaginations of early filmgoers. Its protagonist might be a two-fisted sheriff, a hardworking rancher, or even a bandit reformed by the love of a good woman. Its plot might center on cattle rustling, squabbles over grazing land, a wave of train robberies, or the deliberate fomenting of range war. The short lengths of those primitive

"oaters"—one or two reels of approximately fifteen minutes each—militated against intricate plots and niceties of characterization. Not that viewers cared: what mattered was action . . . the inevitable clash of Good against Evil, the ride to the rescue, the resolution of conflict via blazing guns or smashing fists.

With motion-picture production in the 1910s dominated by firms based in New York and Chicago, it's not surprising that Westerns were shot in the East. New Jersey lacked windswept deserts, roaring rivers, and rugged mountain ranges, but it boasted enough fields, forests, and farmland to provide a reasonable simulacrum of the West—particularly if theatergoers were willing to suspend disbelief. By 1910, the area near Fort Lee, just across the Hudson River from Manhattan, was dotted with studios built by long-forgotten production companies. Coytesville, a less developed suburb of Fort Lee, was home to Rambo's, a combination hotel, saloon, and restaurant featured in countless early Westerns.

After a while, such locations became overly familiar to movie fans. Grassy fields in Jersey substituting for Arizona scrubland eventually invited expressions of scorn and derision. To maintain their competitive edge, a number of filmmakers migrated west. Among the first was a Chicagoan who wanted to produce Westerns that looked authentic—or at least more authentic than those he'd been filming in rural Illinois. Gilbert M. Anderson, a stocky and none-too-prepossessing actor who originally worked for the Edison Company and had

ABOVE: This dynamic poster portrayed *The Great Train Robbery's* eponymous event more effectively than the film itself did, but what mattered was that it proved an irresistible lure to potential theatergoers strolling past their local nickelodeon. The Edison short had no central protagonist; hence the poster's failure to spotlight a specific individual. Once the cowboy hero became firmly entrenched in Western motion pictures, posters invariably gave him prominence at the expense of *mise-en-scène*. In fairly short order, the genre became personality driven.

ABOVE: A candid photo taken during the production of *The Girl from Frisco* (1916), a series of self-contained Western two-reelers often mistaken for a serial. This saloon is an outdoor set at the Kalem studio in Hollywood. That's series director James W. Horne at left, in striped shirt and straw hat. Seated at the table at right are, *from left to right*, principal players Edward Clisbee, Josephine West, Robert N. Bradbury (soon to become a Western director and the father of cowboy star Bob Steele), and series star Marin Sais, who would marry popular Western player Jack Hoxie in 1920.

a bit part in *The Great Train Robbery*, cofounded the Essanay Company with George K. Spoor in 1907. Anderson scouted various areas in California before settling in Niles, a small town located southeast of San Francisco. He created the motion picture Western's first series character, "Broncho Billy," whom he played in some 150 one- and two-reelers. Anderson lacked practically all the qualities that made an effective cowboy hero, yet by virtue of being the first, he achieved a wholly unanticipated degree of success.

The importance of posters to motion-picture exhibitors in this era cannot be understated. Remember, nickelodeons changed their bills on a daily basis. Newspapers neither reviewed nor advertised movies, which at that time were considered crude and vulgar entertainment suitable mainly for immigrants and the marginally literate. Favorable word of mouth would not help, because the next day a different program would be playing. An exhibitor's best hope of attracting trade lay in plastering the outside of his venue with posters—the bigger the better. Standard one-sheets were large enough to grab the attention of passersby, but three-sheets, six-sheets, and banners did a better job. Like circus posters pasted to wooden fences enclosing a vacant lot where the big top would be erected, movie posters framing the entrance of a storefront theater offered what today is called "point-of-purchase marketing."

By 1915, the street-front nickelodeons were dying out, with larger and better-appointed theaters springing up in big and small towns alike. Short-subject

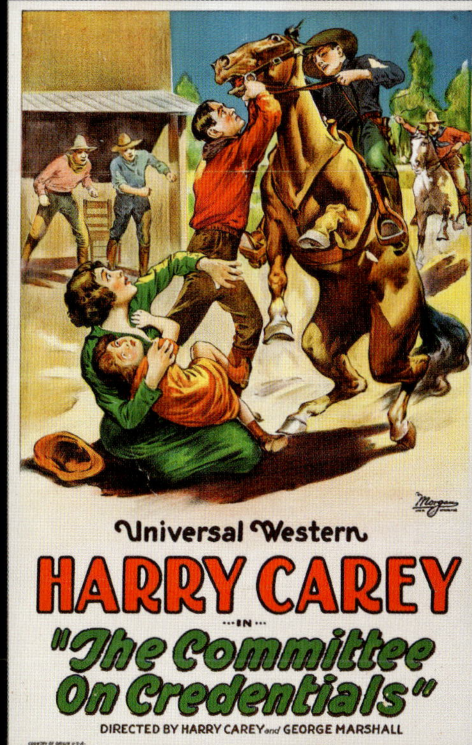

programs receded in importance to "feature" films of five reels or more. Longer running times demanded more expansive plots. Storytelling techniques matured, and technical proficiency improved.

Western stars proliferated during the 1910s. A contemporary of Anderson's, matinee idol J. Warren Kerrigan projected virility and cut a dashing figure in the saddle. He worked for the American Film Company, a Santa Barbara–based outfit whose well-turned out "Flying A" horse operas ranked above most of their contemporaries. Stage favorite William S. Hart, who'd played Messala in the original Broadway production of *Ben-Hur*, wholeheartedly embraced the genre, playing a succession of "good bad men" in short subjects and features alike.

Hart's starring vehicles contained the requisite he-man action but also dripped with treacly displays of self-sacrifice. Meanwhile, Harry Carey, a veteran of touring companies, abandoned stage work altogether and made a name for himself in oaters produced by Carl Laemmle's Universal and directed by a young Irishman named John Ford. And a real-life cowboy named Tom Mix materialized seemingly out of the ether, with no training as an actor, to become a top box-office draw.

Westerns continued to grow in popularity, so much so that accomplished actors with no discernible affinity for the genre allowed themselves to be cast in horse operas to achieve box-office success. These included such prominent stars as Lillian Gish, Douglas Fairbanks, Lionel Barrymore, Charles Ray, Mabel Normond, Robert Edeson, Fritzi Ridgeway, and Taylor Holmes. Even famous opera singer Geraldine Farrar, who had played Joan of Arc for Cecil B. DeMille, took to the saddle in 1918's *The Hell-Cat*.

The floodgates were about to open. ✸

ABOVE LEFT: Opera singer Geraldine Farrar rested her voice by periodically starring in silent movies. She had already played Joan of Arc in a lavish feature film directed by Cecil B. DeMille when she abruptly switched gears to star in this horse opera, one of the earliest motion pictures produced by the soon-to-be-legendary Samuel Goldwyn. Farrar portrays the spirited daughter of an Irish ranch owner.

ABOVE CENTER: A well-rendered poster for an installment of the previously mentioned *Girl from Frisco* series, which was set in a more-or-less-contemporary West and occasionally found leading lady Marin Sais giving her trusty steed a break and traveling by automobile.

ABOVE RIGHT: Stage actor Harry Carey appeared in films of various genres during the 1910s but enjoyed success as a Western hero. He wrote and directed some of his starring vehicles too, including this 1916 Universal three-reeler.

NICKELODEON THRILLS

Westerns featuring historical themes and figures became staples of the nickelodeon era, at least partly because some of the events depicted were still within the memory of older theatergoers. Among the period's biggest successes was the 1912 two-reeler *Custer's Last Fight*, directed by and starring Francis Ford, who also appeared in numerous Civil War dramas for well-regarded producer Thomas H. Ince. Ford played Custer; his frequent costar Grace Cunard appeared as the ill-fated general's wife. Mounted on a lavish scale for such an early film, *Custer's Last Fight* lingered in the memories of those who originally saw it. An outfit called Quality Amusement Corporation acquired the negative in 1925. Quality added footage from other Westerns and incorporated newly written intertitles into the two-reeler, padding it out to five reels and marketing it as a feature attraction. Savvy movie fans recognized the "new" film as a cinematic antique, but the original's quality was such that the reissued version elicited surprisingly favorable reviews and did good business.

PAWNEE BILL'S BUFFALO RANCH
FEATURE FILMS
PRESENTS
MAY LILLIE
QUEEN of the
BUFFALO RANCH
FIVE PARTS

NEW YORK MOTION PICTURE CO.
TRADE MARK
THE
REDMAN'S
WRATH
A FEATURE
BISON
FILM

The
HEART OF THE SHERIFF
Selig
TRADE S MARK
A
WESTERN
DRAMA
Goes
LITHO. CO
CHICAGO

Marian,
THE HOLY TERROR
FORTUITOUS ACCIDENTS
DID YOU HEAR
HIM CHIRP WHEN
I HIT HER?
ON THE SAME
REEL
"DOC YAK
THE MARKSMAN"
S
Selig
COMEDY
Goes
LITHO. CO
CHICAGO

ECLAIR-UNIVERSAL
LIEUT. LANDRIDGE RESCUES THE INJURED MEXICAN GIRL.
THE CABALLERO'S WAY
FROM THE STORY BY
O. HENRY
PRINCIPALS
WM. DUNN
J.W. JOHNSTON
EDNA PAYNE
HAL WILSON
IN 3 PARTS
UNIVERSAL

The Sheriff's Baby
DIRECTED BY
D.W. GRIFFITH
THE CAST INCLUDES
KATE BRUCE
ROBERT HARRON
HARRY CAREY
HENRY B. WALTHALL
LIONEL BARRYMORE
JOSEPH McDERMOTT
"PUT UP YOUR GUN, SHERIFF"
BIOGRAPH

SELIG PRESENTS
WILLIAM FARNUM IN
THE SPOILERS
FROM THE FAMOUS BOOK BY
REX BEACH
A GRIPPING, SENSATIONAL PHOTO-DRAMA OF ALASKAN LIFE
PRODUCED BY
COLIN CAMPBELL
IN 9 REELS 3 ACTS

UNICORN FILM SERVICE CORPORATION
WESTERN DRAMA
THE HOLD-UP AT DEVIL'S PASS
Planning the Hold-Up
BUFFALO

THE GUNFIGHTER
NESTOR
THE OUTLAWS REDEMPTION

IN THREE REELS AND 60 SCENES
AMATA HEARS THE PLOT.
CHEYENNE FEATURE FILM COMPANY
OFFERS
THE CURSE OF THE GREAT SOUTHWEST

THE SATURDAY EVENING POST

THE DIRECT FROM BROADWAY FEATURES
- OFFER -

From the Saturday Evening Post to the Films

AL-JENNINGS
(HIMSELF)
IN

Beating Back,

THE MOST FAMOUS OF THE SATURDAY EVENING POST'S "HUMAN DOCUMENT" SERIALS - A BANDIT STORY FOR RESPECTABLE AUDIENCES

PRODUCED BY
CARROLL FLEMING
LATE OF THE
NEW YORK
HIPPODROME

COMPLETE
IN
6
REELS

AL. JENNINGS AT THE FIGHT AT SPIKE S RANCH

How the most famous of modern Bandits --- A Real Jean Valjean --- Sent to the penitentiary and pardoned by A President of the United States, 'Beat Back' at society until it recognized and honored him. Shows all of Al. Jennings' thrilling life, including his hairbreadth escapes from death at the hands of the law.

COPYRIGHTED 1914 BY GREENWICH LITHO. CO. N.Y.

WILLIAM S. HART, THE FIRST MAJOR WESTERN STAR

In the twentieth century's first decade, practically any Western found a ready audience by virtue of the genre's overall popularity. But what eventually became known as the "star system" was nascent as early as 1912, as film fans began taking notice of the players they most enjoyed. Gilbert M. "Broncho Billy" Anderson attained fame during the prewar years, but the first true Western star was stage veteran William S. Hart, who in his early movie appearances established a persona that audiences eagerly embraced: the Good Bad Man, a stern, stony-faced gent of dubious moral character who in the last reel always redeemed himself with a heroic act of self-sacrifice (usually at the urging of a pretty leading lady). For many years, Hart's film output maintained remarkably consistent, largely because he worked with the same people and established a cohesive filmmaking unit: Thomas H. Ince produced or supervised, C. Gardner Sullivan scripted, Joe August photographed, and Lambert Hillyer directed on those relatively few occasions Hart chose not to.

ARTCRAFT PICTURES
Morgan
THOMAS H. INCE
PRESENTS
WILLIAM S. HART
IN
"BRANDING BROADWAY"
BY C. GARDNER SULLIVAN
DIRECTED BY WILLIAM S. HART
PHOTOGRAPHED BY JOE AUGUST
SUPERVISION OF THOMAS H. INCE
AN ARTCRAFT PICTURE

ARTCRAFT PICTURES
THOMAS H. INCE Presents
WILLIAM S. HART
IN
"Wolves of the Rail"
BY DENISON CLIFT
DISTRIBUTED BY
ARTCRAFT PICTURES
CORPORATION

ARTCRAFT PICTURES
AN ARTCRAFT PICTURE
THOMAS H. INCE
PRESENTS
WILLIAM S. HART
IN
"RIDDLE GAWNE"
BY CHARLES ALDEN SELTZER
DIRECTED BY WILLIAM S. HART
PHOTOGRAPHED BY JOE AUGUST
SUPERVISION OF THOMAS H. INCE

S-A-LYNCH ENTERPRISES, INC.
PRESENT
WM S-HART
IN
THE COLD DECK
A SUPERLATIVE PRODUCTION

ARTCRAFT PICTURES
An ARTCRAFT Picture
SELFISH YATES FORGETS HIMSELF.
Thomas H. Ince
presents
WILLIAM S. HART
IN
"Selfish Yates"
By C. GARDNER SULLIVAN
Directed by WILLIAM S. HART
Photographed by JOE AUGUST
Supervision of THOMAS H. INCE

WILLIAM S. HART
IN
'TUMBLEWEEDS'
Story by Hal G. Evarts. Adapted for the Screen by C. Gardner Sullivan
DIRECTED BY KING BAGGOT
A WILLIAM S. HART PRODUCTION
- a United Artists Picture -

TRIANGLE PLAYS
"Some day I'm a going to ask you to be my wife"
WILLIAM S. HART
IN
THE RETURN OF "DRAW" EGAN
WRITTEN BY C. GARDNER SULLIVAN THOMAS H. INCE PRODUCTION

A Paramount Picture
Adolph Zukor . . . presents
WILLIAM S.
HART
in
WILD BILL
HICKOK
By William S. Hart
Adapted for the screen by..
J. G. Hawks
Directed by Clifford Smith
a William S. Hart
production

WESTERNS WITH NON-WESTERN STARS

Taking roles in Westerns was practically a rite of passage during the film industry's formative years. The genre was so prominent that—especially prior to the advent of the Roaring Twenties—up-and-coming screen actors regarded appearing in horse operas as an important star-building exercise. During her salad days at Biograph Studios, Lillian Gish made Westerns for directors D. W. Griffith and Christy Cabanne. As a young stage actor, the ebullient Douglas Fairbanks specialized in romantic comedies and was cast in such properties when he began making films in 1915. But he soon found the Western a suitable type of movie for his unbridled athleticism and starred in numerous horse operas before transitioning to the lavish swashbucklers for which he is best remembered. (Doug's first big hit, *The Mark of Zorro*, was a Western of sorts, being set in old California.) It took considerable suspension of disbelief, however, to accept distinguished stage actor Lionel Barrymore as a two-fisted Westerner in *The Quitter* (1916).

DOUGLAS FAIRBANKS
IN
'THE MARK OF ZORRO'
DIRECTED BY FRED NIBLO
FROM THE "ALL STORY WEEKLY" NOVEL
"THE CURSE OF CAPISTRANO"
BY JOHNSTON MCCULLEY

DOUGLAS
FAIRBANKS
in
'ARIZONA'
ADAPTED FROM
AUGUSTUS THOMAS'S PLAY
"ARIZONA"
PRODUCED BY
THE DOUGLAS FAIRBANKS
PICTURE CORP.
ARTCRAFT PICTURES
AN
ARTCRAFT
PICTURE

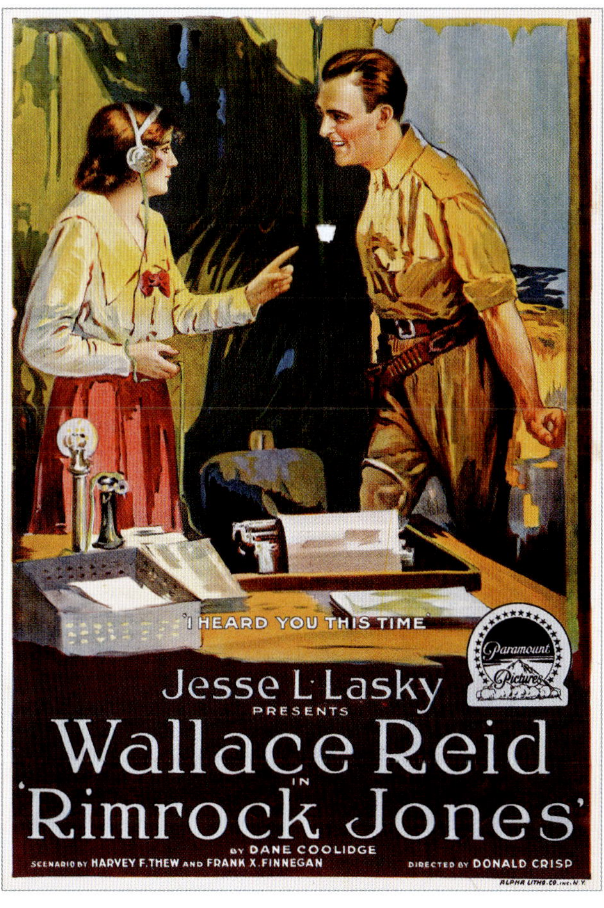
"I HEARD YOU THIS TIME"
Paramount Pictures
Jesse L. Lasky
PRESENTS
Wallace Reid
IN
'Rimrock Jones'
BY DANE COOLIDGE
SCENARIO BY HARVEY F. THEW AND FRANK X. FINNEGAN
DIRECTED BY DONALD CRISP
ALPHA LITHO. CO. INC. N.Y.

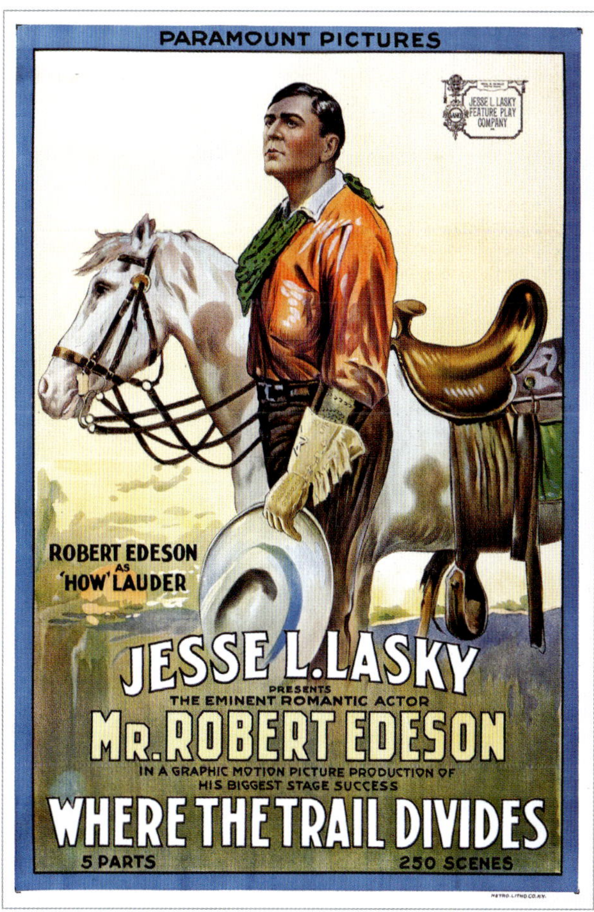
PARAMOUNT PICTURES
JESSE L. LASKY
FEATURE PLAY
COMPANY
ROBERT EDESON
AS
'HOW' LAUDER
JESSE L. LASKY
PRESENTS
THE EMINENT ROMANTIC ACTOR
MR. ROBERT EDESON
IN A GRAPHIC MOTION PICTURE PRODUCTION OF
HIS BIGGEST STAGE SUCCESS
WHERE THE TRAIL DIVIDES
5 PARTS
250 SCENES
METRO. LITHO. CO. N.Y.

A Goldwyn PICTURE
Samuel Goldwyn
presents
Mabel Normand
in
"Pinto"
Written and Directed by
Victor Schertzinger

TUSUN
CAPITAL FILM CO. INC. PRESENTS
BY ARRANGEMENT WITH RUSSELL-GREIVER-RUSSELL
FRITZI RIDGEWAY
THE GIRL WITH A THOUSAND PERSONALITIES
IN
The Sheriff's Daughter
Supported by ROBERT BURNS and an All Star Cast
STORY BY
W.M. PIGOTT
a Doubleday Production
DIRECTED BY
HARRY MOODY

METRO PICTURES
ROLFE PHOTOPLAYS (INC.)
PRESENTS
LIONEL BARRYMORE
IN
"The Quitter"
BY IZOLA FORRESTER
PRODUCED BY
CHAS. HORAN
METRO PICTURES

THOMAS H. INCE--- presents
CHARLES RAY
IN
"THE SHERIFF'S SON"
By WILLIAM McLEOD RAINE
Scenario by J. G. HAWKS ~~~ Directed by VICTOR L. SCHERTZINGER
Photographed by CHESTER LYONS ~~ Produced by THOMAS H. INCE
A PARAMOUNT PICTURE
Morgan

TRIANGLE PLAYS
BELLE BENNETT
IN
ASHES OF HOPE
THE STORY OF A WOMAN SIDE-TRACKED
ON THE ROAD TO GLORY
RELEASED BY
TRIANGLE DISTRIBUTING CORP.

WARTIME WESTERNS

The motion-picture Western evolved at a near-exponential pace during the years that Europe was embroiled in the Great War (1914–18). Crude one- and two-reelers shot in New Jersey forests and farmland disappeared completely as film production became centralized in California. Pioneering companies such as Selig, Kalem, Edison, and Essanay withered and eventually died, while former maverick producers William Fox, Carl Laemmle, and Jesse L. Lasky built mighty organizations that still dominate the movie business: Fox Film Corporation (now 20th Century Studios), the Universal Film Manufacturing Company (now Universal Pictures), and Famous Players-Lasky (now Paramount Pictures). Former serial queens Grace Cunard and Helen Gibson drifted into Westerns, and horse operas were so ubiquitous that one could find a few starring African American cowboys, such as rodeo champion Bill Pickett. By the end of the war years, it was not only possible but relatively easy for even moderately talented performers to forge a career as a Western star.

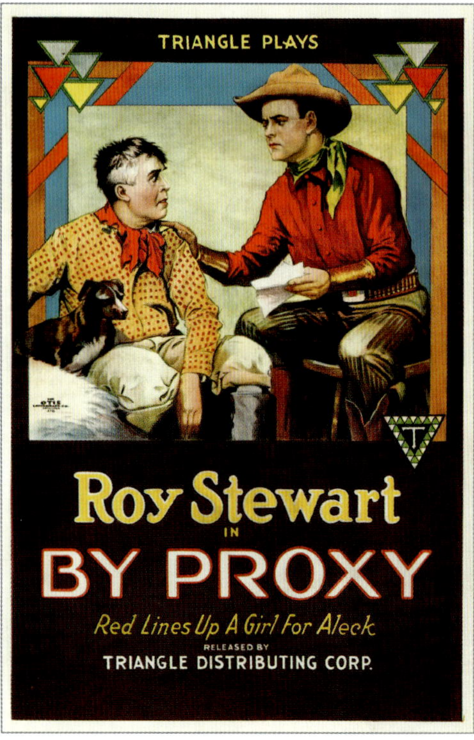

PHIL GOLDSTONE PRESENTS
GRACE CUNARD
IN
CARMEN OF THE BORDER
5 REELS
DIRECTED BY W.B. PEARSON
ADAPTED FROM HELL'S CRATER

SPECIAL ADDED ATTRACTION
CAPITAL FILM CO. PRESENTS
HELEN GIBSON
FILMDOM'S FOREMOST DARE-DEVIL IN
PAYROLL PIRATES
A Thrilling Dramatic Story Of A Woman's Invincible Courage

THE NORMAN FILM MFG. CO.
PRESENTS
BILL PICKETT
World's Colored Champion IN
"THE BULL-DOGGER"
STEVE REYNOLDS
BENNIE TURPIN
ANITA BUSH
BILL PICKETT FIGHTING A WILD MEXICAN BULL
Death Defying Feats of Courage and Skill
THRILLS! LAUGHS TOO!
Produced by NORMAN FILM MFG. CO. Jacksonville, Fla.

"Be my Crusader"
William Fox
PRESENTS
WILLIAM RUSSELL
IN
"The CRUSADER"
STORY BY ALAN SULLIVAN
DIRECTED BY
HOWARD MITCHELL

UNIVERSAL
TWO FROM TEXAS
A Western Masterpiece
Featuring
J. FARRELL McDONALD
Directed by EDWARD FEENEY

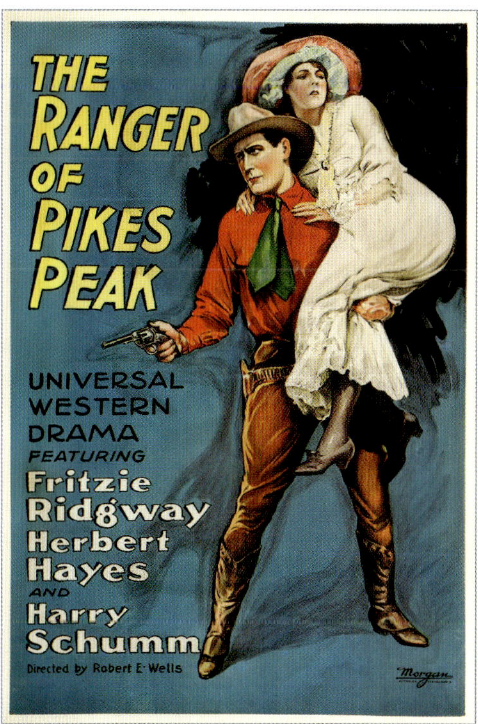
THE RANGER OF PIKES PEAK
UNIVERSAL WESTERN DRAMA
FEATURING
Fritzie Ridgway
Herbert Hayes
AND
Harry Schumm
Directed by Robert E. Wells

THE EVOLUTION OF THE COWBOY HERO

Early genre favorites such as Broncho Billy Anderson and J. Warren Kerrigan faded early, primarily because they didn't transition effectively to feature films. During the 1910s, William S. Hart was indisputably the preeminent Western star, but he faced increasingly stiff competition by decade's end. The big gun, so to speak, would be Tom Mix. He broke into pictures in 1910 shorts for Selig, initially supporting the brawny Scottish star William Duncan. Mix was an expert horseman and a crack shot, but he also had a pleasant personality and a surprising aptitude for comedy. With the Selig brand losing box-office potency, Mix signed with Fox in 1917, debuting in *Hearts and Saddles*. He would peak in the twenties. Other Western players whose screen images evolved during this period were Harry Carey (who distinguished himself in 1919's *Marked Men*, a John Ford–directed adaptation of Peter B. Kyne's oft-filmed *Three Godfathers*), William Farnum (who starred in a slew of Zane Grey adaptations for Fox), and a pair of young cowboys: Charles "Buck" Jones and Edmund "Hoot" Gibson.

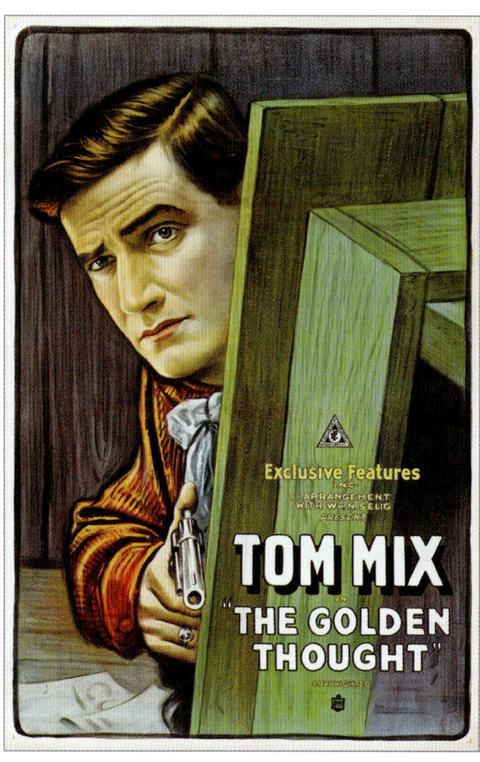

Foxfilm Comedy
TWO REELS
HEARTS AND SADDLES

— WITH —
TOM MIX
DIRECTED BY TOM MIX AND BOB EDDY
FOX FILM CORPORATION

ALPHA LITHO. CO. INC. N.Y.

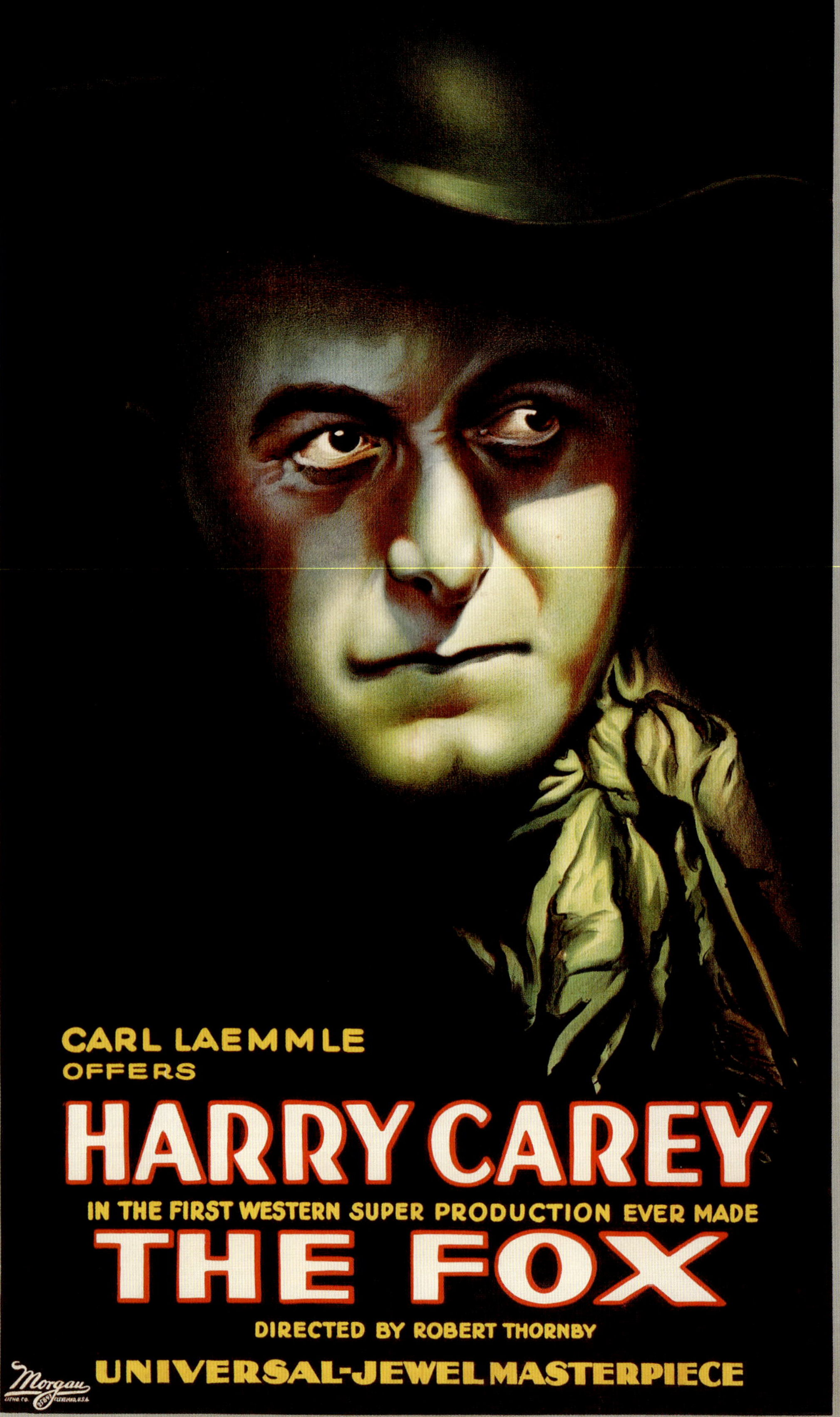
CARL LAEMMLE
OFFERS
HARRY CAREY
IN THE FIRST WESTERN SUPER PRODUCTION EVER MADE
THE FOX
DIRECTED BY ROBERT THORNBY
Morgan
UNIVERSAL-JEWEL MASTERPIECE

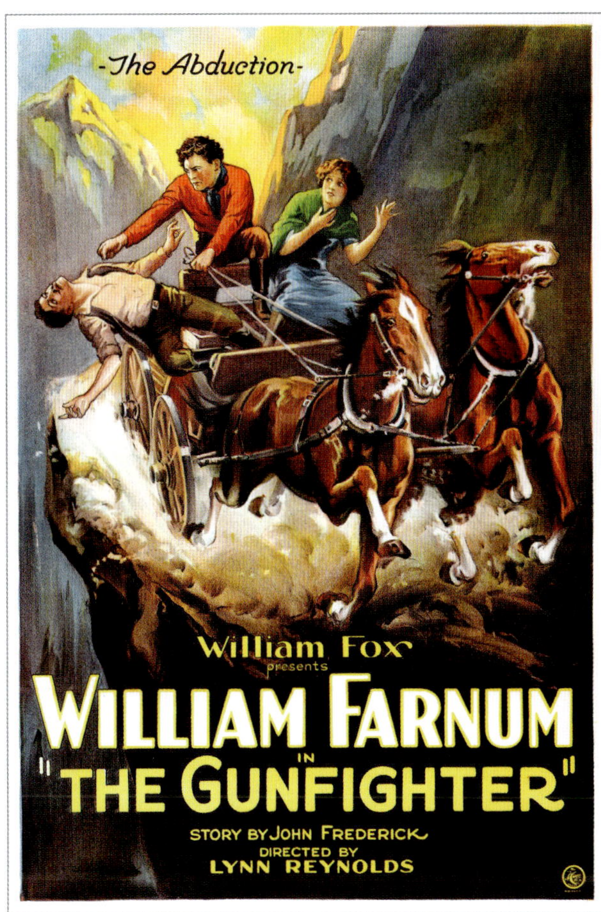
-The Abduction-
William Fox presents
WILLIAM FARNUM
IN
"THE GUNFIGHTER"
STORY BY JOHN FREDERICK
DIRECTED BY
LYNN REYNOLDS

BULLETIN
FLASH IT!
WILLIAM FOX PRESENTS
WILLIAM FARNUM
IN
"BRASS COMMANDMENTS"
BY CHARLES ALDEN SELTZER
DIRECTED BY LYNN REYNOLDS

WILLIAM FOX PRESENTS
CHARLES JONES
IN
'PARDON MY NERVE!'
STORY BY WILLIAM PATTERSON WHITE
DIRECTED BY
REEVES EASON

It's A Universal Western
Hoot Gibson
AND
VIRGINIA FAIRE
IN
"RUNNIN' STRAIGHT"
DIRECTED BY ARTHUR FLAVEN

2
THE
DAWN OF
THE COWBOY
STARS

WESTERNS BECOME BIG BUSINESS

The motion-picture Western comes of age during the 1920s, achieving widespread acceptance by audiences of all stripes. With old-fashioned Indian and Civil War stories now relics of the film industry's past, action-oriented star vehicles dominate the genre. This is the age of the hard-riding, straight-shooting cowboy hero. But the stereotypical shoot-'em-up occasionally takes a back seat to epic Westerns with historical themes and lavish production values . . .

BELOW: Fox Film Corp.'s *The Iron Horse* (1924), about the building of the transcontinental railroad, capitalized on the newly minted vogue for epic Westerns. More importantly, it made a star of first-time leading man George O'Brien and established John Ford as a major director.

OPPOSITE: The first "epic" Western, Paramount's *The Covered Wagon* (1923) impressed moviegoers with its authenticity. No expense was spared in secu ring or creating sets, props, and costumes appropriate to the period covered by this sprawling historical saga.

As the Roaring Twenties began, an America badly rattled by World War I and several years of deep recession increasingly embraced motion pictures as escapist entertainment. The storefront nickelodeons had faded away, replaced in big cities by cavernous "picture palaces" and in small towns by modest but clean and comfortable theaters of three to five hundred seats. By mid-decade, even tiny rural hamlets boasted at least one venue for movie screenings.

By 1920, feature-length films of five reels (with running times of sixty to sixty-five minutes) had replaced the daily potpourri of short subjects previously offered by the old storefront nickelodeons. Shorts were still produced, of course, but they were relegated to secondary positions on a theater's bill of fare. Moving pictures had long since passed beyond the novelty phase; film was now taken seriously as a medium for storytelling. Even in the teens, movie producers had licensed stage plays and popular literary works for adaptation, but that practice intensified as filmmakers refined techniques for visual development of narrative and performers moved past the wild gesticulations that had earlier passed for effective screen acting. Middle- and upper-class consumers who had previously scorned nickelodeon-era films as crude fodder for immigrants and the marginally literate now became regular patrons of their local picture palaces as films gradually improved and achieved respectability.

Throughout this evolutionary process, the Western not only retained popularity but expanded in it. In the late nineteenth century, when magic-lantern operators exhibited the first moving pictures using primitive devices, the Wild West still existed. Texas ranchers still drove their cattle north on the 1,000-mile-long Chisholm Trail; outlaws on horseback still robbed stagecoaches in remote areas

JESSE L. LASKY *Presents a*

JAMES CRUZE
PRODUCTION

THE COVERED WAGON

ADAPTED BY
JACK CUNNINGHAM
FROM THE NOVEL BY
EMERSON HOUGH

a
Paramount
Picture

Morgan

Paramount Pictures
FAMOUS PLAYERS-LASKY CORP.

1-A "COUNTRY OF ORIGIN, U.S.A."

THIS POSTER LEASED FROM FAMOUS PLAYERS-LASKY CORP.

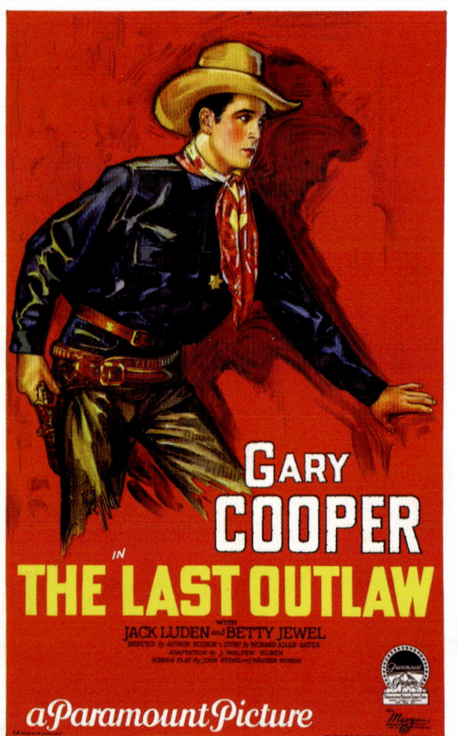

ABOVE: Real-life Montana cowboy and erstwhile art student Gary Cooper was a stunt rider and bit player whose brief supporting turn in *The Winning of Barbara Worth* (1926) persuaded Paramount to try him out in several modestly budgeted Westerns the following year.

BELOW: Ken Maynard had already worked as a trick rider for rodeos, circuses, carnivals, and Wild West shows before crashing Hollywood. His first starring Westerns were six Poverty Row productions that helped him build a loyal fan base, despite their shortcomings.

not yet serviced by railroads. Statehood was still years in the future for Arizona, Oklahoma, and New Mexico. Western films produced in New Jersey during the 1910s did a poor job of representing the historical reality of frontier life, but they found enthusiastic audiences, nonetheless.

By the twenties, things had changed considerably. America no longer depended on agrarian activity for economic growth and prosperity; the country was thoroughly industrialized, and its population no longer adhered to the binary model of city or rurality. The spread of public transit and the affordability of automobiles were major factors in the growth of suburbs—communities that were part commercial, part residential—outside most major cities. In the span of a single generation, life in the United States changed dramatically. Technological innovation occurred rapidly and resulted in consumer products that simplified everyday life for millions of Americans. Suddenly the Old West seemed long ago and faraway. Motion pictures dramatizing the wild-and-woolly exploits of cowboy heroes surged in popularity because, with each passing year, the way of life they personified was receding into history.

Of course, Hollywood—which is where motion-picture production was now centralized—demonstrated scant willingness to depict the Wild West accurately, even though it was still within living memory for many moviegoers. In keeping with the trend that had developed a decade or more previously, the cowboy hero was a mythical figure. He followed a strict moral code: women and children were to be revered and protected; adversaries were always to be given "an even break" in the climactic showdown, no matter how perfidious their previous behavior. More often than not, the hero (especially when played by a beloved Western star) eschewed tobacco and liquor and the company of women of loose morals.

Given the genre's popularity, it was not surprising that producers specializing in Westerns sprang up like weeds along the streets of Hollywood, particularly in an area that came to be known as Poverty Row. Its epicenter, tagged "Gower Gulch" by industry wags, was the intersection of Gower Street and Sunset Boulevard. A reconstituted roadhouse on the northwest corner had become Hollywood's first permanent movie studio, with several others erected nearby. Performers in Western garb congregated every morning at Gower Street's Columbia Drug Store, which had a pay phone. Studio casting departments looking for horse-opera day players need only call the drugstore to get as many as required within minutes.

The fraternity of Western-movie actors and stuntmen largely comprised circus, rodeo, and Wild West Show performers, with a sprinkling of real cowboys who migrated to California as the era of big cattle drives drew to a close. Most of the silent era's stars came from this group, among them Tom Mix, Buck Jones, Hoot Gibson, and Ken Maynard.

In 1923, Paramount Pictures released the first "epic" Western, *The Covered Wagon*, a ten-reel historical saga about pioneers trekking from Kansas to Oregon. Twice as long as the average oater, it cost a record-breaking $782,000 and took

months to shoot on locations in Utah and Nevada as well as California. Early Western star J. Warren Kerrigan was the leading man of this wildly successful opus, which brought prestige to the genre and inspired other filmmakers to emulate it.

Encouraged by *The Covered Wagon*'s success, producer William Fox hired John Ford to direct a large-scale Western that would appeal to sophisticated audiences. *The Iron Horse* (1924) dramatized the construction of America's first transcontinental railroad during the 1860s. Running two and a half hours, it employed hundreds of extras and featured such historical figures as Abraham Lincoln, Wild Bill Hickok, and Buffalo Bill Cody. It ultimately earned a million dollars at the nation's box offices. Young leading man George O'Brien, a former Navy man and son of San Francisco's police chief, turned in a strikingly effective performance and won instant stardom. He specialized in Westerns and closed out his career in Ford's *Cheyenne Autumn* (1964).

Whether big or small, genre entries were marketed in the same way. Western posters from the twenties look remarkably similar, with those for personality-driven films boasting elaborately rendered portraits of the stars. Also, the names of cowboy heroes were lettered to assume more prominence in the design. Posters for the large-scale epics tended to feature imagery reflective of a film's theme: the *Iron Horse* one-sheet, for example, shows an Indian perched on a cliff, spying on the railroad construction gang far below. ✶

ABOVE LEFT: Maynard clowning around with frequent director Albert S. Rogell while on location for one of his well-mounted Westerns distributed by First National in the late twenties. Their effective collaboration—especially on *The Red Raiders* (1927)—made Ken one of the era's top cowboy stars.

ABOVE RIGHT: Taking a break during filming of *The Vanishing Pioneer* (Paramount, 1928) are leading man Jack Holt, principal heavy William Powell, and leading lady Sally Blane (sister of Loretta Young). Within a year, Powell would become a star and leave Westerns behind him.

METROPOLITAN THEATRE
WATERTOWN, S. DAK.
October 29-30-31 November 1-2
FIRST TIME AT POPULAR PRICES
JESSE L. LASKY Presents a
JAMES CRUZE
PRODUCTION
THE
COVERED WAGON
ADAPTED BY JACK CUNNINGHAM
FROM THE NOVEL BY EMERSON HOUGH
a Paramount Picture

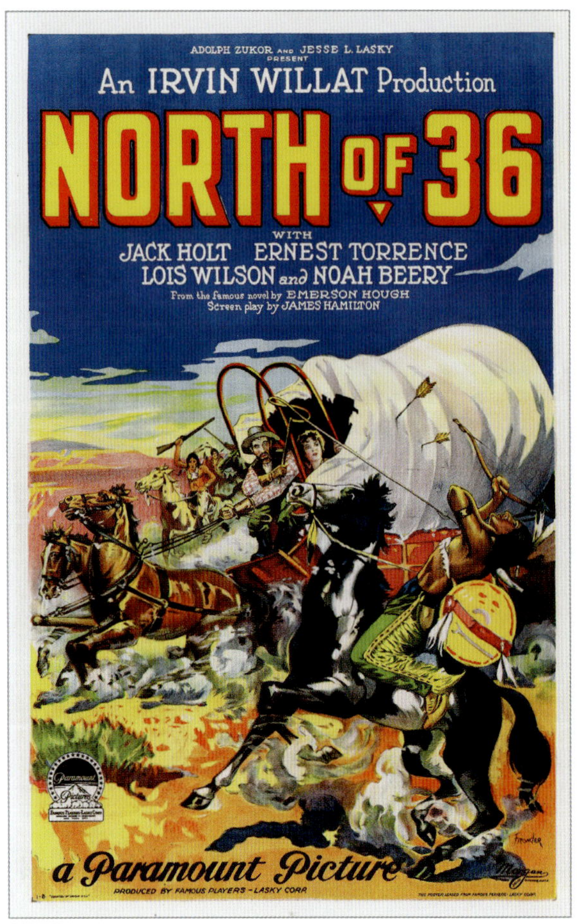
ADOLPH ZUKOR AND JESSE L. LASKY
PRESENT
An IRVIN WILLAT Production
NORTH OF 36
WITH
JACK HOLT ERNEST TORRENCE
LOIS WILSON and NOAH BEERY
From the famous novel by EMERSON HOUGH
Screen play by JAMES HAMILTON
a Paramount Picture
PRODUCED BY FAMOUS PLAYERS-LASKY CORP.

a Paramount Picture
JESSE L. LASKY presents a
JAMES CRUZE
production
The
Covered
Wagon
Adapted by Jack Cunningham
from the novel by Emerson Hough
"COUNTRY ORIGIN U.S.A."
THIS LOBBY DISPLAY LEASED FROM FAMOUS PLAYERS-LASKY CORP.

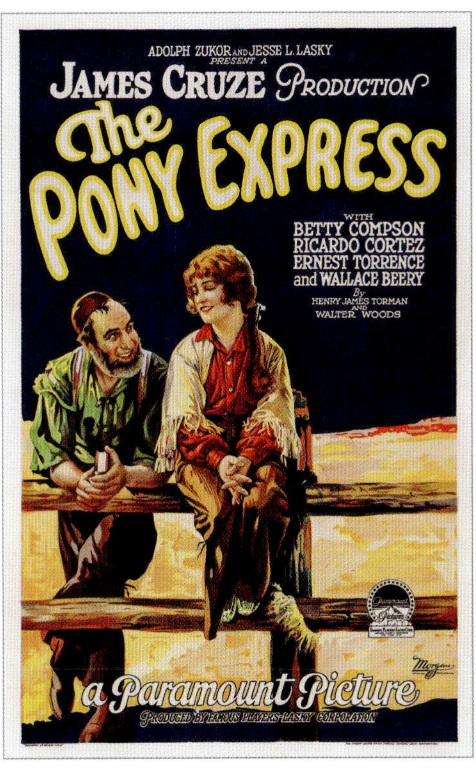
ADOLPH ZUKOR AND JESSE L. LASKY PRESENT A
JAMES CRUZE PRODUCTION
The PONY EXPRESS
WITH
BETTY COMPSON
RICARDO CORTEZ
ERNEST TORRENCE
and WALLACE BEERY
a Paramount Picture

UNIVERSAL PRODUCTION
CARL LAEMMLE Presents
"The FLAMING FRONTIER"
With HOOT GIBSON, DUSTIN FARNUM
ANNE CORNWALL, NOBLE JOHNSON
A Spectacular and Thrilling Drama of The Glorious West
AN EDWARD SEDGWICK PRODUCTION

Samuel Goldwyn presents
THE HENRY KING PRODUCTION
"The WINNING of BARBARA WORTH"
Adapted by Frances Marion from the novel by HAROLD BELL WRIGHT
RONALD COLMAN and VILMA BANKY
RELEASED BY UNITED ARTISTS CORP.

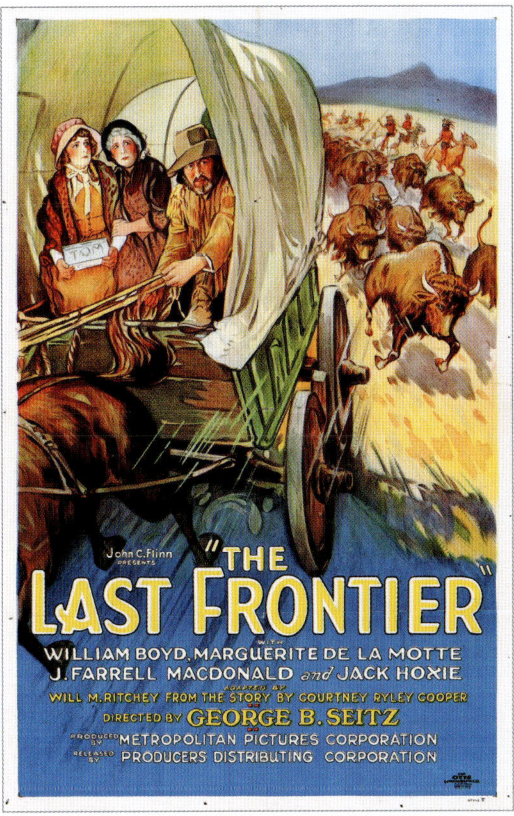
John C. Flinn PRESENTS
"THE LAST FRONTIER"
WILLIAM BOYD, MARGUERITE DE LA MOTTE
J. FARRELL MACDONALD and JACK HOXIE
WILL M. RITCHEY FROM THE STORY BY COURTNEY RYLEY COOPER
DIRECTED BY GEORGE B. SEITZ
METROPOLITAN PICTURES CORPORATION
PRODUCERS DISTRIBUTING CORPORATION

WILLIAM FOX Presents
3 BAD MEN

WRITER OF THE PURPLE PAGE

Ohio-born dentist Zane Grey began writing Western fiction during the twentieth century's first decade, and by the 1920s he was one of America's most popular authors, his novels routinely appearing in yearly lists of top-ten bestsellers. Hollywood began licensing movie rights to his yarns in 1917, and the twenties found competing studios Fox and Paramount producing film adaptations featuring such popular stars as Tom Mix, Gary Cooper, Richard Dix, and Jack Holt. Grey's contract with Paramount stipulated that their celluloid versions of his works had to be shot on location where the stories took place, pushing budgets above the $200,000 mark. The studio's 1924 adaptation of *Wanderer of the Wasteland* was filmed using the recently introduced Technicolor process, making it a prestige release and reinforcing Grey's status as an important box-office draw.

ADOLPH ZUKOR AND JESSE L. LASKY PRESENT
ZANE GREY'S
THE THUNDERING HERD
WITH
JACK HOLT, LOIS WILSON
NOAH BEERY and RAYMOND HATTON
SCREEN PLAY BY
LUCIEN HUBBARD
DIRECTED BY
WILLIAM HOWARD
a Paramount Picture
PRODUCED BY FAMOUS PLAYERS-LASKY CORP.
Morgan
Paramount Pictures
FAMOUS PLAYERS-LASKY CORP.
THIS POSTER LEASED FROM FAMOUS PLAYERS-LASKY CORP.

ADOLPH ZUKOR AND JESSE L. LASKY PRESENT
ZANE GREY'S
THE LIGHT OF WESTERN STARS
WITH
JACK HOLT, NOAH BEERY and BILLIE DOVE
SCREEN PLAY BY LUCIEN HUBBARD
DIRECTED BY WILLIAM K. HOWARD
a Paramount Picture
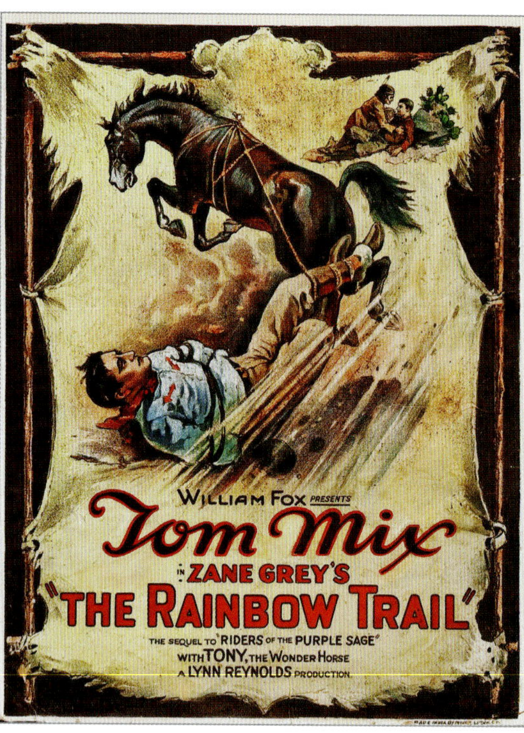
WILLIAM FOX PRESENTS
Tom Mix
IN ZANE GREY'S
"THE RAINBOW TRAIL"
THE SEQUEL TO "RIDERS OF THE PURPLE SAGE"
WITH TONY, THE WONDER HORSE
A LYNN REYNOLDS PRODUCTION
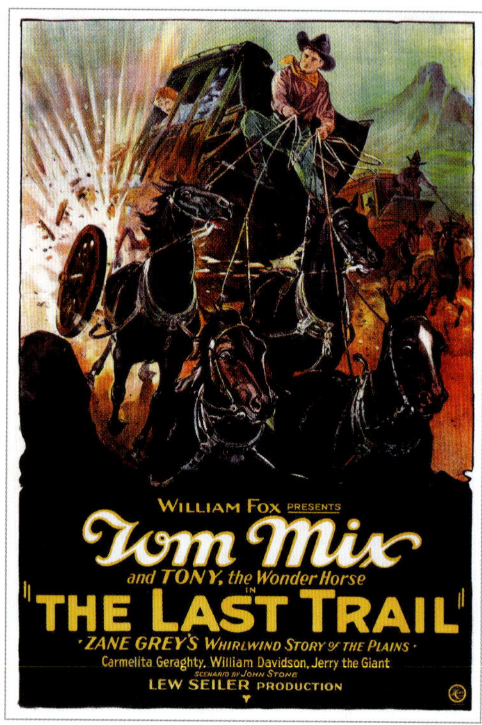
WILLIAM FOX PRESENTS
Tom Mix
and TONY, the Wonder Horse
IN
"THE LAST TRAIL"
ZANE GREY'S WHIRLWIND STORY OF THE PLAINS
Carmelita Geraghty, William Davidson, Jerry the Giant
SCENARIO BY JOHN STONE
LEW SEILER PRODUCTION

ADOLPH ZUKOR AND JESSE L. LASKY PRESENT
ZANE GREY'S
THE VANISHING AMERICAN
WITH
RICHARD DIX
LOIS WILSON, NOAH BEERY and MALCOLM McGREGOR
DIRECTED BY GEORGE B. SEITZ
ADAPTED BY LUCIEN HUBBARD
SCREEN PLAY BY ETHEL DOHERTY
a Paramount Picture
PRODUCED BY FAMOUS PLAYERS-LASKY CORP.

ZANE GREY'S "NEVADA"
a Paramount Picture
WITH GARY COOPER, THELMA TODD, WILLIAM POWELL AND PHILLIP STRANGE

A TALE OF THE WEST
AS ONLY ZANE GREY
CAN WRITE IT

TEEMING WITH THRILLS
—ROMANCE
—EXCITEMENT.

Adolph Zukor and Jesse L. Lasky
present

ZANE GREY'S

NEVADA

WITH

GARY COOPER, THELMA TODD,
WILLIAM POWELL and PHILLIP STRANGE

DIRECTED BY JOHN WATERS
FROM A NOVEL BY ZANE GREY
SCREEN PLAY BY JOHN STONE AND L.G. RIGBY.

Paramount Pictures

a Paramount Picture

RELEASED BY
FAMOUS LASKY FILM SERVICE LIMITED
Paramount Pictures
302 PITT ST SYDNEY AUSTRALIA
BRANCHES IN ALL STATES
N-Z FAMOUS LASKY FILM SERVICE (N.Z.) LTD
73 CUBA ST WELLINGTON.

THIS POSTER PRODUCED BY RICHARDSON STUDIO.

PRINTED BY W.E. SMITH LTD SYDNEY.

ZANE GREY'S

'UNDER THE TONTO RIM'

WITH

RICHARD ARLEN and MARY BRIAN

DIRECTED BY HERMAN C. RAYMAKER
FROM A NOVEL BY ZANE GREY
SCREEN PLAY BY J. WALTER RUBEN

A Paramount Picture

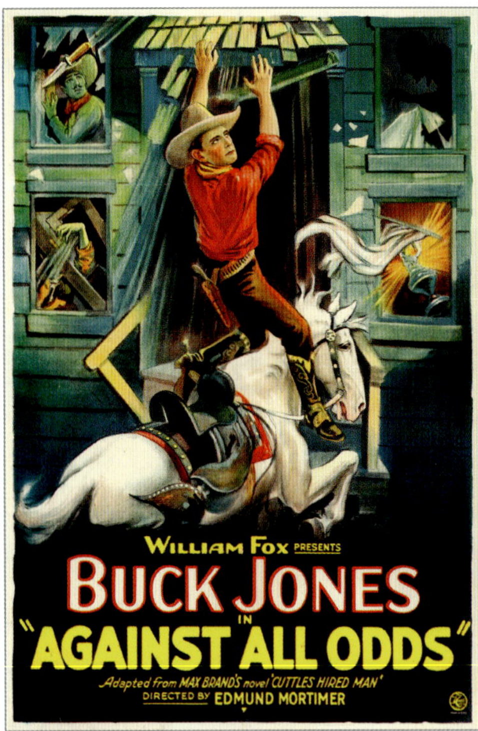

TOP HANDS

Although Tom Mix was the undisputed king of the Hollywood range, the Roaring Twenties saw the rise of many other cowboy stars eager to usurp his throne. Race car driver and Wild West show performer Charles Gebhart was rechristened Buck Jones and signed by William Fox as a possible replacement for Mix. Jones exhibited a flair for comedy and often made lighthearted Westerns. Former US Cavalry officer Tim McCoy, on the other hand, had a somewhat dour screen presence but impressed horse-opera fans with his sober attitude and military bearing. He started with MGM but was dropped by the studio when talkies came in and briefly depressed the market for outdoor action pictures. The aforementioned Ken Maynard hit his stride while associated with First National, his popularity surpassed only by that of Mix and Jones; Hoot Gibson became one of Universal's top stars, and his jocular Westerns often secured bookings in prestige big-city theaters.

William Fox presents
Buck Jones
in
'The Timber Wolf'
A Romance of a Man Feared and Loved
Story by Jackson Gregory
Directed by W. S. Van Dyke

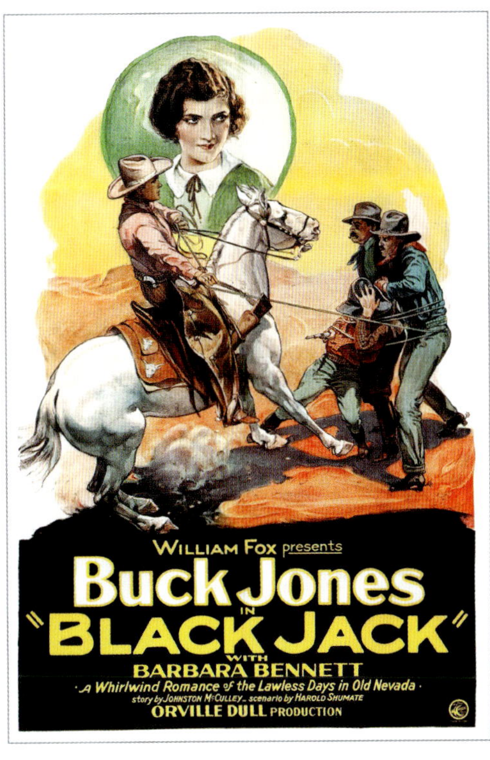
WILLIAM FOX presents
Buck Jones
IN
"BLACK JACK"
WITH
BARBARA BENNETT
A Whirlwind Romance of the Lawless Days in Old Nevada
ORVILLE DULL PRODUCTION

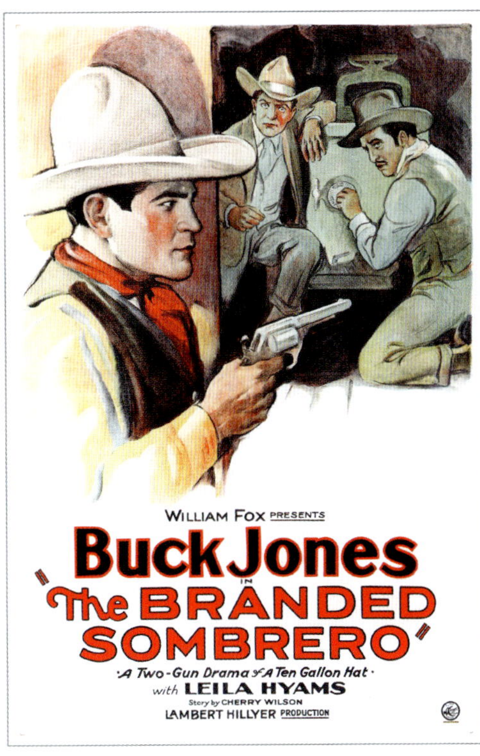
WILLIAM FOX PRESENTS
Buck Jones
IN
"The BRANDED SOMBRERO"
A Two-Gun Drama of A Ten Gallon Hat
with LEILA HYAMS
Story by CHERRY WILSON
LAMBERT HILLYER PRODUCTION

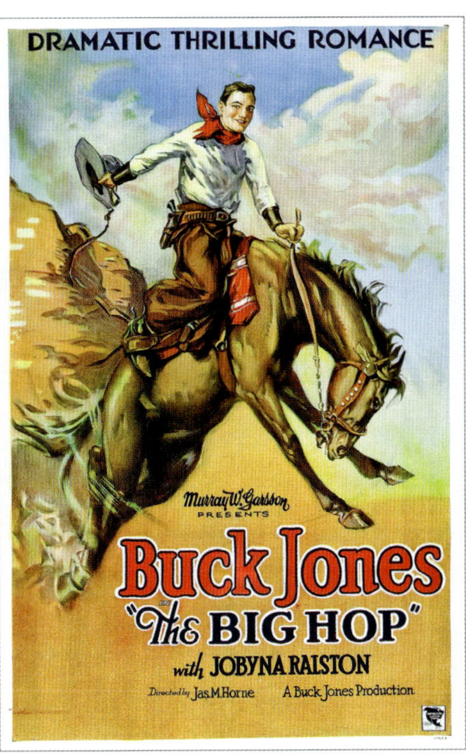
DRAMATIC THRILLING ROMANCE
Murray W. Garsson
PRESENTS
Buck Jones
"The BIG HOP"
with JOBYNA RALSTON
Directed by Jas. M. Horne
A Buck Jones Production

PETER B. KYNE'S
WAR PAINT
Continuity by
CHARLES MAIGNE
Titles by
JOE FARNHAM
with
TIM McCOY
PAULINE STARKE
KARL DANE
Directed by
W. S.
VAN DYKE
A
Metro-Goldwyn-Mayer
PICTURE

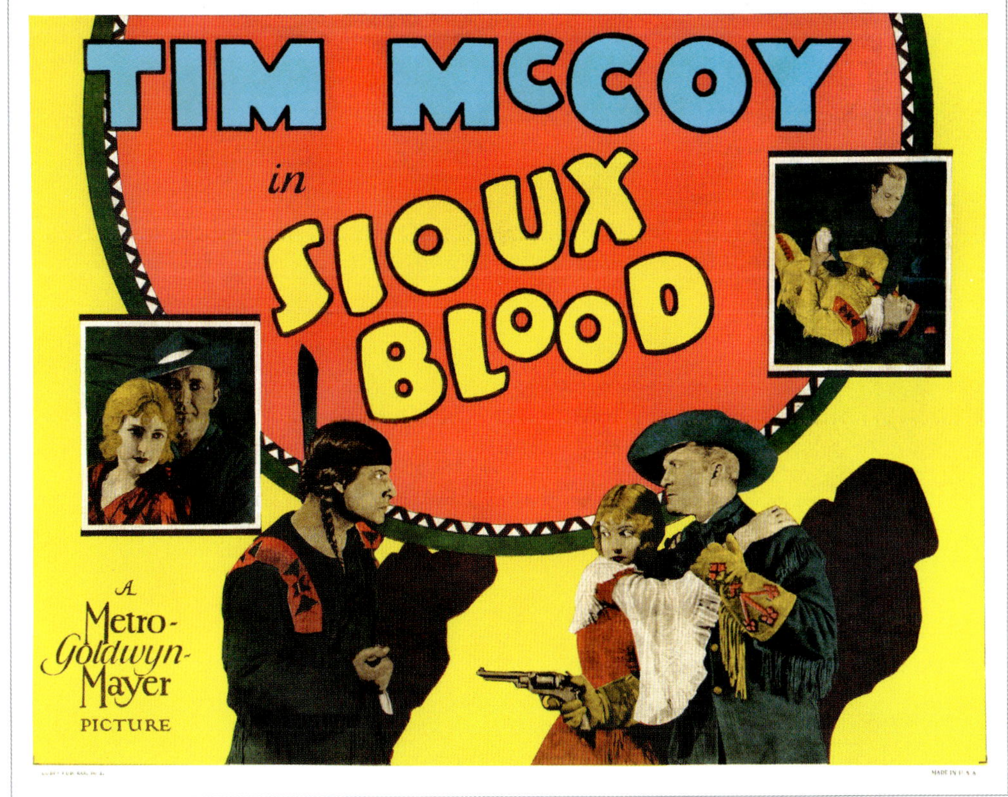
TIM McCOY
in
SIOUX BLOOD
A
Metro-Goldwyn-Mayer
PICTURE

A FIRST NATIONAL PICTURE
CHARLES R·ROGERS presents
KEN MAYNARD
IN
The UNKNOWN CAVALIER
With KATHLEEN COLLINS Screen adaptation by MARION JACKSON
FROM THE STORY "RIDE HIM, COWBOY" by KENNETH PERKINS
Directed by ALBERT ROGELL
Produced under management _ HARRY J·BROWN

KEN MAYNARD
Presented by CHARLES R·ROGERS
IN
The GLORIOUS TRAIL
Story by MARION JACKSON
Directed by ALBERT ROGELL
Supervised by HARRY J·BROWN
A First National Picture

CHARLES R·ROGERS presents
Ken Maynard
IN
THE LAND BEYOND THE LAW
Story and Adaptation by MARION JACKSON
Directed by .... HARRY J·BROWN
A FIRST NATIONAL PICTURE . . .

CHARLES R. ROGERS presents
KEN MAYNARD
IN
The Overland Stage
With
KATHLEEN COLLINS
Story by
MARION JACKSON
DIRECTED BY
ALBERT ROGELL
PRODUCED UNDER MANAGEMENT
HARRY J. BROWN
A FIRST NATIONAL PICTURE

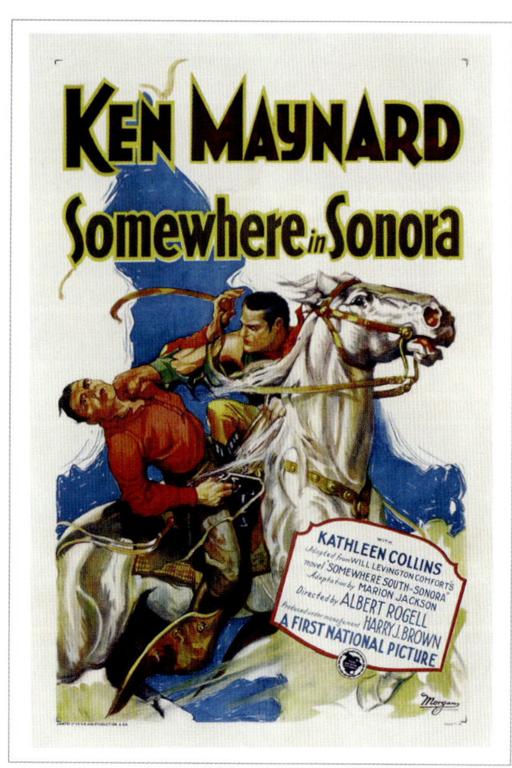
KEN MAYNARD
Somewhere in Sonora
WITH
KATHLEEN COLLINS
Adapted from WILL LEVINGTON COMFORT'S
novel "SOMEWHERE SOUTH in SONORA"
Adaptation by MARION JACKSON
Directed by ALBERT ROGELL
Produced under management HARRY J. BROWN
A FIRST NATIONAL PICTURE
Morgan

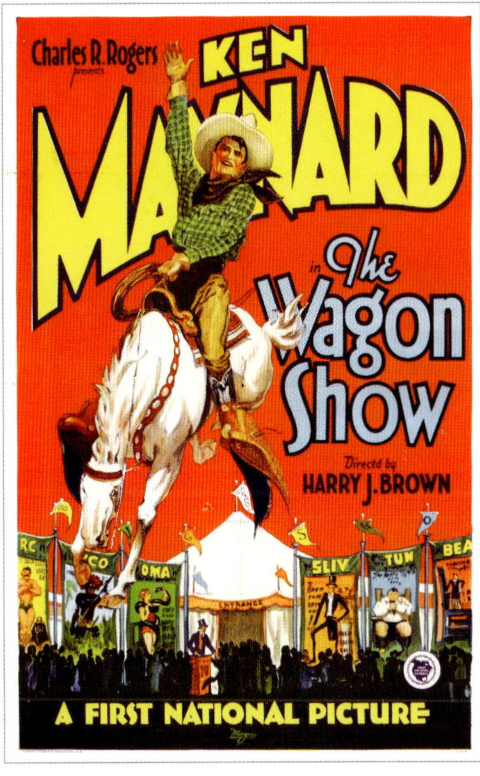
Charles R. Rogers presents
KEN MAYNARD
in The Wagon Show
Directed by HARRY J. BROWN
A FIRST NATIONAL PICTURE

CARL LAEMMLE Presents
HOOT GIBSON
-IN-
"The SAWDUST TRAIL"
FROM A SATURDAY EVENING POST STORY "COURTIN' CALAMITY" by Wm DUDLEY PELLEY
DIRECTED BY EDWARD SEDGWICK
UNIVERSAL GIBSON PRODUCTION

UNIVERSAL-WESTERN
Hoot Gibson
IN
SOME SHOOTER
Directed by HOOT GIBSON

UNIVERSAL-WESTERN
HOOT GIBSON
in THE SHOOTIN' KID
DIRECTED BY HOOT GIBSON

CARL LAEMMLE
presents
HOOT GIBSON
in "The Denver Dude"
Story by Earle Snell
Directed by Reeves Eason
UNIVERSAL-JEWEL

HOOT GIBSON
AS THE SMILING TERROR
IN
"The DOUBLE HOLD-UP"
WITH JOSEPHINE HILL
DIRECTED BY PHIL ROSEN
It's A Universal Western

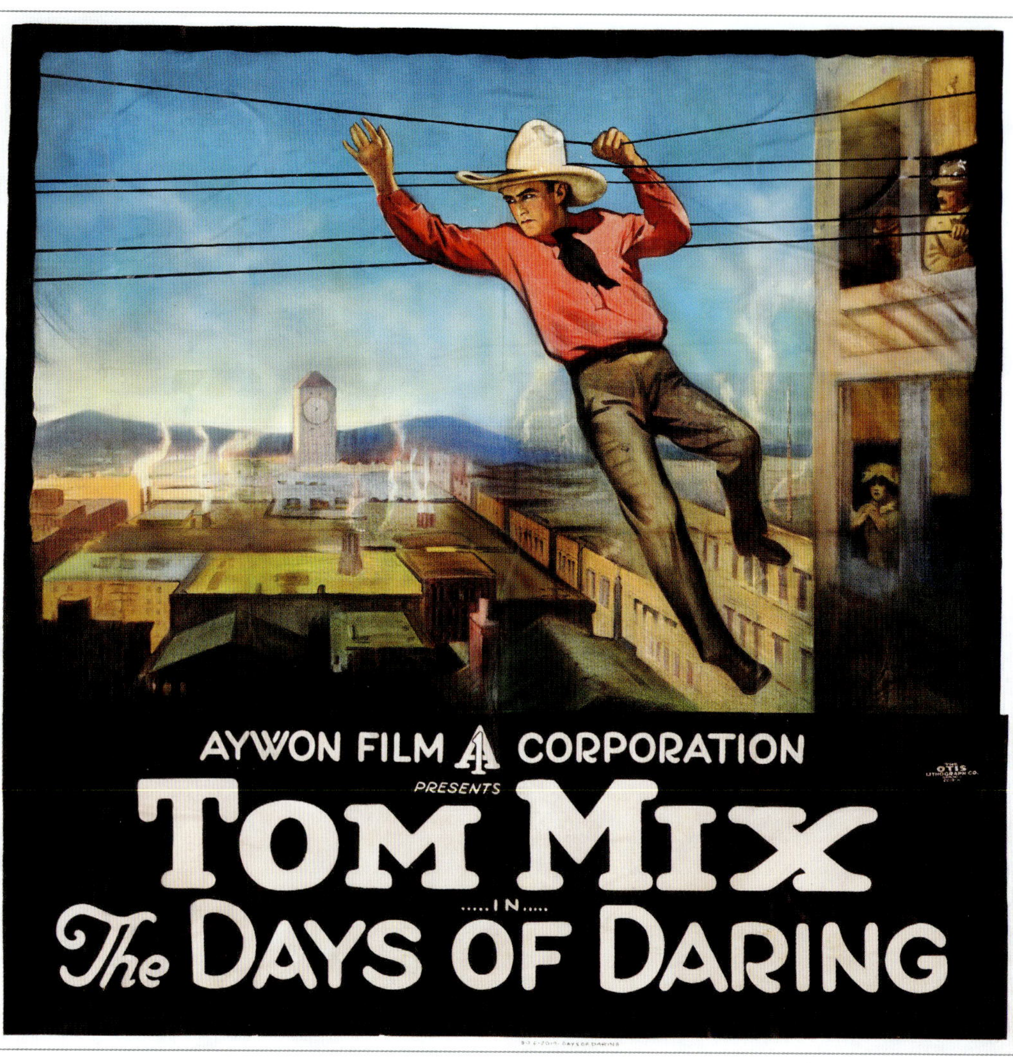

TOM MIX, KING COWBOY

The 1920s were Mix's golden age. With the steady fading of William S. Hart's star in the decade's early years, Tom increased his hold on the nation's moviegoers—especially the young ones. The budgets for his pictures steadily increased, eventually reaching $200,000 per film. This allowed for extensive location shooting, artistic cinematography, and the purchase of top-drawer literary properties for adaptation, including novels by Zane Grey and Max Brand, the two most popular Western fictioneers. Notwithstanding their lavish production values, the main attraction in a Tom Mix film was always Tom Mix, whose outsized personality and flamboyant stunting kept him in a class of his own. No other cowboy star eclipsed him in popularity during the silent-movie era; for several years, he drew a weekly salary of $10,000. Leaving Fox Film Corp. in 1928 for minor studio FBO was a miscalculation, but it was the coming of sound that finally dislodged the King Cowboy from his throne.

WILLIAM FOX
PRESENTS
Tom Mix
and Tony-the Wonder Horse ~ in
THE ARIZONA WILDCAT
with DOROTHY SEBASTIAN
BEN BARD — CISSY FITZGERALD
Story by ADELA ROGERS ST. JOHNS
Scenario by JOHN STONE
R. WILLIAM NEILL PRODUCTION

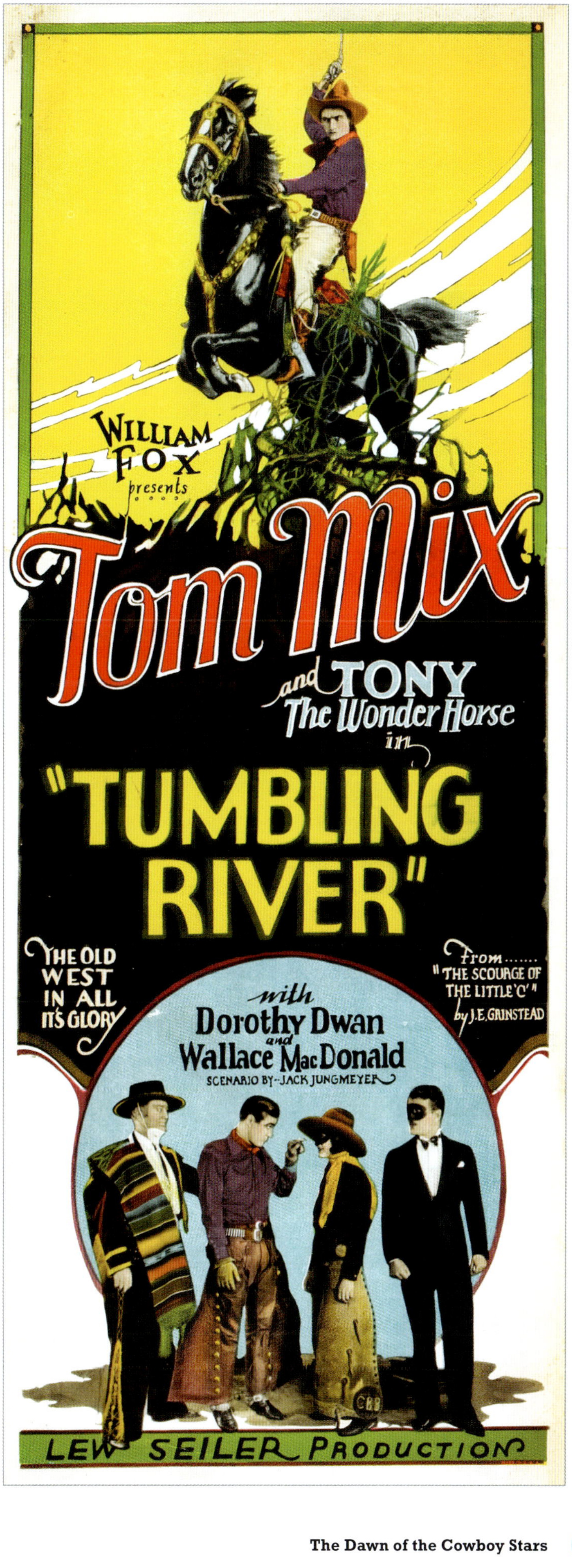

WILLIAM FOX
presents
Tom Mix
and TONY
The Wonder Horse
in
"TUMBLING RIVER"
THE OLD WEST IN ALL ITS GLORY
From "THE SCOURGE OF THE LITTLE 'C'" by J.E. GRINSTEAD
with
Dorothy Dwan
and
Wallace MacDonald
SCENARIO BY JACK JUNGMEYER
LEW SEILER PRODUCTION

WILLIAM FOX
PRESENTS
Tom Mix
and TONY, the Wonder Horse
in
"PAINTED POST"
Powder Puffs Win Against Six Shooters in a Battle of Love
with NATALIE KINGSTON
Story by HARRY SINCLAIR DRAGO — Scenario by BUCKLEIGH S. OXFORD
GENE FORDE PRODUCTION

WILLIAM FOX PRESENTS
Tom Mix
and TONY, the Wonder Horse in
"HELLO CHEYENNE!"
A Daredevil Cowboy Helps Modernize the West
Story by HARRY SINCLAIR DRAGO — Scenario by FRED KENNEDY MYTON
GENE FORDE PRODUCTION

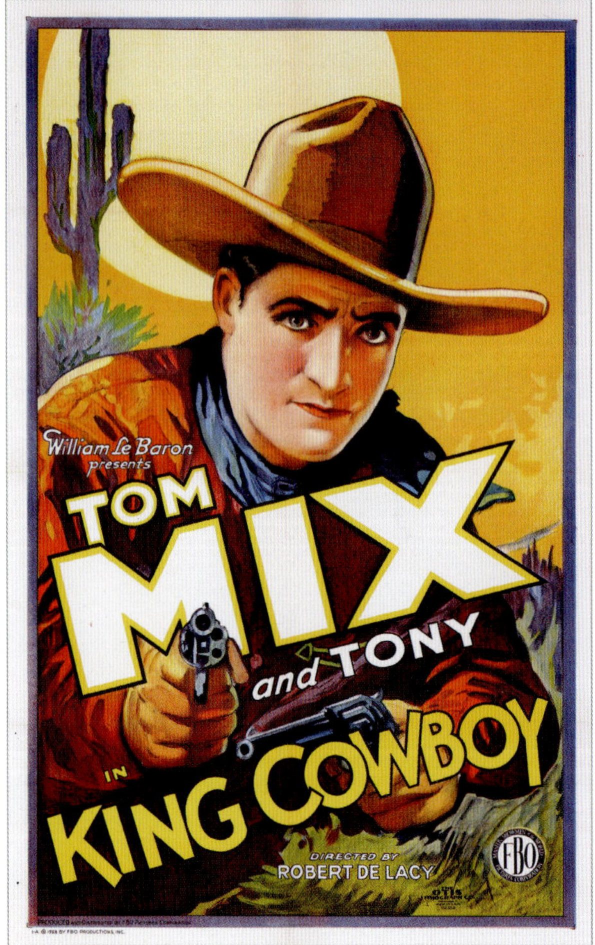
William Le Baron
presents
TOM
MIX
and TONY
IN
KING COWBOY
DIRECTED BY
ROBERT DE LACY
FBO

TOM
MIX CIRCUS
TOM MIX "himself" and TONY
WILL POSITIVELY APPEAR AT EACH PERFORMANCE

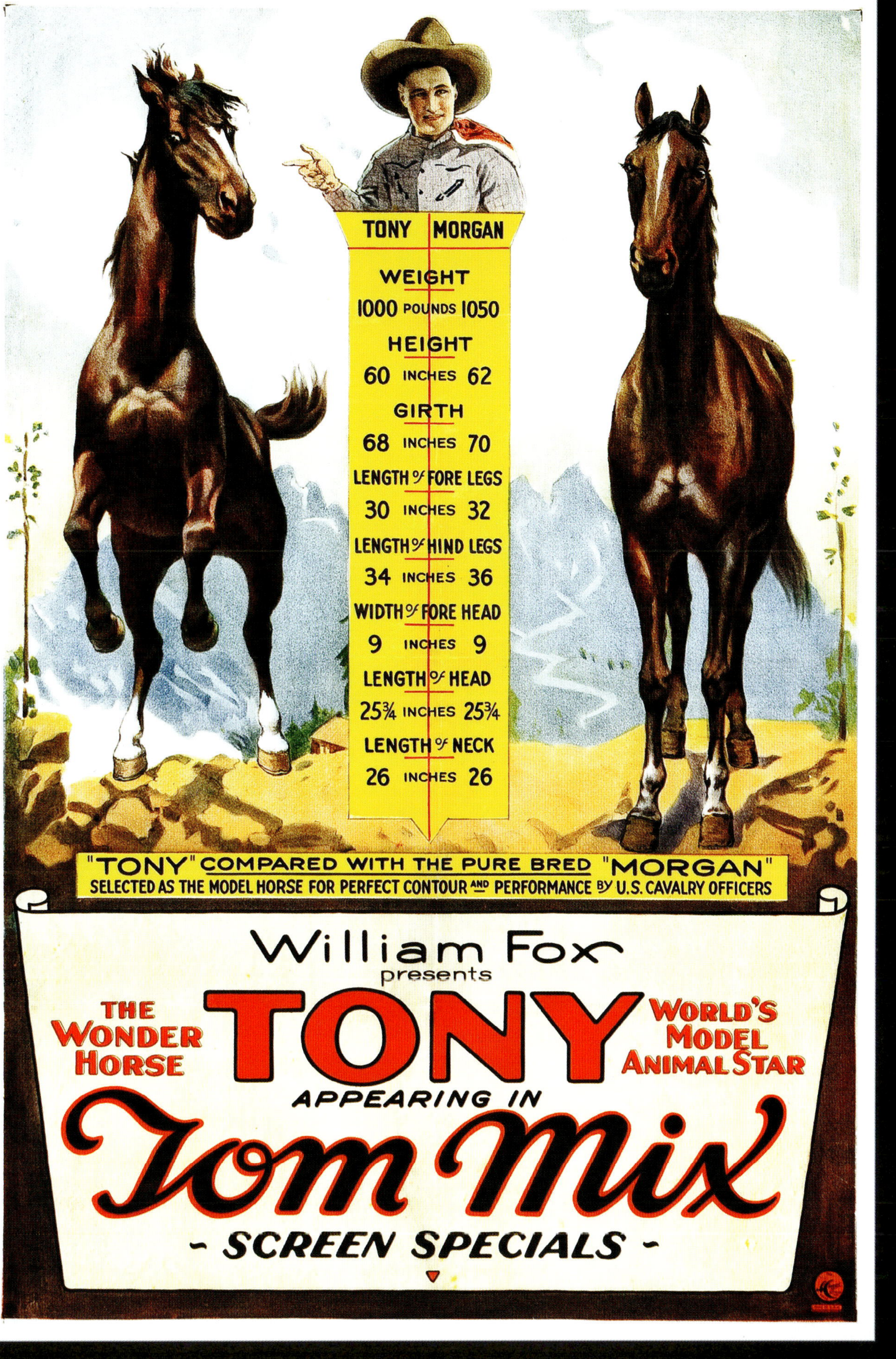
TONY
MORGAN
WEIGHT
1000 POUNDS 1050
HEIGHT
60 INCHES 62
GIRTH
68 INCHES 70
LENGTH OF FORE LEGS
30 INCHES 32
LENGTH OF HIND LEGS
34 INCHES 36
WIDTH OF FORE HEAD
9 INCHES 9
LENGTH OF HEAD
25¾ INCHES 25¾
LENGTH OF NECK
26 INCHES 26
"TONY" COMPARED WITH THE PURE BRED "MORGAN"
SELECTED AS THE MODEL HORSE FOR PERFECT CONTOUR AND PERFORMANCE BY U.S. CAVALRY OFFICERS
William Fox
presents
THE WONDER HORSE
TONY
WORLD'S MODEL ANIMAL STAR
APPEARING IN
Tom Mix
- SCREEN SPECIALS -

MEMBERS OF THE POSSE

While Mix, Jones, Maynard, et al. dominated the marketplace for Western movies, the demand for sagebrush sagas was so enormous during the twenties that even the most modestly talented performers could find work as long as they looked good in a Stetson and could sit a horse without toppling from the saddle. Among the second tier of cowboy stars, Fred Thomson was easily the most promising. Handsome and athletic, the former college football star and US Army chaplain supported Mary Pickford in a 1922 film before signing with FBO to star in low-budget oats operas. Thomson eventually became a Western star for Paramount but died prematurely in 1928. None of his competitors—among them screen veterans Harry Carey, Neal Hart, and Leo Maloney, as well as newcomers Tom Tyler, Bob Steele, Bob Custer, and Buddy Roosevelt—achieved the same degree of success, although many worked in the genre for several decades.

Pathé
presents
LEO MALONEY in
Two-Gun of the Tumbleweed
by
ROBERT J. HORTON
Screen Version by
FORD I. BEEBE
Pathépicture

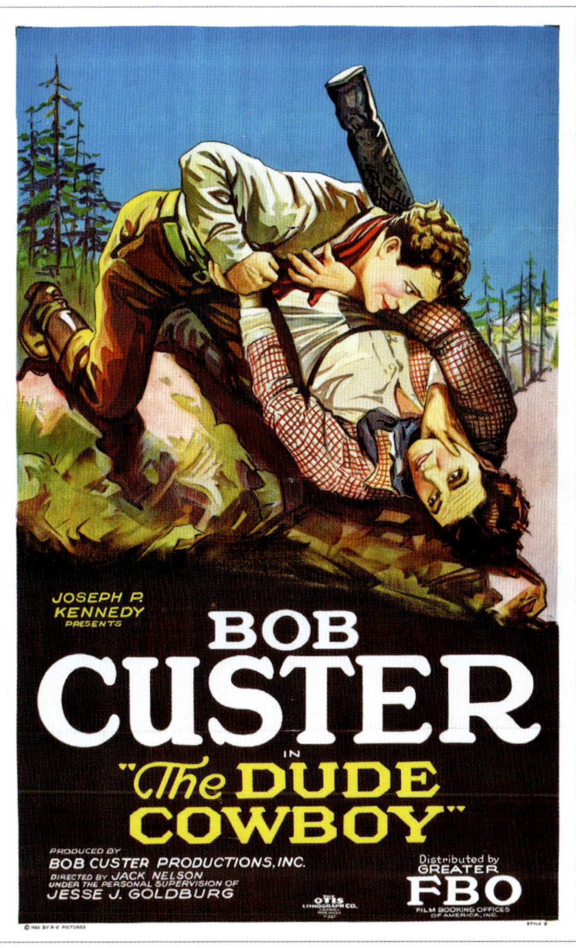
JOSEPH P. KENNEDY PRESENTS
BOB CUSTER
IN
"The DUDE COWBOY"
PRODUCED BY
BOB CUSTER PRODUCTIONS, INC.
DIRECTED BY JACK NELSON
UNDER THE PERSONAL SUPERVISION OF
JESSE J. GOLDBURG
Distributed by
GREATER
FBO
FILM BOOKING OFFICES OF AMERICA, INC.

LESTER F. SCOTT, JR.
PRESENTS
BUDDY ROOSEVELT
IN
"CODE OF THE COW COUNTRY"
Directed by OSCAR APFEL ~ Story by WILTON WEST ~ Continuity by BETTY BURBRIDGE
Produced by ACTION PICTURES, INC.
Pathépicture

A BLUE STREAK WESTERN
JACK HOXIE
WITH HIS WONDER-HORSE "SCOUT"
AND HIS DOG-PAL "REX"
in
"The WILD HORSE STAMPEDE"
Directed by CLIFFORD SMITH
Story by CHAS. LOGUE

THE WESTERN WHIRLWIND AND HIS WHIZZING PALS IN HIS FASTEST ACTION PICTURE!
FBO PRESENTS
TOM TYLER WITH HIS PALS
IN
"The COWBOY COP"
STORY BY FRANK RICHARDSON PIERCE
DIRECTED BY ROBERT DE LACEY

W. RAY JOHNSTON presents
Jack Perrin
IN
"SILENT SHELDON"
A "WHIRLWIND WESTERN" with
JOSEPHINE HILL, MARTIN TURNER and "STARLIGHT"
A Harry Webb Production

WILLIAM STEINER PRODUCTIONS
PRESENTS
NEAL HART
IN
TANGLED TRAILS
THE TIGER – GETS HIS PREY
A STIRRING TALE OF THE GREAT NORTHWEST

Farrah
JOSEPH P. KENNEDY presents
BOB Steele
IN
The RIDING RENEGADE
DIRECTED BY WALLACE FOX
FROM THE STORY BY FRANK HOWARD CLARK

Hunt Stromberg
presents
THE OTIS LITHOGRAPH CO.
HARRY CAREY
IN
"THE NIGHT HAWK"
A HUNT STROMBERG PRODUCTION
Directed by STUART PATON
Produced by
STELLAR PRODUCTIONS, INC.
CHARLES R. ROGERS, VICE PRES.
Distributed by
HODKINSON PICTURES

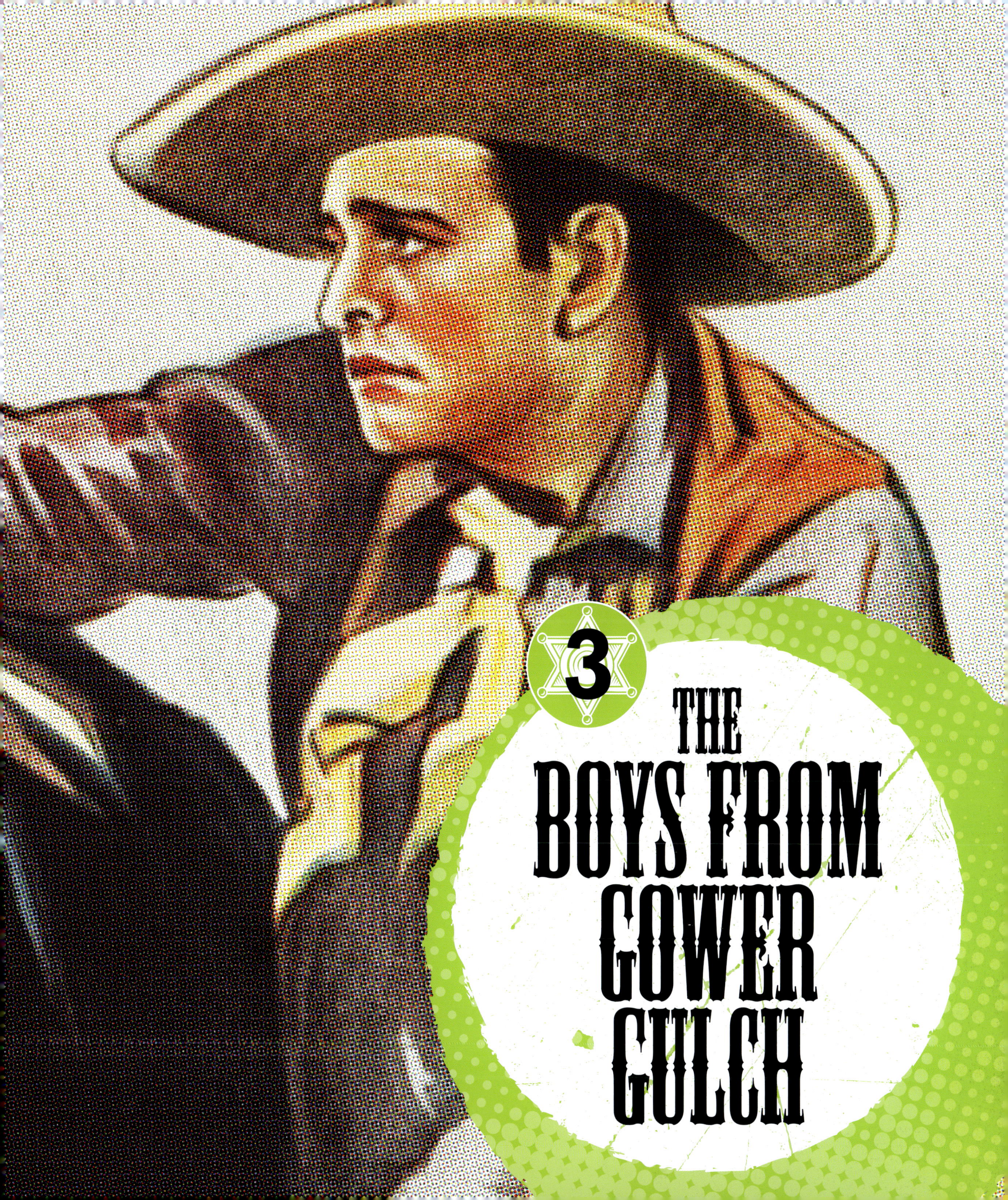
3
THE
BOYS FROM
GOWER
GULCH

THE POVERTY ROW COWBOYS

The talking-picture era is ushered in along with the Great Depression. Cash-strapped patrons want more for their money, so exhibitors are forced to adopt a "double feature" policy, pairing a more expensive "A" movie with a less expensive "B." Small-town theaters, catering to a working-class clientele, obtain many of their Westerns from the shoestring producers operating along Hollywood's "Poverty Row," home to cowboy heroes of minor stature . . .

BELOW: Jack Perrin top-lined Western movies as far back as 1919, but true stardom eluded him, even though he occasionally played leads in Poverty Row horse operas well into the thirties. But at the same time, he took bit parts for little money and no billing, a reflection of Depression-induced anxiety.

OPPOSITE: Lane Chandler's career started promisingly—he played opposite "it girl" Clara Bow at Paramount—but 1931 found him on Poverty Row, making ultracheap oaters for indie producer Willis Kent. The abortive 1934 *Phantom Rider* series (two entries only) finished him as a Western star.

The Depression couldn't have come at a worse time for motion-picture exhibitors. Not only were they losing the patronage of newly unemployed regulars, they also had in recent years spent considerable amounts of money wiring their theaters for sound. A sizable number of them had trouble keeping their heads above water, and indeed thousands of them were submerged beneath waves of debt. By late 1931, some four thousand American movie theaters had shuttered, many for good.

The situation was equally dicey for producers and distributors. Major studios owned large theater chains and managed huge picture palaces in downtown areas of the big cities. Although the likes of MGM, Paramount, Fox, and Warner Bros. were better capitalized, they too had taken on debt related to outfitting their houses for sound. Moreover, in reaction to rapidly deteriorating business conditions, these high-end venues were forced to reduce admission prices, making it increasingly difficult to pay the mortgages on their expensive theaters. In fact, failure to meet their financial obligations drove several majors into receivership. While restructuring their debt, these companies temporarily cut back on production, creating new opportunities for plucky hand-to-mouth independent producers—especially those corralled in a small area of Hollywood known as "Poverty Row."

The Row's original epicenter was the intersection of Gower Street and Sunset Boulevard. On one corner stood the first permanent studio established in Tinseltown, a converted roadhouse where short films were made during the prewar years. On another was the plant for what would become Columbia Pictures. Around the corner sat the old Universal lot, active during the early

EMPIRE FILM DISTRIBUTORS Presents
LANE CHANDLER
IN The "OUTLAW TAMER"
with
JANET MORGAN
CHARLES WHITTAKER
BENNY CORBETT
GEORGE S. HAYES
story by
J. WESLEY PATTERSON
directed by
J. P. McGOWAN
an
H. & H. PRODUCTION
A KINEMATRADE RELEASE
THE PHANTOM RIDER SERIES
EMPIRE FILM DISTRIBUTORS INC.
COPYRIGHT by EMPIRE FILM DISTRIBUTORS INC.
LITHO in U.S.A.

teens before studio president Carl Laemmle bought the 260-acre tract that in 1915 became Universal City. The area was a hotbed of low-budget production activity generated by maverick filmmakers often referred to as "coffee-and-cake producers," because that was about all they could afford to buy on their meager profits.

The largest companies not only had their own exhibition outlets but also maintained worldwide networks of distribution. Nearly three dozen of the largest cities in America boasted major-studio branch offices, known as "exchanges." From these branches flowed the prints projected first in the downtown picture palaces, then in "subsequent-run houses" of progressively smaller size, located in bedroom communities, suburbs, and small towns. Poverty Row producers—lacking the resources of Fox, Paramount, and the other big concerns—couldn't afford their own exchanges and sales staffs, much less a nationwide chain of theaters. So, they contracted with independent regional exchange owners to distribute their product via what was called the "state rights" method. Producers licensed their films to these subdistributors on a territorial basis, granting them exclusive rights to rent movies to theaters within fixed geographical limits. Most territories consisted of complete states, but some—especially west of the Mississippi—were stitched together from parts of several states. Subdistributors paid producers a fixed amount for distribution rights, either in perpetuity or for a contractually specified period of time. Canny producers with proven track records of delivering films on schedule occasionally persuaded state-rights distributors to advance money toward future production, reducing and often eliminating their need to secure short-term bank loans.

At that time, Westerns were the cheapest movies that Poverty Row producers could make. Since they took place mostly outdoors, horse operas seldom required soundstage rentals. And that meant saving money on interior set construction, prop rentals, and elaborate lighting. Most Western-movie bit players wore their own clothes, saving money on costume rentals. Such performers congregated in front of a Gower Street drugstore with a pay phone. Producers needing extras on short notice need only place a call to that pharmacy to get all the extras, riders, and stunt performers they required.

To put the scale of production in proper perspective, in 1932, Metro-Goldwyn-Mayer spent over $700,000 on its all-star drama *Grand Hotel*, which played in the country's best theaters and handily turned a profit even in the depths of the Depression. The most lavish Poverty Row picture made during that same year might cost $40,000–$50,000. The average B Western produced by the denizens of "Gower Gulch" was brought in for $10,000, with many costing far less.

Cheapie Westerns of this period almost exclusively starred second-tier cowboy heroes who had started their careers in the twenties, during the silent era, and weathered the nerve-wracking transition to talking pictures late in the decade. Lacking the star power of a Tom Mix or a Buck Jones, they considered themselves lucky to be employed at all. A few, notably veteran leading man Jack Perrin, took starring roles when they could get them but also accepted

ABOVE: A functional illiterate, Jack Hoxie enjoyed popularity in the silent era, but he was undone in talkies by his inability to properly read scripts and memorize dialogue. He struggled through six Poverty Row quickies (*Gun Law* was the best of a bad lot) before retiring from the screen in 1933.

OPPOSITE TOP: Bill Cody was another marginal Western star who, thanks to the genre's popularity, had opportunities his meager talent didn't really warrant. Here he is with horse Chico in 1934, on location in Lone Pine's Alabama Hills for the shooting of *Frontier Days*.

OPPOSITE BOTTOM: Real-life cowboy Bob Custer starred in mid-twenties Westerns for FBO, skating by on his superficial resemblance to Tom Mix. But the advent of sound revealed that he was a terrible actor who delivered lines in a soporific monotone. He made only two more films after *Ambush Valley* (1936).

character parts if they were offered. Things were tough all over, as a popular saying of the time went, and it was risky to turn down a day's work.

The Row's filmmakers eschewed production niceties and cut corners wherever possible, but they didn't stint on marketing materials. The movies themselves might have looked cheesy, but the posters, pressbooks, and lobby cards were designed and printed carefully. Without the large art departments maintained by the major studios, coffee-and-cake producers were forced to farm out their marketing materials to independent artists and ad agencies specializing in freelance work of that type. In most cases, as you'll see in the coming pages, Poverty Row Western posters equaled those turned out by better-heeled studios. And for good reason.

Poverty Row Westerns generally played at Saturday matinees in small-town venues, especially in the South and Midwest. In larger cities they were most frequently exhibited in "scratch houses" and "shooting galleries"—old, run-down, none-too-clean theaters that charged only a dime for admission and exclusively booked double- and triple-feature programs run all day and in some cases all night as well. Vivid posters were deemed vitally important to lure customers into these marginal houses. And since the Gower Gulch outfits produced hundreds of cheap Westerns during the thirties, it's clear those posters proved effective. ✸

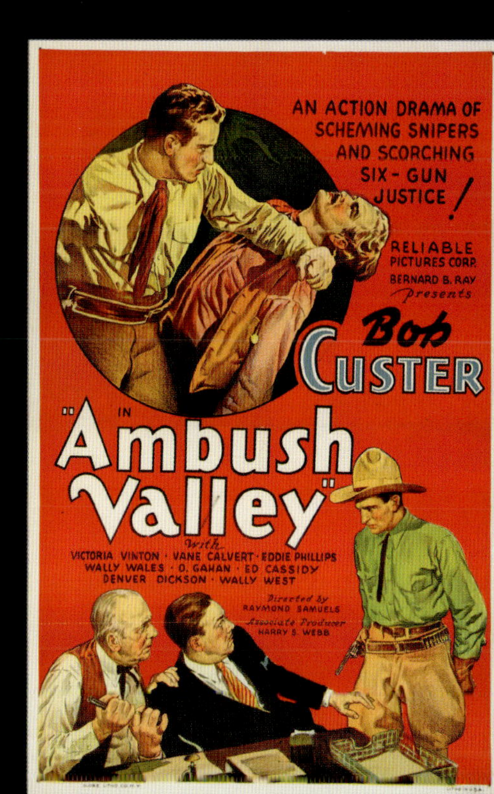

RIDERS OF GOWER GULCH

Poverty Row producers turned out Westerns consistently during the Depression because they didn't cost much to make and could almost always be counted upon to return a small profit, no matter how ineptly they were put together. The stars of such films were generally newcomers on the way up or old-timers on the way down. All had one thing in common: they were willing to work cheap. Boyishly handsome Rex Bell starred in an eight-picture series for Monogram and a six-picture series for Resolute before quitting Hollywood. Noah Beery Jr. and Fred Kohler Jr., sons of well-known Western heavies, had leads in a few films before settling into supporting roles. During the thirties, many genre veterans worked for Gower Gulch impresarios on their descent to the bottom of Hollywood's food chain, among them Hoot Gibson, Tim McCoy, Harry Carey, and Jack Hoxie. Some fared better than others, gradually fading from the public eye with their dignity intact.

SUNSET STUDIOS Ltd.
Presents
Noah
BEERY, JR.
in
"FIVE BAD MEN"
FEATURING
BILL PATTON
BUFFALO BILL Jr.
WALLY WALES
PETE MORRISON
ART MIX
AND AN ALL-STAR CAST
Directed by
CLIFFORD S. SMITH
Photographed by
PAUL EAGLER, A.S.C.

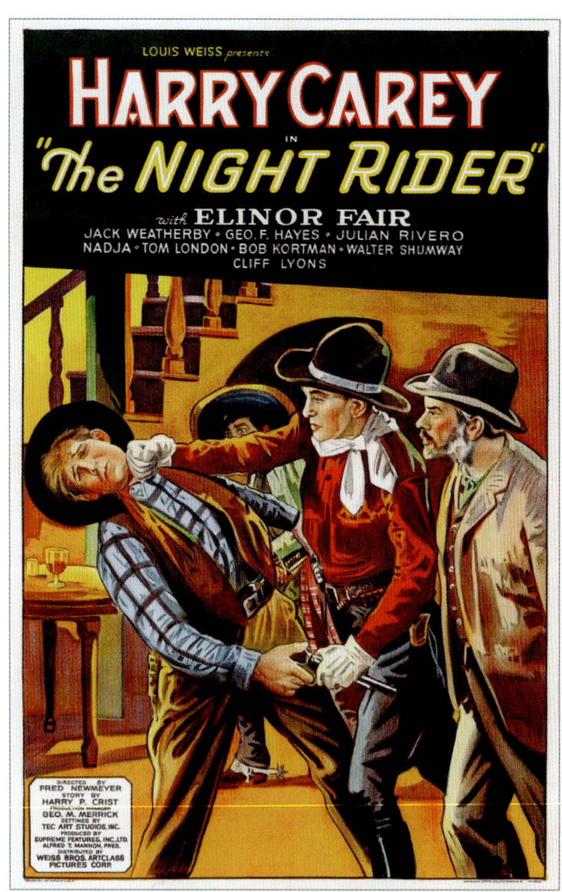
LOUIS WEISS presents
HARRY CAREY
IN
"The NIGHT RIDER"
with ELINOR FAIR
JACK WEATHERBY • GEO. F. HAYES • JULIAN RIVERO
NADJA • TOM LONDON • BOB KORTMAN • WALTER SHUMWAY
CLIFF LYONS
DIRECTED BY
FRED NEWMEYER
STORY BY
HARRY P. CRIST
GEO. M. MERRICK
SETTINGS BY
TEC ART STUDIOS, INC.
PRODUCED BY
SUPREME FEATURES, INC., LTD.
ALFRED T. MANNON, PRES.
DISTRIBUTED BY
WEISS BROS. ARTCLASS
PICTURES CORP.

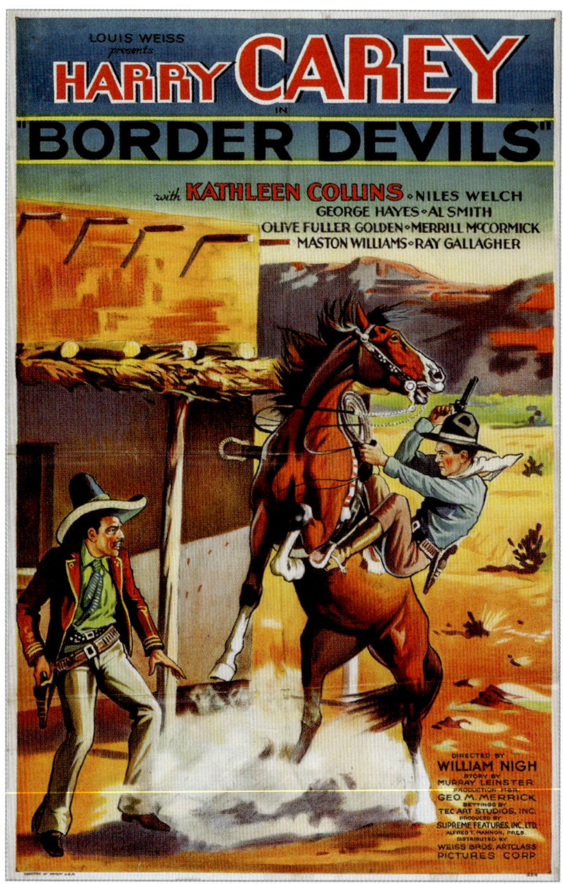
LOUIS WEISS
presents
HARRY CAREY
IN
"BORDER DEVILS"
with KATHLEEN COLLINS • NILES WELCH
GEORGE HAYES • AL SMITH
OLIVE FULLER GOLDEN • MERRILL McCORMICK
MASTON WILLIAMS • RAY GALLAGHER
DIRECTED BY
WILLIAM NIGH
STORY BY
MURRAY LEINSTER
PRODUCTION MGR.
GEO. M. MERRICK
SETTINGS BY
TEC ART STUDIOS, INC.
PRODUCED BY
SUPREME FEATURES, INC., LTD.
ALFRED T. MANNON, PRES.
DISTRIBUTED BY
WEISS BROS. ARTCLASS
PICTURES CORP.

WILLIS KENT presents
Lane CHANDLER
in
"The BATTLING BUCKAROO"
Directed by ...
OLIVER DRAKE

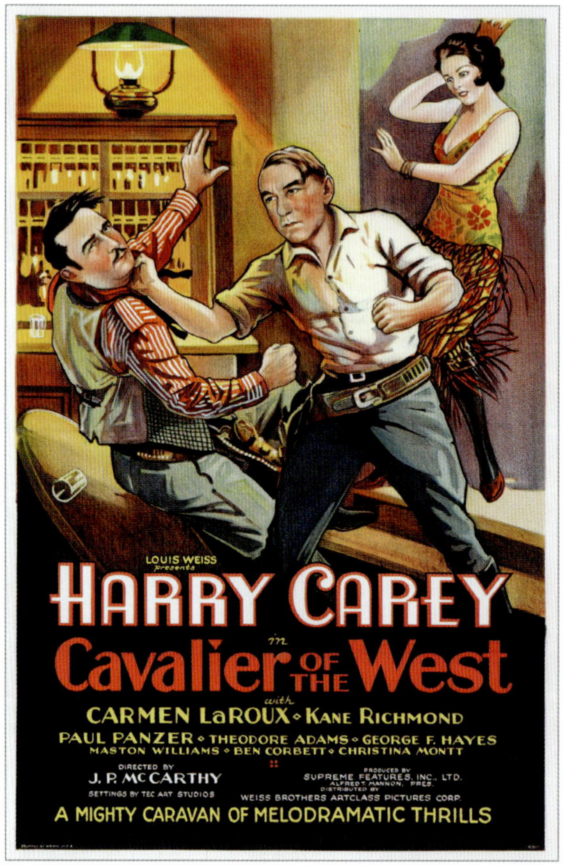
LOUIS WEISS
presents
HARRY CAREY
in
Cavalier OF THE West
with
CARMEN LaROUX • KANE RICHMOND
PAUL PANZER • THEODORE ADAMS • GEORGE F. HAYES
MASTON WILLIAMS • BEN CORBETT • CHRISTINA MONTT
DIRECTED BY
J. P. McCARTHY
SETTINGS BY TEC ART STUDIOS
PRODUCED BY
SUPREME FEATURES, INC., LTD.
ALFRED T. MANNON, PRES.
DISTRIBUTED BY
WEISS BROTHERS ARTCLASS PICTURES CORP.
A MIGHTY CARAVAN OF MELODRAMATIC THRILLS

Willis Kent presents
Lane Chandler
in
THE CHEYENNE CYCLONE
with
Marie Quillan and Frankie Darro
from the "SAGEBRUSH ROMEO" by OLIVER DRAKE
Directed by ARMAND SCHAEFER

M·H·Hoffman, Jr.
presents
HOOT GIBSON
IN
"The
HARD
HOMBRE"
with
LINA BASQUETTE
SCREEN PLAY BY
JACK NATTEFORD
DIRECTED BY
OTTO BROWER
PRODUCED BY
ALLIED PICTURES
CORPORATION
Recorded by RCA PHOTOPHONE

M·H·Hoffman, Jr. presents
HOOT GIBSON
IN
"A MAN'S LAND"
with
MARIAN SHILLING · AL BRIDGE · SKEETER BILL ROBBINS
CHARLES KING · ETHEL WALES · HAL BURNEY · ROBERT ELLIS
BILL NYE and HOOT GIBSON'S COWBOYS
DIRECTED BY
PHIL ROSEN
PRODUCED BY
ALLIED PICTURES
CORPORATION
AP

WALTER FUTTER
presents
HOOT
GIBSON
IN
SWIFTY
with
JUNE GALE
GEORGE F. HAYES
RALPH LEWIS
WALLY WALES
ART MIX
AND
STARLIGHT
THE
WONDER HORSE
FROM THE STORY
"TRACKS" by STEPHEN PAYNE
DIRECTED BY ALAN JAMES
DISTRIBUTED BY
DIVERSION PICTURES, INC.

MAJESTIC
PICTURES
presents
JACK HOXIE
in "LAW AND
LAWLESS"
DIRECTED BY
ARMAND
SCHAEFER

MAJESTIC PICTURES CORP. presents
JACK HOXIE
in
"OUTLAW JUSTICE"
with
DOROTHY GULLIVER
AND
DONALD KEITH

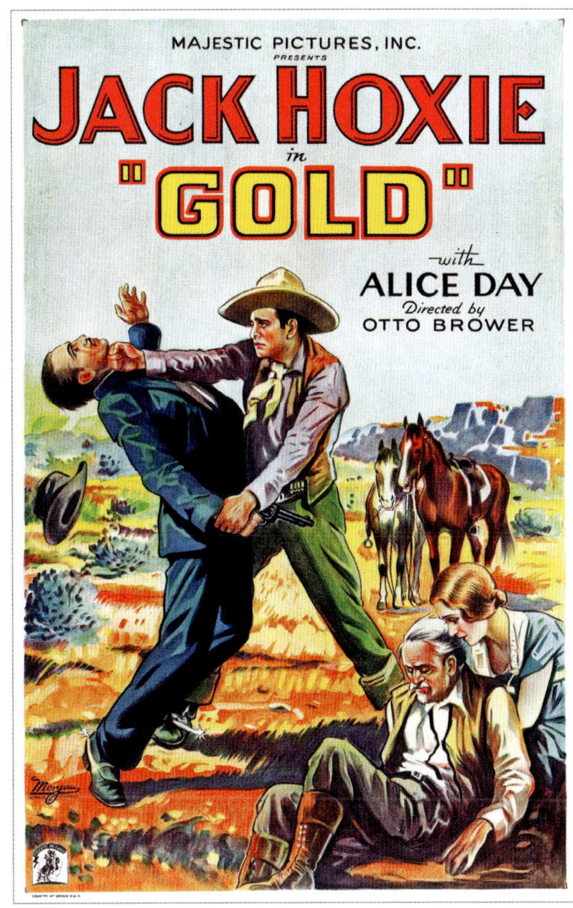
MAJESTIC PICTURES, INC.
PRESENTS
JACK HOXIE
in
"GOLD"
with
ALICE DAY
Directed by
OTTO BROWER

WEBB-DOUGLAS
PRESENTS
The
"LONE TRAIL"
With
REX LEASE-VIRGINIA BROWN FAIRE
BILLY O'BRIEN
DIRECTED BY HARRY WEBB & FORREST DOUGLAS
DISTRIBUTED BY WEBB DOUGLAS PROD. INC.

GEORGE M. MERRICK
presents
CYCLONE
of the SADDLE
featuring
REX LEASE and BOBBY NELSON
with BLACK FOX-THE SCHOLAR HORSE
JANET CHANDLER-YAKIMA CANUTT-GEORGE CHESEBORO-MILBURN MORANTI
THE RANGE RANGLERS BAND AND HUNDREDS OF INDIANS & CAVALRY
DIRECTED BY
ELMER CLIFTON
PRODUCED BY
WEISS PRODUCTIONS, INC.

MAYNARD BROTHERS AND FRIENDS

Ken Maynard and his lookalike younger brother, Kermit, both spent time on Poverty Row. Ken landed there in 1934, following an acrimonious split with Universal, where he'd headed an autonomous production unit. Mascot's Nat Levine snapped him up for a feature, *In Old Santa Fe*, and a serial, *Mystery Mountain*. Levine also contemplated starring him in a series of low-budget oaters, but Ken's drinking problem and abusive behavior cost him that opportunity, and while he continued to find work along the Row, each short-lived series proved worse than the last. The more amiable Kermit, meanwhile, found a home at Maurice Conn's Ambassador Pictures, and between 1934 and 1938 he starred in eighteen outdoor action films, equally divided between Mountie pictures and traditional Westerns. Jack Perrin, Wally Wales, and Buddy Roosevelt—all of them frequently seen in Maynard brothers pictures—toiled in cheapjack series for Gower Gulch outfits when not taking supporting roles.

AMBASSADOR PICTURES, INC. Presents
JAMES OLIVER CURWOOD'S
"WILD HORSE" ROUND-UP
WITH
BETTY LLOYD DICKIE JONES
JOHN MERTON ROGER WILLIAMS
FRANK HAGLEY DICK CURTIS
"ROCKY"
Starring KERMIT MAYNARD
Directed by ALAN JAMES
Produced by MAURICE CONN

BERNARD B. RAY
PRESENTS
JACK PERRIN
IN
RAWHIDE MAIL
WITH
NELSON McDOWELL - CHRIS MARTIN
LILLIAN GILMORE - RICHARD CRAMER
Directed by B.B. RAY
Distributed by WILLIAM STEINER

BERNARD B. RAY presents
Jack PERRIN
IN
"NORTH of ARIZONA"
with
BLANCHE MEHAFFEY · LANE CHANDLER · AL BRIDGE · MURDOCK MACQUARRIE
GEORGE CHESEBRO · ARTIE ORTEGO · BUD BUSTER
Directed by HARRY S. WEBB
Distributed by WILLIAM STEINER

WILLIAM BERKE presents
THE AMAZING EXPLOITS OF A FIGHTER FROM RING TO RANCH!
Jack PERRIN
and STARLIGHT The Wonder Horse
IN
"Wildcat Saunders"
with
WILLIAM GOULD · SNOWFLAKE
BLANCHE MEHAFFEY · ED CASSIDY
TOM LONDON · ROGER WILLIAMS
Directed by HARRY FRASER
Distributed by ATLANTIC PICTURES CORP.
BERKE PERRIN
A BLUE RIBBON FEATURE

Lester F. Scott, Jr.
presents
Buddy Roosevelt
IN
"LIGHTNING RANGE"
PRODUCED BY
CALIFORNIA MOTION PICTURE ENTERPRISES
DISTRIBUTED BY
SUPERIOR TALKING PICTURES

WILLIS KENT presents
Reb RUSSELL
and
REBEL
"The Marvel Horse"
IN A WESTERN ACTION THRILLER!
"OUTLAW RULE"
with
AL BRIDGE - BETTY MACK
YAKIMA CANUTT - JOHN McGUIRE
JOSEPH GIRARD - RALPH LEWIS
HENRY HALL - JACK ROCKWELL
and JACK KIRK
Directed by S. ROY LUBY
Distributed by WILLIS KENT

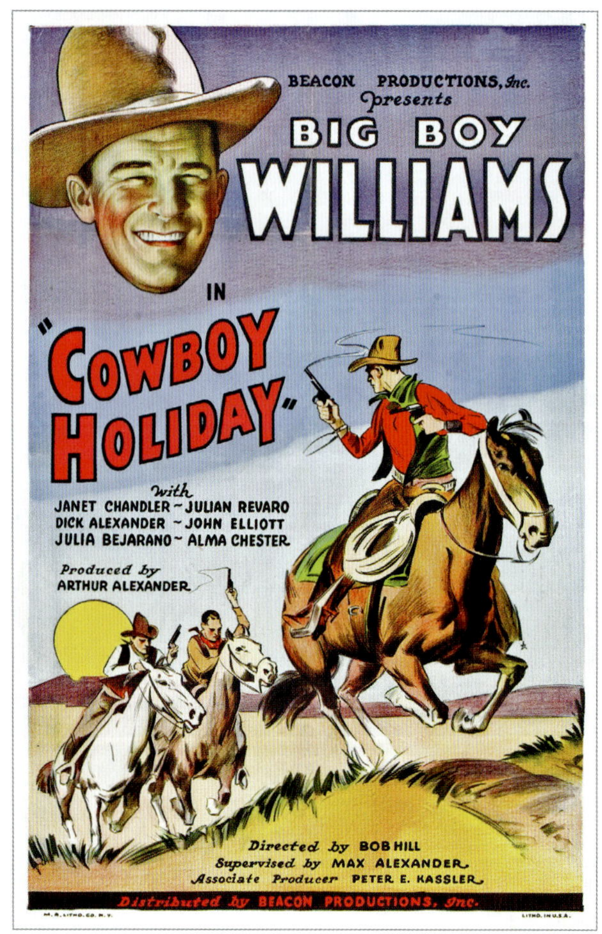
BEACON PRODUCTIONS, Inc.
presents
BIG BOY
WILLIAMS
IN
"COWBOY HOLIDAY"
with
JANET CHANDLER - JULIAN REVARO
DICK ALEXANDER - JOHN ELLIOTT
JULIA BEJARANO - ALMA CHESTER
Produced by
ARTHUR ALEXANDER
Directed by BOB HILL
Supervised by MAX ALEXANDER
Associate Producer PETER E. KASSLER
Distributed by BEACON PRODUCTIONS, Inc.

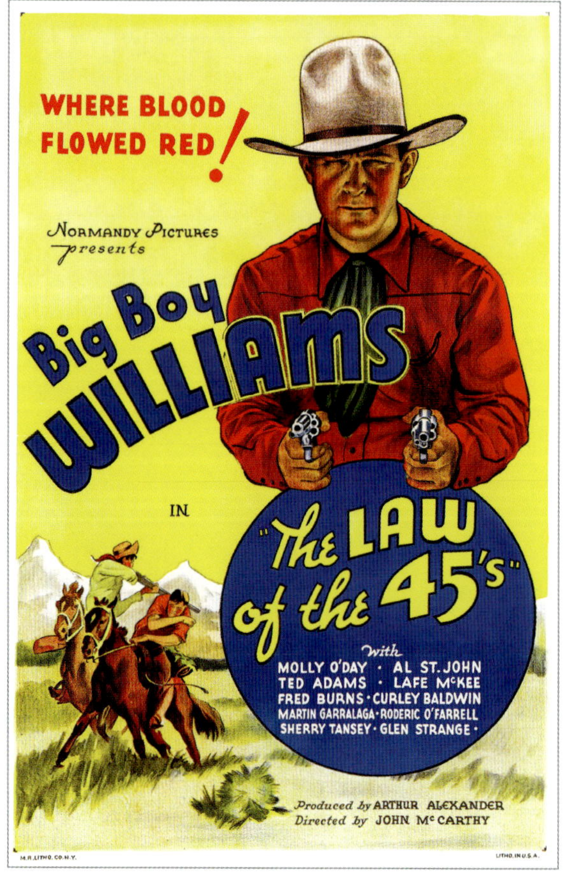
WHERE BLOOD FLOWED RED!
NORMANDY PICTURES
presents
Big Boy
WILLIAMS
IN
"The LAW of the 45's"
with
MOLLY O'DAY · AL ST. JOHN
TED ADAMS · LAFE McKEE
FRED BURNS · CURLEY BALDWIN
MARTIN GARRALAGA · RODERIC O'FARRELL
SHERRY TANSEY · GLEN STRANGE ·
Produced by ARTHUR ALEXANDER
Directed by JOHN McCARTHY

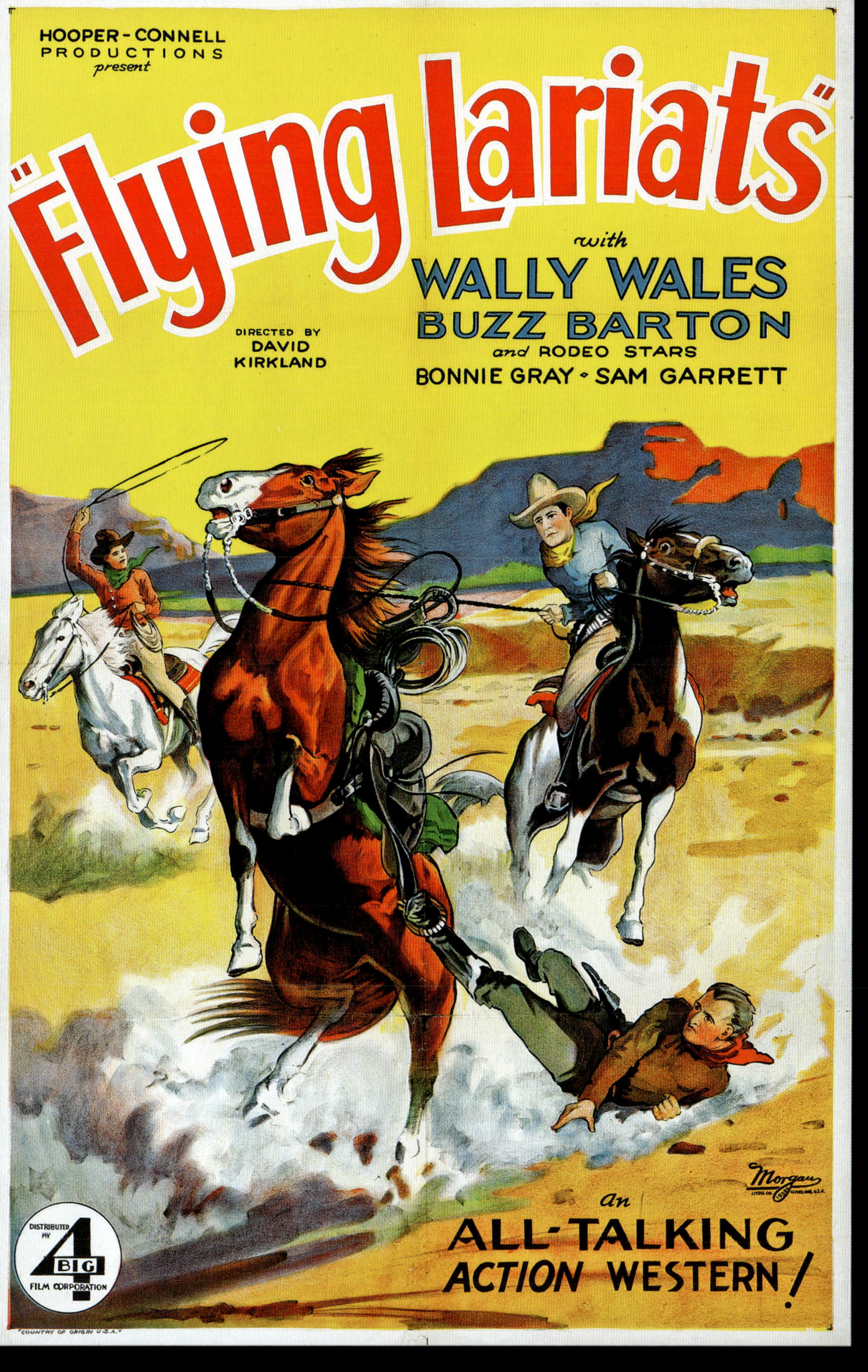
HOOPER-CONNELL
PRODUCTIONS
present
"Flying Lariats"
with
WALLY WALES
BUZZ BARTON
and RODEO STARS
BONNIE GRAY • SAM GARRETT
DIRECTED BY
DAVID
KIRKLAND
Morgan
an
ALL-TALKING
ACTION WESTERN!
DISTRIBUTED BY
4
BIG
FILM CORPORATION
"COUNTRY OF ORIGIN U.S.A."

BATTLING BOB AND TRIGGER TOM

The late twenties saw the emergence of two personable young Western stars from FBO (Film Booking Offices), a small but well-capitalized studio that specialized in horse operas. The first was Tom Tyler (real name: Vincent Markowski), a champion weightlifter whose chiseled features and imposing physique gave him a leg up on the competition. The second was Bob Steele (real name: Robert N. Bradbury Jr.), a bantam scrapper whose father had been directing Westerns and serials since 1918. When FBO was absorbed into the newly formed RKO in 1929, Tyler and Steele were dropped and forced to scrounge for work on Poverty Row. With the coming of sound, Tom was additionally handicapped by his strong Lithuanian accent, which he labored mightily to overcome. Both men worked for a succession of marginal studios—including Syndicate, Monogram, Monarch, Supreme, Reliable, Victory, Metropolitan, and PRC—and retained small but loyal fan bases. Both also drifted into supporting roles and made excellent heavies.

ASTOR PICTURES
presents
TOM TYLER
IN
"VANISHING MEN"
DIRECTED BY HARRY FRAZER

BERNARD B. RAY
Presents
TOM
TYLER
in
"Tracy Rides"
WITH
VIRGINIA BROWN FAIRE - EDMUND COBB
CHARLES K. FRENCH - CAROL SHANDREW
LAFE McKEE
DISTRIBUTED BY
WILLIAM STEINER
DIRECTED BY
HARRY S. WEBB

RELIABLE
PICTURES
CORPORATION
BERNARD B. RAY
Presents
TOM
TYLER
IN
TRIGGER
TOM
WITH
AL ST. JOHN · BERNADINE HAYES
WILLIAM GOULD · JOHN ELLIOTT
BUD OSBORNE · LLOYD INGRAHAM
WALLY WALES
FROM THE LARIAT MAGAZINE STORY THE SWIMMING HERD
ASSOCIATE PRODUCER HARRY S. WEBB • DIRECTED BY HENRI SAMUELS
DISTRIBUTED BY RELIABLE PICTURES CORPORATION

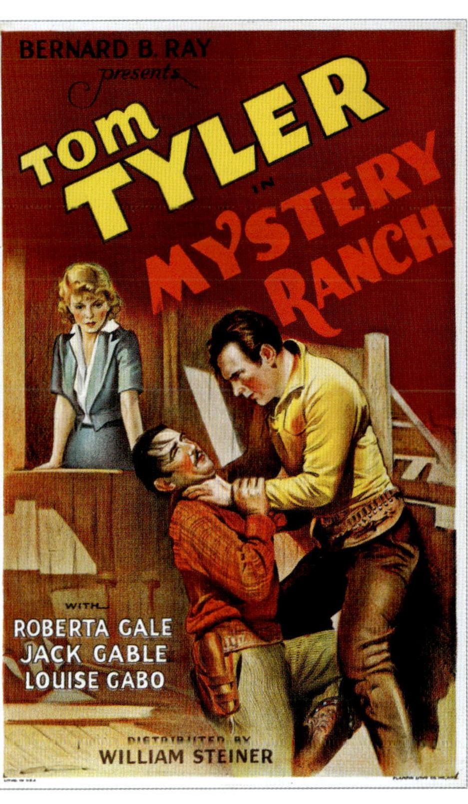
BERNARD B. RAY
presents
TOM
TYLER
IN
MYSTERY
RANCH
WITH
ROBERTA GALE
JACK GABLE
LOUISE GABO
DISTRIBUTED BY
WILLIAM STEINER

VICTORY PICTURES
SAM KATZMAN presents
TOM
TYLER
IN
The PHANTOM
OF THE RANGE
BETH MARION · SAMMY COHEN

FOUR-LEGGED FRIENDS

Warner Bros was a struggling little company in 1923 when it distributed *Where the North Begins*, an outdoor melodrama featuring a highly trained German shepherd named Rin Tin Tin. To the surprise of everyone involved, the picture was a hit, leading Rin Tin Tin to star in nineteen more features for the studio. His popularity encouraged other dog trainers to find producers who would put their mutts in pictures. Kazan, a police dog owned by minor supporting player Jack King, appeared in several Poverty Row productions. Lightning the Super Dog was not to be confused with Lightning the Wonder Dog: the former starred in a series of late-twenties Western two-reelers, the latter in such bottom-of-the-barrel features as *When Lightning Strikes*. And then, of course, there was a Rin Tin Tin Jr. Equine protagonists were less numerous, but they included Rex the Wild Horse (an all-black Morgan stallion with a nasty disposition) and Black King, whom Poverty Row producer tried without success to build into a star attraction.

MITCHELL LEICHTER
Presents
"BLACK★KING"
The HORSE with the HUMAN BRAIN
IN
"GUNNERS AND GUNS"
WITH
EDWIN COBB
EDNA ASLIN
FRANK WALKER
with an
ALL-STAR CAST
Supervised by
Charles Hutchison
Directed by
JERRY CALLAHAN
PRODUCED BY BLACK KING PRODUCTIONS, INC.
DISTRIBUTED by
BEAUMONT PICTURES INC.
HOLLYWOOD, CALIF.

ONE-SHOT ODDITIES

With so many Westerns hewing to tried-and-true formulas, Poverty Row producers occasionally made horse operas with offbeat elements to distinguish them from the thundering herd. Given their minuscule budgets, turning out such pictures entailed nominal risk—and the upside to a surprise hit was considerable. Hence such anomalies as *The Dude Wrangler* (1930, with a comically effeminate leading man), *The Terror of Tiny Town* (1938, with an all-midget cast), and *The Bronze Buckaroo* (1939, with an ostensibly African American leading man revealed decades later to be of Italian and Ethiopian descent). Other oddities included a short-lived series built around aging Conway Tearle, a distinguished and decidedly unathletic stage and screen actor more comfortable in tuxedos than in Stetson hats and batwing chaps. *Tex Takes a Holiday* (1932) was the first of numerous B Westerns shot in color, even if it *was* a cheap process that reduced everything to orange-red or blue-green hues.

PRINCIPAL ATTRACTIONS PRESENTS
Buffalo Bill Jr.
The TEXAN
LUCILLE BROWN
JACK MOWER
LAFE McKEE
BOBBY NELSON
directed by CLIFF SMITH

DANGEROUS TRAILS and DARING DEEDS!
WILLIAM BERKE presents
Fred KOHLER, Jr.
IN
"The Pecos Kid"
with
RUTH FINDLAY
ROGER WILLIAMS
ED CASSIDY
WALLY WALES
EARL DWYER
FRANCIS WALKER
Directed by LESTER WILLIAMS
Distributed by COMMODORE PICTURES CORP.
William Steiner, Pres.

MITCHELL LEICHTER Presents
"TRAILS" END
Starring
CONWAY TEARLE
with
CLAUDIA DELL
FRED KOHLER
STANLEY BLYSTONE
AND
"BLACK KING" The Horse with a Human Brain
Directed by AL HERMAN Supervised by Charles Hutchison
PRODUCED DISTRIBUTED by BEAUMONT PICTURES CORP.

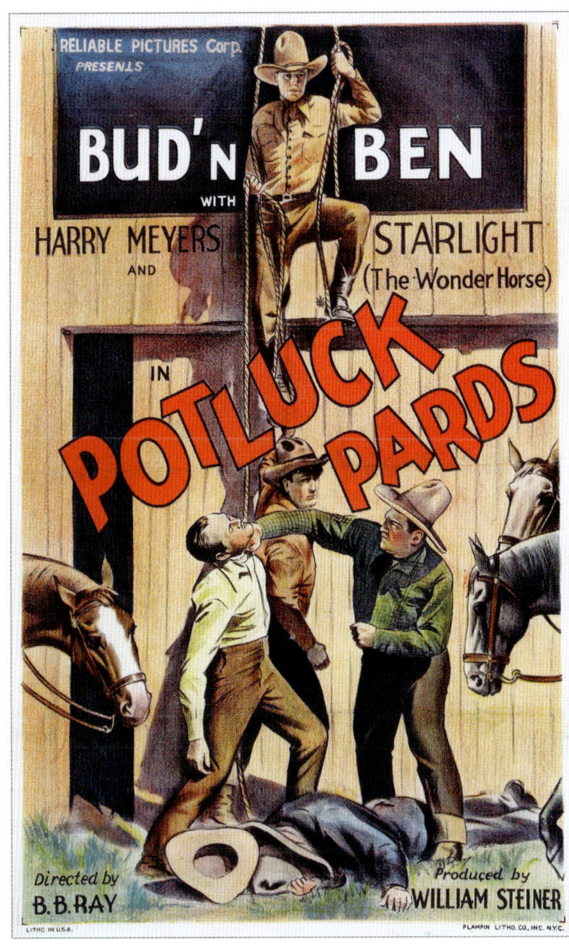
RELIABLE PICTURES Corp. PRESENTS
BUD'N BEN
WITH
HARRY MEYERS
AND
STARLIGHT (The Wonder Horse)
IN
POTLUCK PARDS
Directed by B.B. RAY
Produced by WILLIAM STEINER

THESE TOM THUMBS ARE COLOSSAL!
FIRST TIME ON ANY SCREEN!
JED BUELL'S
MIDGETS
The TERROR
of TINY TOWN
Screen Play by FRED MYTON
Directed by SAM NEWFIELD
ASTOR PICTURES CORP.

DEARHOLT, STOUT AND COHEN PRESENT
THE PHANTOM OF SANTA FE
DIRECTED BY JACQUES JACCARD
with
NINA QUARTARO
CARMELITA GERAGHTY
NORMAN KERRY
FRANK MAYO
in 100% Natural Color
TARZAN PICTURES Inc.

Robert Emmett presents
"COURAGE of the NORTH"
with
JOHN PRESTON as MORTON of the MOUNTED
WILLIAM DESMOND • TOM LONDON • JUNE LOVE • WHITE FEATHER
AND
DYNAMITE THE WONDER HORSE
CAPTAIN KING OF DOGS
PRODUCED BY EMPIRE PICTURES
DISTRIBUTED BY STAGE AND SCREEN PRODUCTIONS, INC.

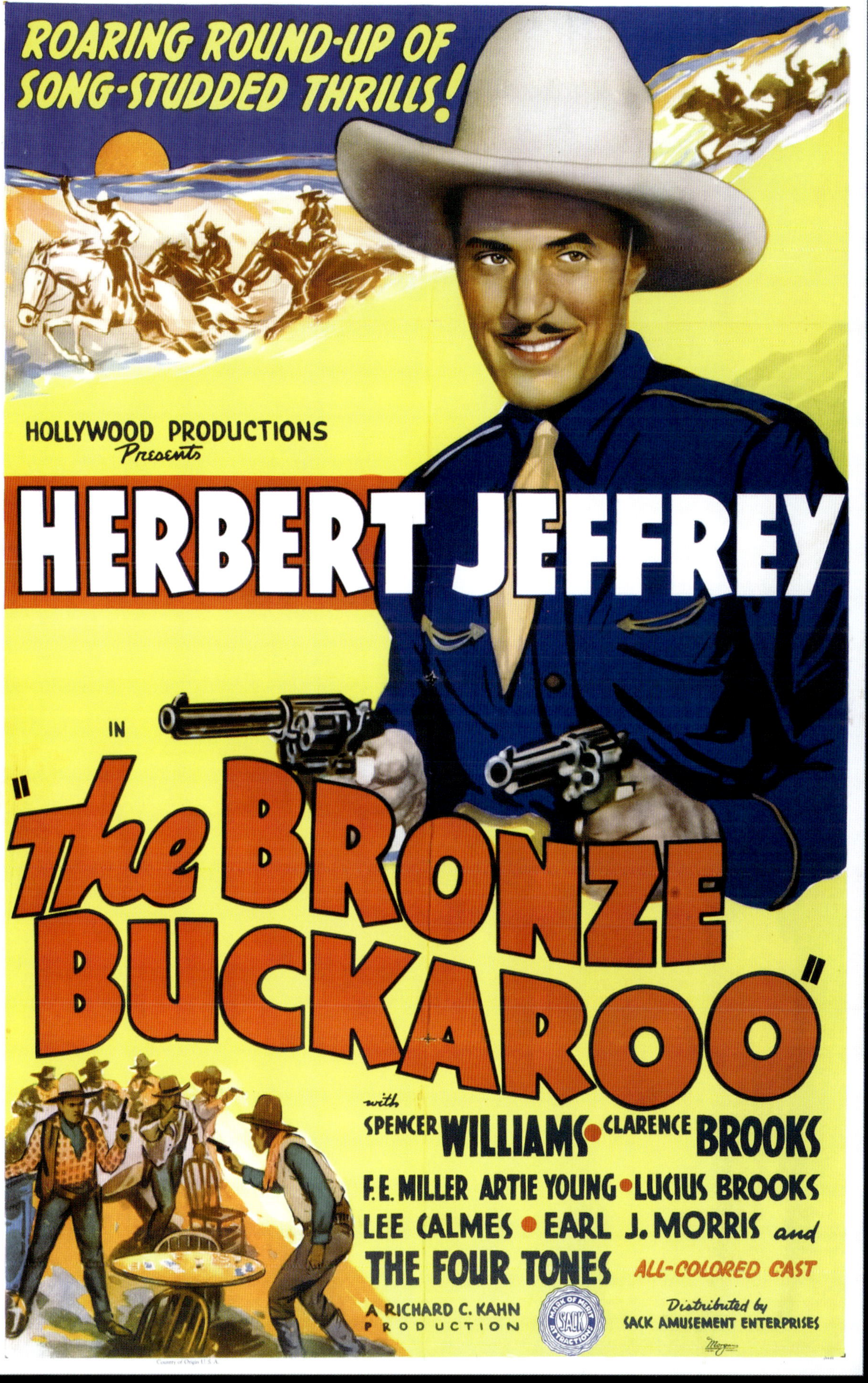
ROARING ROUND-UP OF SONG-STUDDED THRILLS!
HOLLYWOOD PRODUCTIONS Presents
HERBERT JEFFREY
IN
"The BRONZE BUCKAROO"
with
SPENCER WILLIAMS • CLARENCE BROOKS
F.E. MILLER ARTIE YOUNG • LUCIUS BROOKS
LEE CALMES • EARL J. MORRIS and
THE FOUR TONES
ALL-COLORED CAST
A RICHARD C. KAHN PRODUCTION
Distributed by SACK AMUSEMENT ENTERPRISES

4
THE
GOLDEN AGE
OF WESTERN
MOVIES

THE BLOSSOMING OF A GENRE

The 1930s begin promisingly for Westerns as major studios overcome the limitations of early sound-recording technology to supply extravagant outdoor epics to moviegoers. But with the Depression beginning to wrap its crushing tentacles around the world's economy, these ambitious efforts are doomed to financial failure. For much of the decade, it's the B Westerns that keep the genre alive, until 1939 sees a surprising renewal . . .

BELOW: Twentieth Century Fox's *Jesse James*, lavishly produced on a budget of $1.6 million, was the third-highest-grossing film in 1939. Only *Gone with the Wind* and *Mr. Smith Goes to Washington* took in more money at the nation's box offices that year.

At the dawn of the talking-picture era, some Hollywood naysayers predicted sound would decimate the market for Westerns. The technology for outdoor recording was insufficient at best, and it was not expected to improve anytime soon, and it was believed that the mania for "talkies" would compel studios to concentrate on producing stage-bound, dialogue-heavy dramas.

And then, in 1929, along came Fox's *In Old Arizona*.

This adaptation of O. Henry's famous short story "The Cabellero's Way" (already filmed twice as a silent) starred Warner Baxter as the Cisco Kid. True, the exterior sound recording was primitive and not always intelligible, but the film enthralled audiences and silenced the skeptics.

Several major studios, noting *Arizona*'s critical and commercial success, rushed large-scale Westerns into production. Both MGM and Fox Film Corp. expended considerable resources on outdoor epics in 1930. Fox's *The Big Trail*, a wagon-train saga, harked back to 1923's *The Covered Wagon*. Director Raoul Walsh supervised 93 actors, 725 Indian extras, and assorted livestock numbering in the thousands. Principal photography consumed four months, during which time location shooting took place in seven states. The picture was filmed in an early widescreen process called 70 mm Grandeur and cost $1.25 million when all was said and done. The star was a young, untested bit player named Marion Michael Morrison. Walsh renamed him John Wayne.

Unfortunately, when *Big Trail* was released in November 1930, the United States was just beginning to feel the effects of the Great Depression. More importantly, only a handful of theaters had the extra-wide screens and special projectors needed to accommodate Grandeur, and the recently incurred costs of wiring for sound kept most exhibitors from installing the cumbersome equipment. To

ABOVE: When *The Jazz Singer* (1927) created a vogue for talking pictures, the major Hollywood studios believed that recording sound outdoors would present insurmountable technical difficulties. Western movies remained silent until 1929, when *In Old Arizona* proved that outdoor recording was not only possible but actually enhanced horse operas. Sounds of thundering hoofbeats, reverberating gunfire, and creaking saddle leather entranced audiences. Owen Wister's twice-filmed novel *The Virginian* was dusted off in 1929, its success catapulting Gary Cooper to major stardom. *The Big Trail* (1930) failed to recoup its $1.25 million budget but proved Hollywood technicians equal to the task of making elaborate all-talking oaters.

counter this, a panicky Fox Film Corp. hastily prepared a conventional 35 mm version of *The Big Trail*, but despite its obvious entertainment value the picture never came close to recouping its production costs. Its failure doomed John Wayne to a decade of starring in B-grade Westerns.

Released almost simultaneously with *Big Trail*, MGM's lavishly mounted biopic *Billy the Kid* likewise employed a 70 mm widescreen process called "Realife" and boasted picturesque location photography. It too flopped, and for the same reasons as John Wayne's starring debut. Playing the title role was former Alabama footballer Johnny Mack Brown, a Metro contract player who had appeared opposite Greta Garbo and Joan Crawford in silent movies. But his thick southern drawl worked against him once sound became the rage. No longer considered a credible leading man for dress-suit dramas, he, like Wayne, was mired in B Westerns for the thirties and beyond.

RKO, the most recently formed of Hollywood's major studios, gambled a small fortune on its own epic Western, an adaptation of Edna Ferber's novel *Cimarron*, the sprawling saga of Oklahoma's famous land rush and the territory's decades-long struggle for statehood. Silent-era favorite Richard Dix played charismatic pioneer Yancey Cravat and Irene Dunne his long-suffering wife, Sabra. Released in January 1931, it elicited rapturous reviews and became the only Western to win the Academy Award for "Best Picture" until Kevin Costner's *Dances with Wolves* in 1990. But while *Cimarron* grossed more than a million dollars at the nation's box offices, it wasn't enough to cover the picture's $1.4 million cost. The epic Western was, for the time being, dead. But American moviegoers never lost their appetites for horse operas.

In addition to the Poverty Row oaters discussed in the previous chapter, exhibitors during the early and mid-thirties could choose from a range of Westerns budgeted higher than the usual B and made with more care than typical Saturday-matinee fodder. George O'Brien, the brawny Irishman who attained stardom in John Ford's *The Iron Horse* (1924), spent the decade's first half starring in sturdily mounted Fox Film Corp. adaptations of novels by bestselling Western scribes Zane Grey and Max Brand. O'Brien's sparkling personality and devil-may-care approach to action—he was a splendid athlete who insisted on doing all but the most dangerous stunts—turned such films as *The Lone Star Ranger* (1930), *Riders of the Purple Sage* (1931), *The Rainbow Trail* (1932), and *Robbers' Roost* (1932) into profitable attractions for Fox's theater chain. Eventually, his budgets were trimmed, but even such modest efforts as *The Dude Ranger* (1934) and *When a Man's a Man* (1935) proved popular with movie fans.

Another economically made series was Paramount's run of remakes of its silent-era Zane Grey adaptations, which not only vaulted Virginia-born bit player Randolph Scott to stardom but also provided a springboard to A-grade pictures for their director, Henry Hathaway. Paramount also began releasing the Hopalong Cassidy oaters in 1935 and maintained its faith in the commercial viability of big-budget Westerns with a trio of box-office favorites in the decade's second half: *The Texas Rangers* (1936), *Wells Fargo* (1937), and especially *The Plainsman* (also 1937), a Cecil B. DeMille spectacular that returned Gary Cooper to Westerns in the role of Wild Bill Hickok.

The other major studios continued to shy away from Western epics, having been badly burned years earlier. But that all changed in 1939, when John Ford's *Stagecoach* proved that mature, intelligent, character-driven Westerns could attract audiences of all social and economic backgrounds to venues large and small, in the biggest cities as well as the smallest towns. Its box-office totals more than doubled the picture's budget of $531,000. More importantly for the genre, it released leading man John Wayne from B-movie limbo.

ABOVE: The crew sets up a shot for *Jesse James*, the exteriors for which were shot mainly in and around Pineville, Missouri. This small town (population 383 in 1939) was close to Jesse's old stomping grounds and had remained unchanged from the late nineteenth century.

Suddenly the biggest stars were cast in large-scale Westerns, several of them with historical underpinnings. Fox's *Jesse James* featured the studio's resident heartthrob Tyrone Power as the notorious bandit, whose depredations were considerably whitewashed for audience consumption; Paramount's *Union Pacific*, another DeMille deluxer, dramatized the building of the transcontinental railroad and spotlighted Joel McCrea, Barbara Stanwyck, and Robert Preston as its romantic triangle. Warner Bros took the biggest chances, castwise, with *Dodge City* (starring Errol Flynn as an Australian-born cattleman) and *The Oklahoma Kid* (making cowboys of gangster-film leads James Cagney and Humphrey Bogart). James Stewart was an unlikely Westerner in Universal's comedic remake of *Destry Rides Again*, which costarred Marlene Dietrich as an equally unlikely saloon girl.

The latter, released on December 29, 1939, officially closed out thirties oater production. Ironically, the most dismal decade in America's economic history had been the movie Western's golden age. ✮

ABOVE LEFT: Cast members John Wayne (*foreground left*) and Andy Devine (*seated next to him*) watch on during the filming of a scene from *Stagecoach*. Director John Ford, visible over the Duke's left shoulder, closely monitors the action while seated atop the camera platform.

ABOVE RIGHT: The exemplary critical and commercial reception to *Stagecoach* rescued John Wayne from Republic B Westerns—finally boosting him into stardom's top ranks—and inspired a wave of big-budget genre offerings with major stars and adult appeal.

ADULT WESTERNS

The addition of sound to motion pictures freed Westerns from their previous near-total reliance on vivid action and picturesque scenery. With dialogue, filmmakers could tell more intricate stories and limn more interesting characters. Pictorial values still mattered greatly, but screenwriters enjoyed the liberty of establishing mood and fleshing out narratives with talk. The Oscar-winning "Best Picture" of 1931, RKO's *Cimarron*, boasted a spectacular visualization of 1889's Oklahoma Land Rush, but audiences were equally captivated by the depictions of charismatic pioneer Yancey Cravat (Richard Dix) and his indomitable wife, Sabra (Irene Dunne), which would have been woefully incomplete without their emotion-drenched conversations. *Gun Smoke* (also 1931) eschewed the simple-minded action of Saturday-matinee horse operas in portraying the conflict between modern-day Westerners and big-city racketeers. *Law and Order* (1932) skillfully adapted W. R. Burnett's novel *Saint Johnson*, a thinly disguised fictionalization of the notorious Earp–Clanton feud in old Tombstone. It demonstrated just how effective dialogue could be when tersely written and parsimoniously deployed. The early thirties vogue for gritty Westerns didn't last long, but it produced some of the genre's most memorable films.

BILLY
THE
KID
A Metro-Goldwyn-Mayer ALL TALKING PICTURE

HERE IT IS..TO THRILL
YOU AGAIN!
WORLD'S MIGHTIEST SHOW!
EDNA
FERBER'S
COLOSSAL
CIMARRON
RICHARD DIX
IRENE DUNNE
ESTELLE TAYLOR .. WILLIAM COLLIER, JR.
NANCE O'NEIL .. EDNA MAY OLIVER
RKO-RADIO PICTURE

TERRIFIC AS ALL CREATION
THE TALKIES
REBORN
MIGHTIEST
DRAMA OF
THE AGES
EDNA
FERBER'S
COLOSSAL
CIMARRON
RICHARD
DIX
IRENE DUNNE ESTELLE TAYLOR
WM. COLLIER, JR. AND A GRAND AS-
SEMBLAGE OF SUPERLATIVE ARTISTS
WESLEY RUGGLES PRODUCTION

NOT
EXACTLY
GENTLEMEN
with
Victor McLAGLEN
Fay WRAY ... Lew CODY
Eddie GRIBBON
FOX
Movietone
Directed by BENJAMIN STOLOFF

Bill Boyd
IN THE
PAINTED
DESERT
with
HELEN TWELVETREES
and WILLIAM FARNUM
Directed by
HOWARD HIGGIN
A PATHÉ feature
PRODUCED BY E. B. DERR

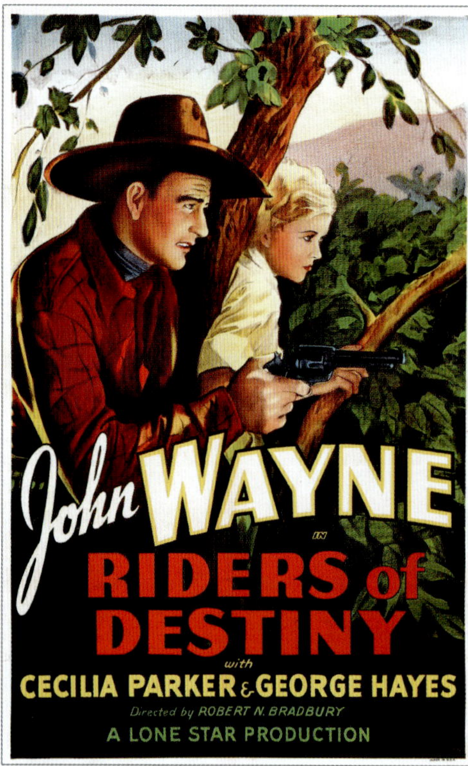

ENTER THE DUKE

The Big Trail's resounding thud at the nation's box offices forced its young leading man, John Wayne, to scramble for work. After several turns supporting Buck Jones and Tim McCoy in Columbia oaters, the Duke in 1932 secured a berth at Warner Bros., starring in six low-budget Westerns built around stock footage from old Ken Maynard silents. Dumped by Warner in 1933, Wayne wound up at Monogram Pictures, a small outfit one step above Poverty Row. Over the next two years, he starred in sixteen "Lone Star Westerns," produced by Trem Carr for $8,000 to $12,000. They were shot in five days each, and Wayne got a thousand bucks per picture. Crude but vigorous, the action-packed Lone Stars enabled the Duke to hone his craft and helped build him a following. When Monogram was absorbed into the newly formed Republic Pictures in 1935, he went along too and began in earnest his climb to stardom.

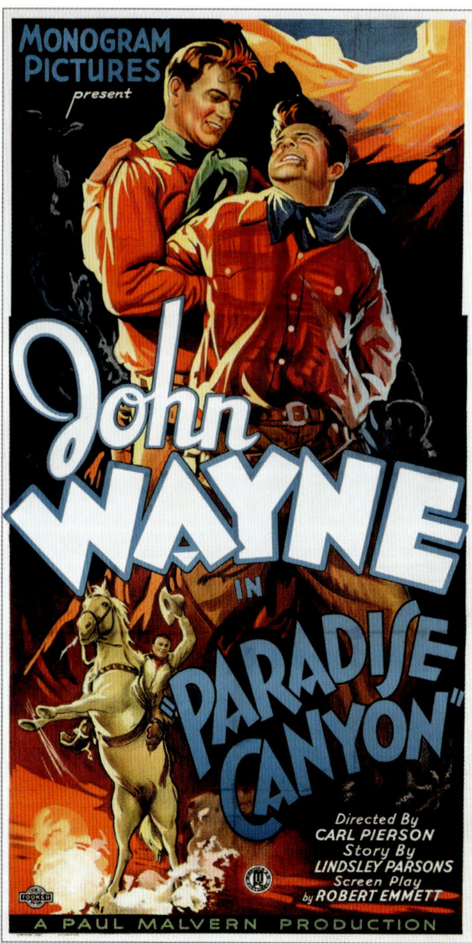

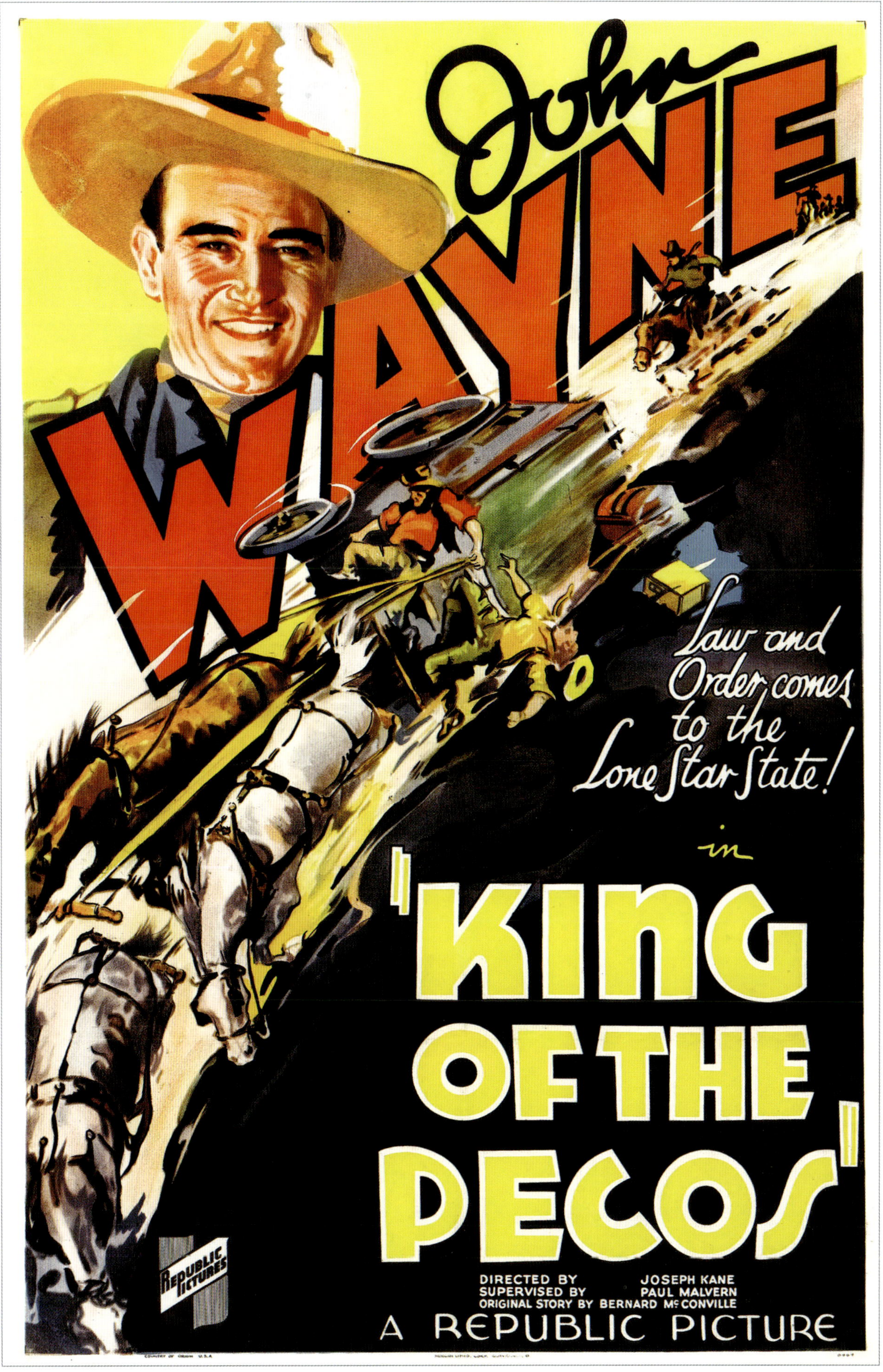
John
WAYNE
Law and
Order comes
to the
Lone Star State!
in
"KING
OF THE
PECOS"
REPUBLIC PICTURES
DIRECTED BY JOSEPH KANE
SUPERVISED BY PAUL MALVERN
ORIGINAL STORY BY BERNARD McCONVILLE
A REPUBLIC PICTURE

ZANE GREY RIDES AGAIN

Hollywood continued to recycle Grey's best-known yarns during the 1930s. Two major studios—Fox and Paramount—held long-term licenses on most of his novels. The early thirties saw Fox remake *The Lone Star Ranger*, *The Last of the Duanes*, *Riders of the Purple Sage*, and *The Rainbow Trail*, and others with brawny George O'Brien as their star. (William Farnum had appeared in the 1910s versions and Tom Mix in their twenties remakes.) Paramount made up-and-coming Randolph Scott the star of its Zane Grey retreads, which were built around stock footage from twenties adaptations that had starred Jack Holt and Richard Dix. In 1933 alone, Scott top-lined new celluloid editions of *To the Last Man*, *Man of the Forest*, *The Thundering Herd*, and *Sunset Pass*. His director was Henry Hathaway, who expertly blended new and stock footage to good effect. When Scott and Hathaway moved up to "A" movies in 1935, the Zane Grey series began to lose steam, but Paramount kept it going until decade's end with stars including Tom Keene, Buster Crabbe, and even John Wayne.

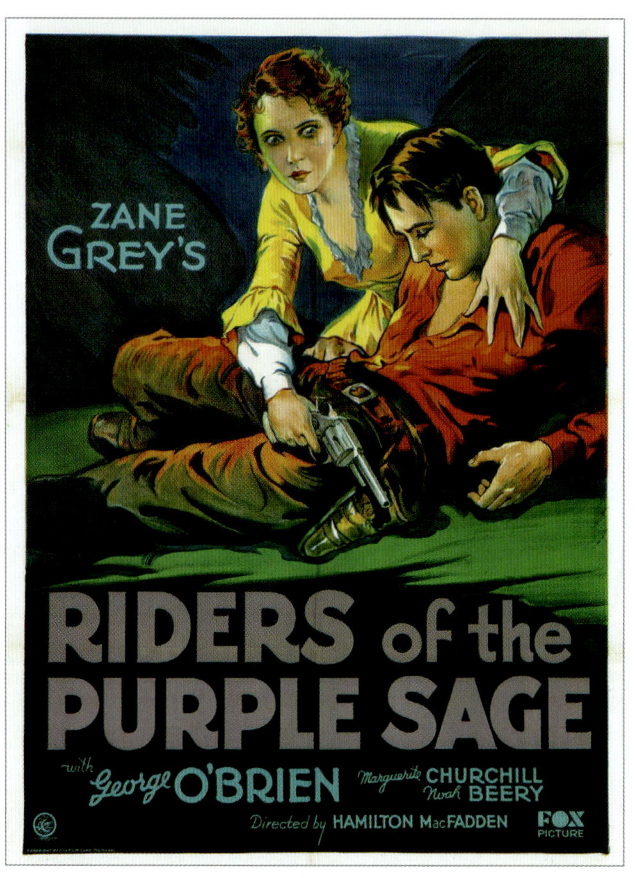

ZANE GREY'S
'WILD HORSE MESA'
WITH
RANDOLPH SCOTT
SALLY BLANE and
FRED KOHLER
a Paramount Picture

Zane GREY'S
"MAN OF THE FOREST"
WITH
RANDOLPH SCOTT
HARRY CAREY, NOAH BEERY
VERNA HILLIE
a Paramount Picture

ZANE GREY'S
TO THE LAST MAN
With
RANDOLPH SCOTT
ESTHER RALSTON
BUSTER CRABBE
JACK LARUE
NOAH BEERY
a Paramount Picture

ADOLPH ZUKOR presents
ZANE GREY'S
"Wagon Wheels"
with
RANDOLPH SCOTT, GAIL PATRICK
MONTE BLUE, RAYMOND HATTON
BILLY LEE
A PARAMOUNT PICTURE

George O'BRIEN
IN Zane Grey's
THUNDER MOUNTAIN
with
Barbara Fritchie · Frances Grant
Morgan Wallace · Directed by DAVID HOWARD
A FOX RELEASE
LITHO IN U.S.A. #6833
THIS POSTER IS THE PROPERTY OF THE FOX FILM CORP. IT IS LEASED - NOT SOLD. COPYRIGHT BY FOX FILM CORP. MCMXXXV
TOOKER-MOORE LITHOGRAPH CO. INC., N.Y.

ADOLPH ZUKOR PRESENTS
ZANE GREY'S
BORN TO THE WEST
with JOHN WAYNE · MARSHA HUNT · JOHN MACK BROWN
JOHN PATTERSON
MONTE BLUE ·
LUCIEN LITTLEFIELD
NICK LUKATS ·
a Paramount Picture
Directed by Charles Barton
Screen Play by Stuart Anthony and Robert Yost · From the Novel by Zane Grey

THE OLD GUARD

The silent era's top Western stars all made the transition to talking pictures. After several years off the screen altogether, Tom Mix returned in 1932 with a highly anticipated series distributed by Universal. The earliest entries—*Destry Rides Again* and *Rider of Death Valley*—were top notch, but later ones were uneven. After completing nine pictures, Mix retired again. His berth at Universal was next occupied by Ken Maynard (1933–34) and Buck Jones (1934–38). The latter was then at the peak of his popularity; his fan club, the Buck Jones Rangers, boasted a million members. He had previously starred in an excellent series for Columbia, where Tim McCoy also spent the early thirties. Maynard wound up there too, gradually losing popularity in a mediocre series made by independent producer Larry Darmour. He would soon languish on Poverty Row. The same fate befell Hoot Gibson, whose starring career was over by 1937. All these old-timers would continue to work, albeit in greatly diminished circumstances.

Shooting! Riding! Fighting!
THRILLING!
Buck JONES
in
"The TEXAS RANGER"
with
CARMELITA GERAGHTY
DIRECTED BY
D. ROSS LEDERMAN
a Columbia Picture

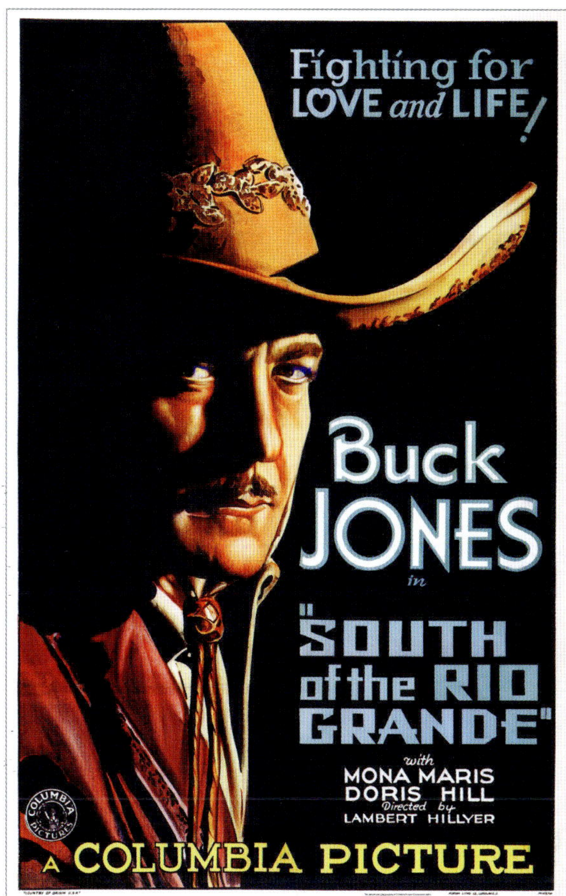
Fighting for LOVE and LIFE!
Buck JONES
in
"SOUTH of the RIO GRANDE"
with
MONA MARIS
DORIS HILL
Directed by
LAMBERT HILLYER
A COLUMBIA PICTURE

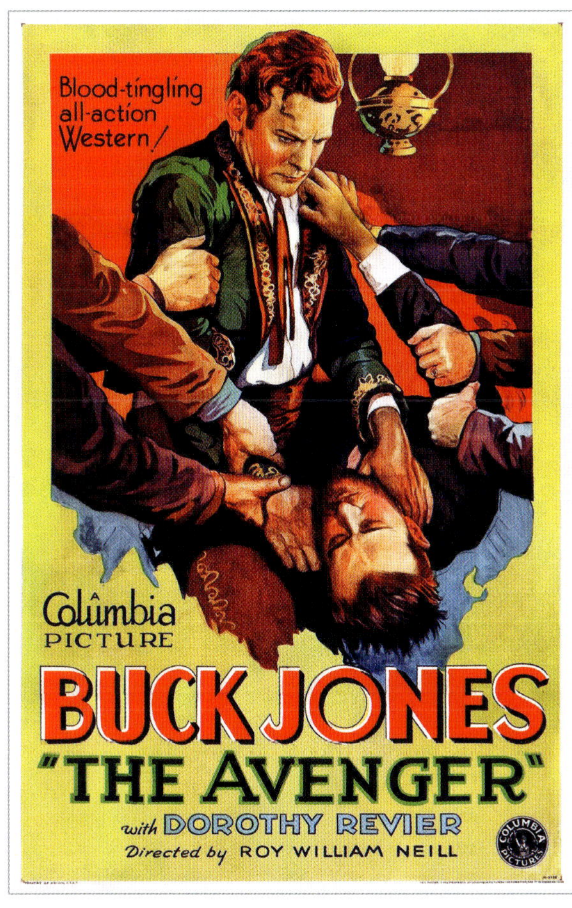
Blood-tingling all-action Western!
Columbia
PICTURE
BUCK JONES
"THE AVENGER"
with DOROTHY REVIER
Directed by ROY WILLIAM NEILL

UNIVERSAL
presents
The great
Buck Jones
IN
OUTLAWED GUNS
a
UNIVERSAL
PICTURE

Duty or FRIENDSHIP ?
Tim McCOY
IN
"CORNERED"
with
SHIRLEY GREY • NOAH BEERY
RAYMOND HATTON
DIRECTED BY B. REEVES EASON
A COLUMBIA PICTURE

TIM McCOY
in
"MAN of ACTION"
with CARYL LINCOLN
Directed by GEORGE MELFORD
a COLUMBIA PICTURE

CARL LAEMMLE presents
Ken MAYNARD in
"HONOR OF THE RANGE"
with Cecilia PARKER
and Fred KOHLER
A UNIVERSAL PICTURE

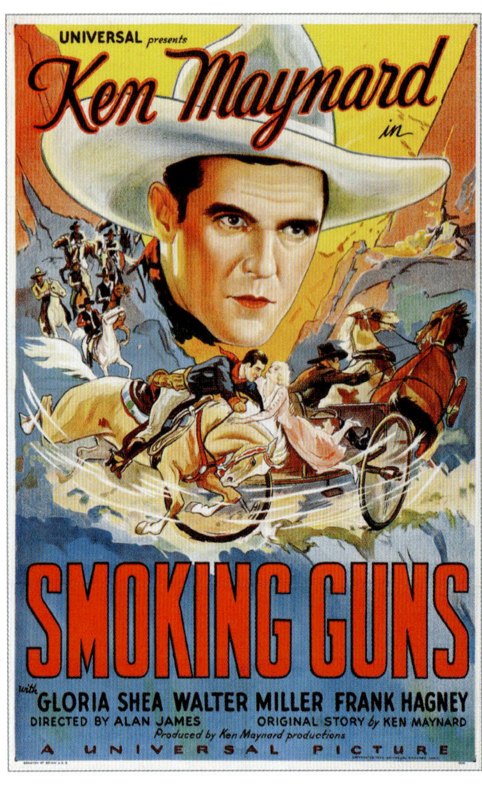
UNIVERSAL presents
Ken Maynard
in
SMOKING GUNS
with
GLORIA SHEA WALTER MILLER FRANK HAGNEY
DIRECTED BY ALAN JAMES ORIGINAL STORY by KEN MAYNARD
Produced by Ken Maynard productions
A UNIVERSAL PICTURE

HARRY CAREY ★ HOOT GIBSON
IN
THE LAST OUTLAW
WITH
TOM TYLER
Henry B. WALTHALL
Margaret CALLAHAN
DIRECTED BY CHRISTY CABANNE
ASSOCIATE PRODUCER ROBERT SISK

Gambling with Life for Love!
Tim McCoy
in
"The ONE WAY TRAIL"
with DORIS HILL
DIRECTED BY RAY TAYLOR
a COLUMBIA PICTURE

Roaring into the Bandit's nest....... UNARMED!
KEN MAYNARD
IN
WESTERN COURAGE
WITH
GENEVA MITCHELL
DIRECTED BY SPENCER GORDON BENNET
COLUMBIA PICTURES
A COLUMBIA PICTURE
COUNTRY OF ORIGIN U.S.A.

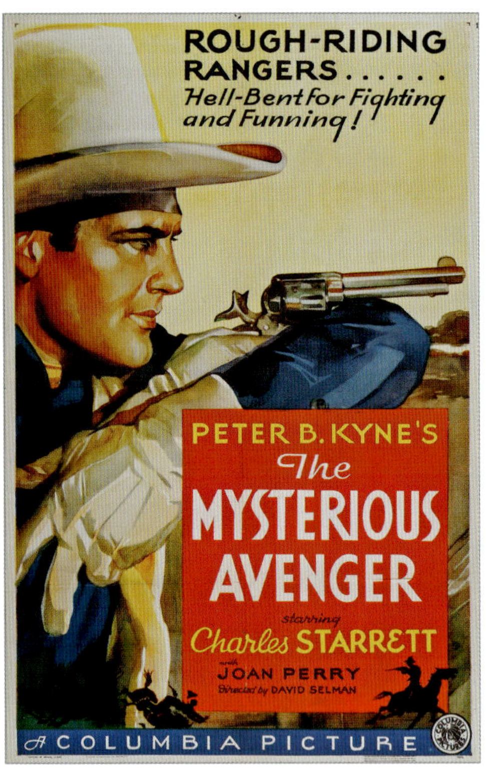

THE COLUMBIA COWBOYS

Columbia Pictures, basically a Poverty Row outfit in the twenties, attained a measure of respectability in the thirties as a result of hits generated by contract director Frank Capra. But the studio still relied on its B Westerns, low-budget crime films, serials, and short subjects to remain profitable. So, when one cowboy star departed, another was hired immediately. Charles Starrett, the scion of a wealthy New England family, had been in pictures for five years without making much of an impression when, in 1935, he agreed to take Tim McCoy's place on Columbia's release schedule. He was a better actor than most cowboy stars, and he stayed at the studio until it shut down B-Western production in 1952. Gordon Elliott, nicknamed "Wild Bill" after he clicked in the 1938 Columbia serial *Great Adventures of Wild Bill Hickok*, subsequently graduated to feature films and established a loyal following that stayed with him when he moved to Republic in 1943.

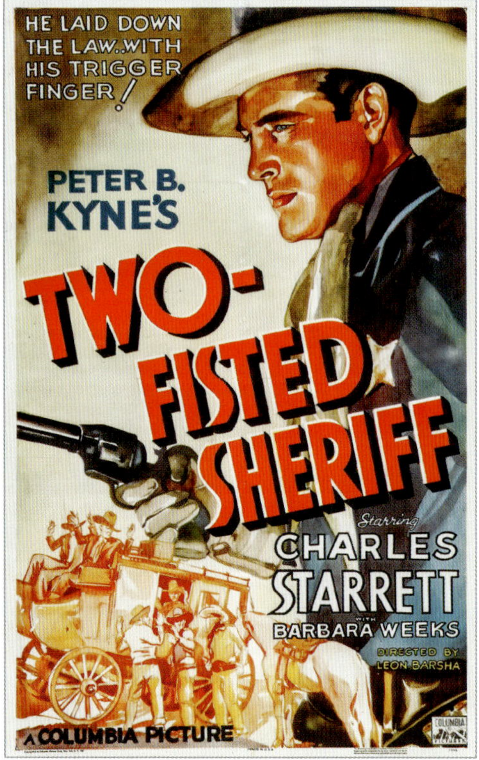

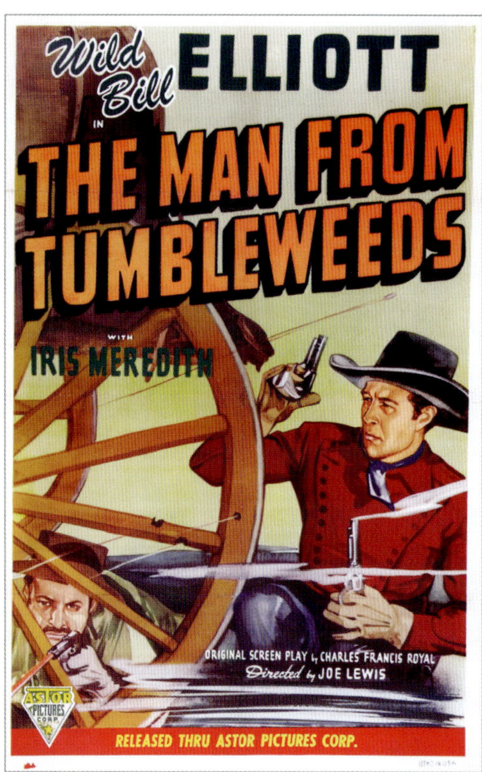

SIX-GUNS
BARK THE
DOOM OF
BAD-MEN!
BILL
ELLIOTT
IN
PIONEERS OF THE FRONTIER
with
LINDA WINTERS
ORIGINAL SCREEN PLAY BY FRED MYTON
DIRECTED BY SAM NELSON
A COLUMBIA PICTURE
A WILD BILL SAUNDERS
Adventure
Country of Origin U.S.A.

THE EPIC WESTERN RETURNS

After four years in the doldrums, big-budget, adult-oriented Westerns suddenly flooded the nation's movie theaters. Paramount led the pack with three epics produced in two years: *The Texas Rangers*, *The Plainsman* (both 1936), and *Wells Fargo* (1937). All three had historical backgrounds and narratives of broad scope. Cecil B. DeMille's *The Plainsman* starred Gary Cooper as an absurdly whitewashed Wild Bill Hickok, and Jean Arthur made a ridiculously glamorous Calamity Jane, but that didn't stop the film from grossing nearly $2.3 million—more than double its huge budget. DeMille returned to the genre a few years later with *Union Pacific* (1939), another smash hit. That same year, Universal remade Tom Mix's *Destry Rides Again*, based on the bestselling Max Brand novel. Producer Joe Pasternak threw out the book and commissioned a seriocomic screenplay, casting Marlene Dietrich and James Stewart in the leading roles. Big-budget Westerns with major stars were here to stay.

Paramount's Thundering Romance Of The Winning Of The West!
ADOLPH ZUKOR presents
FRANK LLOYD'S
WELLS FARGO
FEATURING
JOEL McCREA
BOB BURNS
FRANCES DEE
WITH
LLOYD NOLAN
HENRY O'NEILL
PORTER HALL
ROBERT CUMMINGS
RALPH MORGAN
MARY NASH
JOHN MACK BROWN
BARLOWE BORLAND
A PARAMOUNT PICTURE
Produced and Directed by FRANK LLOYD Associate Producer HOWARD ESTABROOK Screen Play by Paul Schofield, Gerald Geraghty and Frederick Jackson Based on a Story by Stuart N. Lake
Country of Origin U. S. A.
This Poster leased from Paramount Pictures Inc. it must not be traded, sold, given away or sub-leased.
All Rights Reserved

Adolph Zukor presents
JOAN BENNETT
RANDOLPH SCOTT
in
THE TEXANS
with
MAY ROBSON · WALTER BRENNAN
ROBERT CUMMINGS · ROBERT BARRAT
A LUCIEN HUBBARD Production
Screen Play by Bertram Millhauser, Paul Sloane and William Wister Haines · Based on a Story by Emerson Hough
Directed by JAMES HOGAN · A Paramount Picture

CECIL B. DeMILLE'S
UNION PACIFIC
BARBARA STANWYCK and JOEL McCREA
with AKIM TAMIROFF · ROBERT PRESTON · LYNNE OVERMAN · BRIAN DONLEVY
PRODUCED AND DIRECTED BY CECIL B. DeMILLE
A PARAMOUNT PICTURE

JAMES
MARLENE
DIETRICH · STEWART
DESTRY RIDES AGAIN
with
Charles WINNINGER
Mischa AUER · Brian DONLEVY
IRENE HERVEY · UNA MERKEL · ALLEN JENKINS
WARREN HYMER · BILLY GILBERT
A JOE PASTERNAK PRODUCTION
Directed by GEORGE MARSHALL

ERROL FLYNN
DODGE CITY
in TECHNICOLOR
OLIVIA de HAVILLAND · ANN SHERIDAN
ALAN HALE · FRANK McHUGH · BRUCE CABOT
Directed by MICHAEL CURTIZ
A WARNER BROS. PICTURE

WEST OF CHICAGO
THERE WAS NO LAW!
WEST OF DODGE CITY
THERE WAS NO GOD!
WARNER BROS.
PICTURES INC. PRESENTS
ERROL FLYNN
DODGE CITY
in TECHNICOLOR
OLIVIA de HAVILLAND · ANN SHERIDAN
ALAN HALE · FRANK McHUGH · BRUCE CABOT
Directed by MICHAEL CURTIZ

5
"GUNS ON THEIR HIPS, SONGS ON THEIR LIPS"

THE SINGING-COWBOY CRAZE

The demand for B Westerns remains strong throughout the thirties, but halfway through the decade even the most confirmed horse-opera fans grow restive. By now there has been so much plot repetition and uniformity of production style that they know what to expect as soon as they plunk down their dimes and quarters. Enter maverick producer Nat Levine, who inadvertently revitalizes the genre by hiring an unassuming singer more at home with a guitar pick than a six-shooter . . .

BELOW: Autry's first starring feature, *Tumbling Tumbleweeds* (1935), performed way above expectations, earning Republic several hundred thousand dollars—most of it realized from flat-rate bookings averaging $15. His tyro effort was particularly well received in small towns in the South and Midwest.

Twenty-six-year-old Orvon Grover Autry—known to his friends as Gene—was a modestly successful songwriter, radio vocalist, and recording artist when, in July 1934, he accepted an invitation from Mascot Pictures producer Nat Levine to appear in a Hollywood Western. *In Old Santa Fe* was to star popular cowboy hero Ken Maynard, but the script called for a "dude ranch" entertainer, and Levine felt Autry—at that time one of the leading exponents of "hillbilly music," today known as country and western—would fill the bill neatly.

With his wife, Ina Mae, and fellow performer Lester "Smiley" Burnette, Gene drove west from Oklahoma to California through blazing summer heat. He met Levine and sold the producer on using Smiley in the lengthy square-dance sequence for which he'd been hired. Effectively a screen test, Gene's segment of *In Old Santa Fe* registered solidly with Western fans and persuaded Levine that a singing cowboy was just the novelty he needed to lure customers into theaters at a time when there was a surfeit of B Westerns on the market.

The canny producer signed Autry to a one-year contract at $100 per week—and, seeing how well his new hire worked with the jovial, rotund Burnette, signed Smiley as well. Their first starring vehicle was a twelve-chapter serial titled *The Phantom Empire*—a bizarre fusion of Western, musical, and science fiction. Released in early 1935, it enjoyed great success and vindicated Levine's rather controversial decision to promote Gene as an up-and-coming cowboy star.

Why Autry immediately clicked with moviegoers is still hotly debated by Western-movie aficionados. He was pleasant looking but not ruggedly handsome, as were most horse-opera leading men. He didn't seem particularly

virile, and he could barely stay in a saddle. His dialogue delivery suggested that English might not be his first language. But his screen presence was soothing: Gene radiated optimism and wholesomeness—qualities that weary Depression audiences appreciated. His singing was folksy and untutored, and he was shrewd about the songs he chose to include in his films. Levine decided his new star could take acting lessons and riding lessons, but he couldn't fake the simplicity and sincerity that attracted theater patrons.

ABOVE LEFT: The screen's first singing-cowboy star, Gene Autry, is seen here performing a song in one of his early films for Republic Pictures. A shrewd businessman, Autry parlayed his success as Republic's first homegrown cowboy hero into a multimedia empire eventually worth millions of dollars.

ABOVE RIGHT: The newly christoned Roy Rogers made his starring debut in *Under Western Stars* (1938), a contemporary Western originally planned for Gene Autry, who went on strike not long before shooting was to commence. Roy temporarily inherited Gene's longtime sidekick Smiley Burnette.

Gene's first solo feature, *Tumbling Tumbleweeds* (1935), was released under the auspices of Herbert Yates's newly formed Republic Pictures, with which Levine had merged Mascot. Produced for a modest $18,800, it generated more than ten times that much in revenue within a few short months—the lion's share coming from small-town and rural venues that rented the picture for $15. Some viewers already knew Gene from his radio appearances as "Oklahoma's Yodeling Cowboy." Others had purchased his recordings. But a majority were encountering him for the first time, and they liked what they saw.

In short order, Autry became Republic's top box-office draw. His starring vehicles became more elaborate. Many of their songs were written by Gene, Smiley, and composer Fred Rose, but "America's Singing Cowboy" (as he was often billed) also licensed successful Western tunes written and recorded by others, including such hits as "The Last Roundup," "South of the Border," and "Take Me Back to My Boots and Saddles."

ABOVE: Shooting *Under Western Stars* in the High Sierras, March 1938: Roy at left, director Joe Kane in sunglasses and dark coat. Smiley Burnette seems distracted. Character actor Jack Rockwell, supposedly on horseback, stands on an apple box to deliver his lines.

From 1936 onward, Autry placed high on the annual lists of "Top Ten Western Stars," but his popularity transcended the genre, and from 1940 to 1942 he also occupied positions on the list of "Top Ten Money-Making Stars" industrywide, putting him in the company of such Hollywood heavyweights as Clark Gable, Bing Crosby, Bette Davis, Bob Hope, Betty Grable, and Spencer Tracy. It was almost incomprehensible that a B-Western star from lowly Republic Pictures could have risen to such heights, but Gene did.

Of course, during his ascent to the cinematic stratosphere, Gene had been challenged by imitators from studios big and small. The first was Warner Bros. contract player Dick Foran, a former Princeton footballer and big-band singer. This handsome redheaded Irishman from New Jersey was no more a cowboy than Gene Autry had been, but Warners schooled him in the Western arts, so to speak, and gave his films good production mounting. Unfortunately, he never really caught on with Saturday-matinee audiences, and his series was curtailed in 1937 after twelve entries.

The next entrant in Hollywood's singing-cowboy sweepstakes was Woodward Maurice "Tex" Ritter, born and raised in the Lone Star State. Tall and lanky, Tex had studied law at Northwestern prior to being bitten by the show-business bug. He moved to New York City and found work both on Broadway and in various Western-themed radio programs. At the urging of newly minted movie producer Ed Finney, Ritter moved to Los Angeles in 1936 and made his film debut in *Song of the Gringo*. Never considered a top cowboy star, Ritter nonetheless managed to stay constantly employed, bouncing from one studio to another for nine years. He retired from acting in 1945, but in 1952 he made what likely was his greatest contribution to Western movies by singing "The Ballad of High Noon," which played over the credits of the Gary Cooper classic.

There were other competitors to Gene Autry: Fred Scott, Jack Randall, Bob Baker, Smith Ballew, and even a one-hit wonder named Tex Fletcher, who dragged a print of his sole starring oater, *Six-Gun Rhythm* (1939), with him for a quarter century, habitually projecting it at personal appearances. Ironically, though, the biggest threat to Autry's dominance of the singing-cowboy subgenre came from a fellow Republic contractor.

Leonard Slye of Duck Run, Ohio, was an original member of the Sons of the Pioneers, a well-known group of hillbilly vocalists renowned for their amazing harmonies. Len left the group in 1937, determined to make a name for himself as a solo performer. Republic signed him, changed his name to Dick Weston, and gave him a couple of bit parts.

When Autry went on strike in early 1938, Republic management decided to promote a new singing cowboy, rather than immediately capitulate to Gene's demands. Dick Weston became Roy Rogers and was reintroduced to Western fans as the leading man in that year's *Under Western Stars*, a film originally intended for Autry. The film was good, and Rogers clicked. Republic eventually came to terms with Gene, but Roy was given his own starring series too. More would be heard from him later. ✡

ABOVE: Like most of the singing cowboys, Tex Ritter at first seemed lacking in virility and ruggedness, up to then essential qualities for Western-movie heroes. But he improved dramatically in short order, holding his own in bruising brawls and developing an impressive snap-draw.

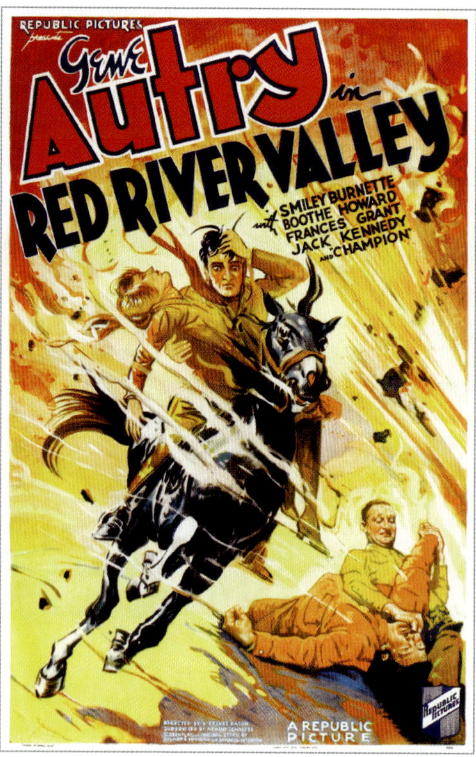

GENE AUTRY

Autry wasn't the first cowboy star to warble on screen—that honor belongs to Ken Maynard—but he was the first whose films were specifically designed as vehicles to accommodate his musical talents. Republic Pictures groomed Gene for stardom and developed the formula that quickly made him the most popular Western personality in the business. With very few exceptions, his films were contemporary horse operas. Gene always played himself, and scripts often called for him to be a radio vocalist or recording star (or both). Since he had difficulty projecting virility and forcefulness, scriptwriters frequently made his leading lady a spitfire who clashed with the mild-mannered cowpoke but always required his help to extricate her from some difficult situation. No matter how knotty the problem, Gene found time to perform a handful of songs in each picture, many of them already made famous by other recording artists. And he engaged in typical Western action—riding, fighting, shooting—as plots demanded.

REPUBLIC PICTURES presents
GENE AUTRY
in
"YODELIN' KID FROM PINE RIDGE"
with
SMILEY BURNETTE · BETTY BRONSON
The TENNESSEE RAMBLERS
Directed by JOE KANE
Screen play by JACK NATTEFORD, STUART McGOWAN, DORRELL McGOWAN
Original Story by JACK NATTEFORD
ASSOCIATE PRODUCER ARMAND SCHAEFER
REPUBLIC PICTURES
A REPUBLIC PICTURE

REPUBLIC PICTURES presents
Gene
AUTRY
in
"ROOTIN' TOOTIN' RHYTHM"
with SMILEY BURNETTE
ARMIDA
Directed by
MACK V. WRIGHT
Screen Play by
JACK NATTEFORD
Original Story By
JOHNSTON McCULLEY
Associate Producer
ARMAND SCHAEFER
A REPUBLIC PICTURE

Gene AUTRY
IN
MAN from MUSIC MOUNTAIN
with
SMILEY BURNETTE
CAROL HUGHES ★ POLLY JENKINS
AND HER PLOWBOYS
Directed by JOE KANE
Associate Producer CHARLES E. FORD
A Republic
PICTURE

Gene AUTRY
RHYTHM OF THE SADDLE
SMILEY BURNETTE ★ PERT KELTON
DIRECTED BY GEORGE SHERMAN
ASSOCIATE PRODUCER-HARRY GREY
A Republic PICTURE

Gene AUTRY
in
HOME ON THE PRAIRIE
with
Smiley BURNETTE
JUNE STOREY
SHERVEN BROTHERS
RODEOLIERS
Directed by JACK TOWNLEY
Associate Producer HARRY GREY
A Republic
PICTURE

GENE AUTRY
WITH SMILEY BURNETTE
IN
COLORADO SUNSET
AND
JUNE STOREY
BARBARA PEPPER
LARRY "BUSTER" CRABBE
ROBERT BARRAT
PATSY MONTANA
THE CBS-KMBC
TEXAS RANGERS
Directed by
GEORGE SHERMAN
A Republic PICTURE
REPUBLIC PICTURES

SOUTH OF THE BORDER
SCREEN SENSATION!
A
STARRING
Gene AUTRY
WITH SMILEY BURNETTE
JUNE STOREY
LUPITA TOVAR
MARY LEE
DUNCAN RENALDO
A Republic PICTURE

MELODY RANCH
A REPUBLIC PICTURE
GENE AUTRY ★ JIMMY DURANTE
ANN MILLER ★ BARTON MacLANE · BARBARA ALLEN (VERA VAGUE)
GEORGE "Gabby" HAYES · JEROME COWAN · MARY LEE · JOSEPH SANTLEY · Director

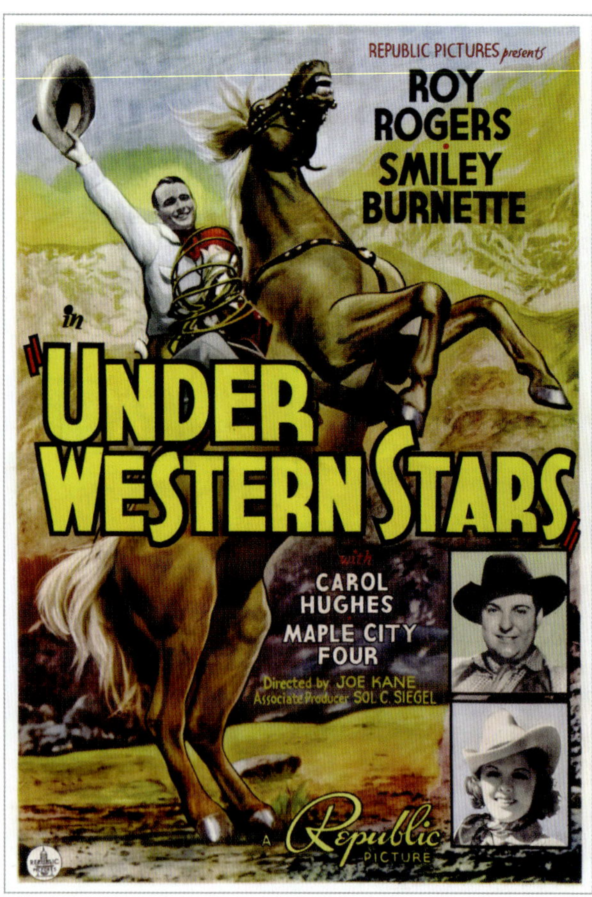

ROY ROGERS

After several years and numerous movie appearances with the Sons of the Pioneers singing group, Ohio native Leonard Slye struck out on his own. He wangled a contract at Republic Pictures and played a few bit parts, for which he was billed as Dick Weston. Then, when Gene Autry went on strike in early 1938, the Republic brass changed young Leonard's name to Roy Rogers and hastily shunted him into a film that had been prepared for Autry. *Under Western Stars* proved a big success, and its newly minted star was duly awarded his own series. Roy's Westerns were period pieces, and he often played youthful historical figures, including Buffalo Bill, Billy the Kid, and Wild Bill Hickok. With George "Gabby" Hayes as his sidekick, Rogers built a reliable fan following. When Gene went into military service the following year, Republic crowned Roy "King of the Cowboys," boosted his budgets, and increased the musical content of his films to appeal to family audiences.

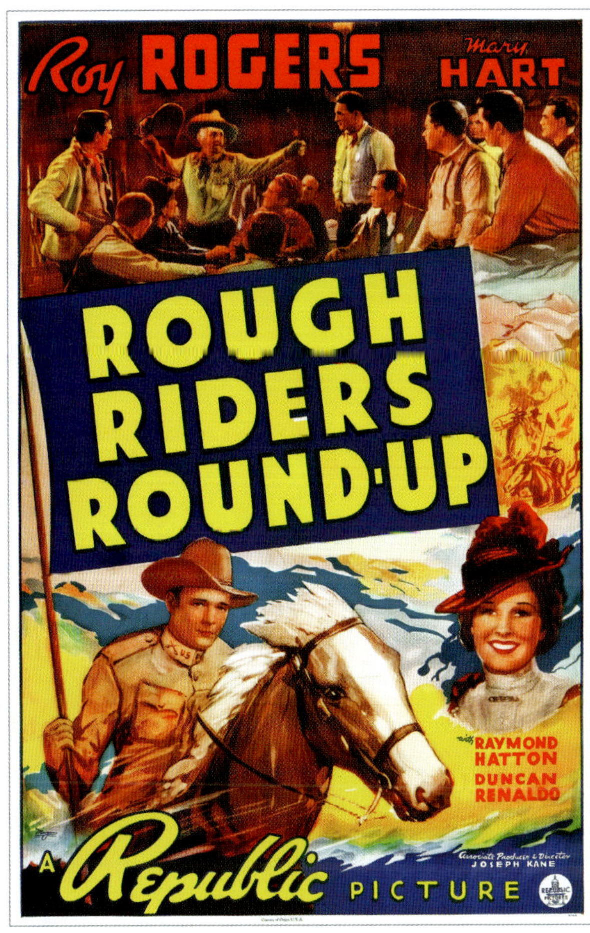
Roy ROGERS
Mary HART
ROUGH
RIDERS
ROUND-UP
with RAYMOND HATTON
DUNCAN RENALDO
A Republic PICTURE

ROY ROGERS
MARY HART
FRONTIER
PONY EXPRESS
with RAYMOND HATTON
Associate Producer & Director JOSEPH KANE
A Republic PICTURE

ROY ROGERS
MARY HART
IN OLD CALIENTE
with GEORGE "GABBY" HAYES
JACK LA RUE
KATHERINE DeMILLE
A Republic PICTURE

ROY ROGERS
in
WALL STREET
COWBOY
with
GEORGE "GABBY" HAYES
RAYMOND HATTON
ANN BALDWIN · LOUISIANA LOU
JACK ROPER
Associate Producer Director JOSEPH KANE
A Republic PICTURE

ROY ROGERS
as
THE ARIZONA KID
with
GEORGE "Gabby" HAYES
and
SALLY MARCH · STUART HAMBLEN
Associate Producer-Director JOSEPH KANE
A Republic PICTURE

Roy ROGERS
in
SAGA of DEATH VALLEY
WITH
GEORGE "GABBY" HAYES
DONALD BARRY
DORIS DAY
FRANK M. THOMAS
Associate Producer-Director JOSEPH KANE
A Republic PICTURE

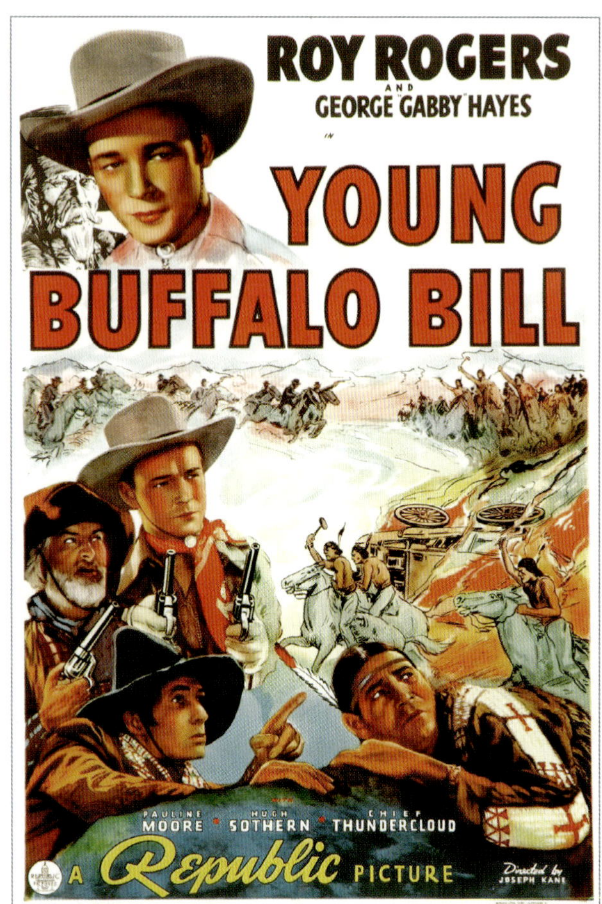
ROY ROGERS
AND
GEORGE "GABBY" HAYES
in
YOUNG BUFFALO BILL
PAULINE MOORE · HUGH SOTHERN · CHIEF THUNDERCLOUD
A Republic PICTURE
Directed by JOSEPH KANE

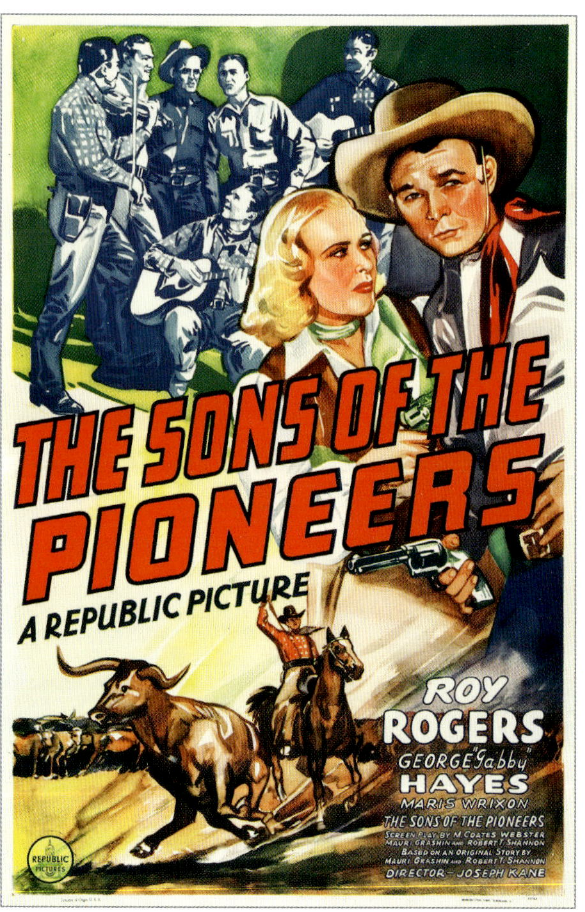
THE SONS OF THE PIONEERS
A REPUBLIC PICTURE
ROY ROGERS
GEORGE "Gabby" HAYES
MARIS WRIXON
THE SONS OF THE PIONEERS
SCREEN PLAY BY M. COATES WEBSTER MAURI GRASHIN AND ROBERT T. SHANNON
BASED ON AN ORIGINAL STORY BY MAURI GRASHIN AND ROBERT T. SHANNON
DIRECTOR—JOSEPH KANE

ROY ROGERS
King of the Cowboys
'TRIGGER'
SMARTEST HORSE IN THE MOVIES
AND
SMILEY BURNETTE
SILVER SPURS
A REPUBLIC PICTURE
JOHN CARRADINE
PHYLLIS BROOKS
JEROME COWAN JOYCE COMPTON
BOB NOLAN and
THE SONS OF THE PIONEERS
JOSEPH KANE — DIRECTOR
ORIGINAL SCREEN PLAY BY
JOHN K. BUTLER J. BENTON CHENEY
REPUBLIC PICTURES
Country of Origin U.S.A.
MORGAN LITHO. CORP. CLEVELAND, O.

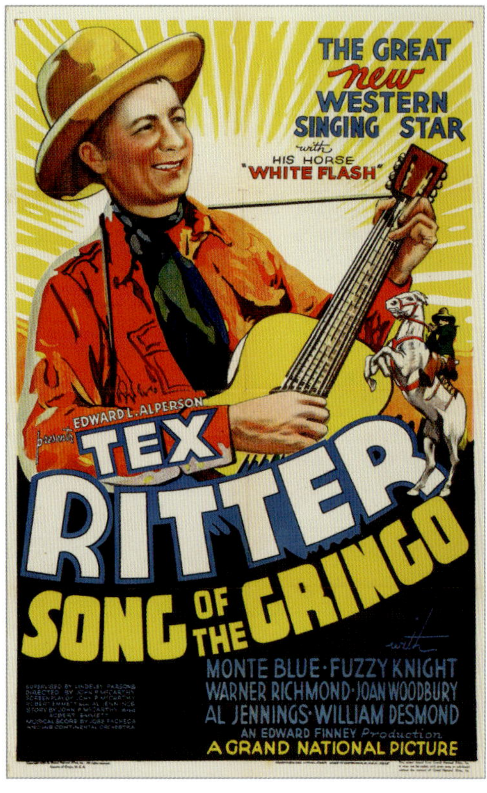

TEX RITTER

While he never reached the heights that Autry and Rogers did, Tex Ritter enjoyed a fairly substantial career. He was discovered by Republic publicity director Ed Finney, who signed the lanky Texan to a contract in 1936 and took him to the newly formed Grand National. Eager to capitalize on Gene Autry's meteoric rise to fame, the company agreed to let Finney produce a Tex Ritter series. Tex lacked virility and, like Autry, needed extensive lessons in riding and fighting to make himself presentable as a Western he-man. Vocally he was more than qualified, and he often included authentic cowboy songs in his pictures. After two years, Finney took Tex to Monogram Pictures and endowed his starring vehicles with slightly better production values. Their partnership dissolved in 1941, and Ritter moved on. He worked steadily in B Westerns for the next four years, although never again in a series of his own.

EDWARD L. ALPERSON
presents
TEX
RITTER
and his horse "WHITE FLASH" in
"TEX RIDES
WITH THE
Boy Scouts"
An EDWARD F. FINNEY Production
DIRECTED BY RAY TAYLOR
SUPERVISED BY LINDSLEY PARSONS
SCREENPLAY BY EDMUND KELSO
A GRAND
NATIONAL PICTURE

Edward L. Alperson presents
Tex
Ritter
and his horse "White Flash" in
"Frontier Town"
An Edward F. Finney Production
Directed by Ray Taylor
Supervised by Lindsley Parsons
Screenplay by Edmond Kelso
A Grand National Picture

Monogram Pictures presents
Tex Ritter
in "Starlight over Texas"
with the Northwesterners
Directed by Al Herman
Screen play by John Rathmell
An Edward Finney Production

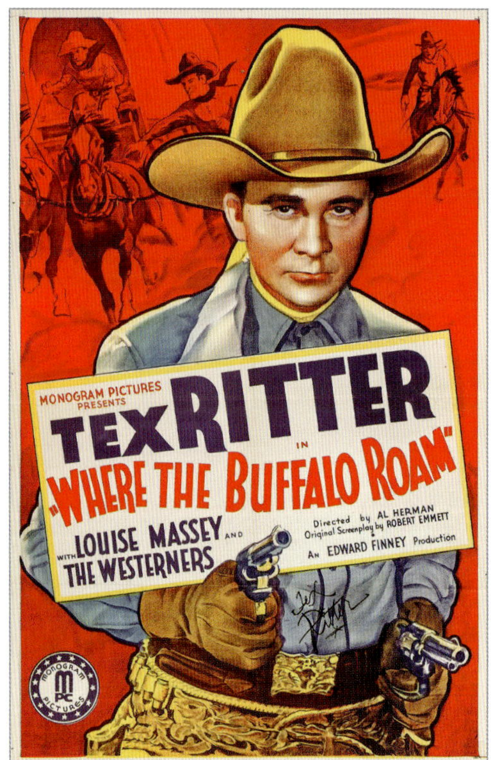
Monogram Pictures presents
Tex Ritter
in
"Where the Buffalo Roam"
with Louise Massey and The Westerners
Directed by Al Herman
Original Screenplay by Robert Emmett
An Edward Finney Production

Tex
RITTER
WITH HIS HORSE
WHITE FLASH
IN
"WESTBOUND STAGE"
AN EDWARD FINNEY PRODUCTION
DIRECTED BY
SPENCER GORDON BENNET
Screenplay by ROBERT EMMETT
Story by JOHN FOSTER
A Monogram PICTURE

MONOGRAM PICTURES
PRESENTS
Tex RITTER IN
"Pals OF THE SILVER SAGE"
SUGAR DAWN
MUSICAL "SLIM" ANDREWS
WITH HIS HORSE WHITE FLASH
AN EDWARD FINNEY PRODUCTION
DIRECTED BY AL HERMAN SCREENPLAY BY ROBERT EMMETT

TEX
RITTER
"RIDERS OF THE FRONTIER"
AND HIS HORSE
"WHITE FLASH"
Directed by SPENCER BENNET
Story & Screenplay by JESSE DUFFY JOSEPH LEVERING
AN
EDWARD FINNEY
PRODUCTION
A MONOGRAM PICTURE

SECOND-STRING COWBOYS

The singing-cowboy phenomenon took Hollywood by storm: within two years of Gene Autry's *Tumbling Tumbleweeds*, a half-dozen competitors were making musical Westerns for major and minor studios alike (and several more soon to come). Most lacked authenticity, though: Warner Bros.' Dick Foran and Principal Pictures' Smith Ballew were radio vocalists and big-band singers, Spectrum's Fred Scott sang in opera and other theatrical productions, and Monogram's Jack Randall didn't sing professionally at all. Only Universal's Bob Baker could lay claim to being a genuine son of the West, having worked as a cowboy and competed in rodeos before entering films. But in the wake of Autry's success, practically anyone who could carry a tune and looked good in a Stetson was considered a potential rival. The Sons of the Pioneers, who supported Charles Starrett in the late thirties and Roy Rogers in the forties, came closest to duplicating an authentic Western sound.

The
SINGING, FIGHTING SON of THE PLAINS!
Dick
FORAN
in
BLAZING
SIXES
with
HELEN
VALKIS

Here he is! THE NEWEST and GREATEST WESTERN STAR
THE New UNIVERSAL Presents
Bob BAKER
"COURAGE of the WEST"
with
LOIS JANUARY · J. FARRELL McDONALD
FUZZY KNIGHT · HARRY WOODS · CARL STOCKDALE
BUDDY COX · FORREST TAYLOR
Original Story and Screen Play by J. Norton Parker
Directed by Joseph H. Lewis
A New UNIVERSAL Picture

THE New UNIVERSAL presents
Bob
BAKER
"The Singing Outlaw"
with
JOAN BARCLAY · FUZZY KNIGHT
HARRY WOODS · CARL STOCKDALE
ROY MASON · GEORGIA O'DELL
RALPH LEWIS
A New UNIVERSAL Picture

A
NEW UNIVERSAL
PICTURE
Bob Baker
in
THE LAST STAND!
with CONSTANCE MOORE
FUZZY KNIGHT · EARL HODGINS · GLENN STRANGE

BOB
BAKER
GHOST TOWN
RIDERS
with FAY SHANNON · GEORGE CLEVELAND · FORREST TAYLOR

BOB
BAKER
THE
PHANTOM
STAGE
with
Marjorie REYNOLDS · Forrest TAYLOR
Reed HOWES · Glenn STRANGE
A NEW UNIVERSAL PICTURE

SPECTRUM PICTURES CORP. presents
FRED SCOTT
WITH HIS FIERY STALLION "WHITE KING"
SILVERY VOICED BARITONE
in
"THE SINGING BUCKAROO"
with
WILLIAM FAVERSHAM
VICTORIA VINTON
CLIFF NAZARRO
AND THE SINGING BUCKAROOS
DIRECTED BY TOM GIBSON
A CALLAGHAN-BUELL PRODUCTION

SPECTRUM PICTURES CORP. Presents
FRED SCOTT
The SILVERY VOICED BARITONE
in
"The RANGERS' ROUNDUP"
A STAN LAUREL PRODUCTION
DIRECTED BY SAM NEWFIELD
PRODUCED BY JED BUELL
with AL ST. JOHN
CHRISTINE McINTYRE
EARL HODGINS

SPECTRUM PICTURES CORP. presents
FRED SCOTT
SILVERY VOICED BARITONE
in
MOONLIGHT ON THE RANGE
AL ST. JOHN
LOIS JANUARY
DICK CURTIS
FRANK LA RUE
Directed by SAM NEWFIELD
A CALLAGHAN-BUELL PRODUCTION

SPECTRUM PICTURES Presents
FRED SCOTT
(SILVERY VOICED BARITONE)
WITH HIS FLAMING STALLION
WHITE KING
MELODY OF THE PLAINS
with
LOUISE SMALL
AL ST. JOHN
DAVID SHARPE
LAFE McKEE
BUD JAMESON
and a troupe of dare-devil riders..
Directed by SAM NEWFIELD
A CALLAGHAN-BUELL Production

SPECTRUM PICTURES CORP. presents
FRED SCOTT
SILVERY VOICED BARITONE
WITH HIS FLAMING STALLION "WHITE KING"
IN "ROMANCE RIDES THE RANGE"
WITH
CLIFF NAZARRO — MARION SHILLING
STORY BY TOM GIBSON - DIRECTED BY HARRY FRAZER
A BUELL-CALLAGHAN PRODUCTION

SPECTRUM PICTURES CORP.
presents
FRED SCOTT
SILVERY VOICED BUCKAROO
in
CODE of the FEARLESS
WITH CLAIR ROCHELLE
JOHN MERTON RAWLINS·WALTER McGRAIL·HARRY HARVEY
DIRECTED BY RAYMOND K. JOHNSON ··· A C.C. BURR PRODUCTION

THE ROUGH-AND-READY WEST ROARS INTO ROMANTIC HAWAII....

SOL LESSER presents

HAWAIIAN BUCKAROO

with

Smith BALLEW · Evelyn KNAPP

Pat O'BRIEN · Harry WOODS

DIRECTED by RAY TAYLOR

ORIGINAL STORY AND SCREENPLAY by DAN JARRETT

RELEASED by GUARANTEED PICTURES CO. INC.

A PRINCIPAL Production

Country of Origin U.S.A.

MORGAN LITHO. CORP. CLEVELAND, O.

MONOGRAM PICTURES presents
Jack RANDALL
THE NEW SINGING COWBOY STAR IN
IN RIDERS OF THE DAWN
with
WARNER RICHMOND · GEORGE COOPER · PEGGY KEYS
PRODUCED and DIRECTED BY R.N. BRADBURY
ORIGINAL STORY BY ROBERT EMMETT
MONOGRAM MPC PICTURES

MONOGRAM PICTURES presents
Jack RANDALL IN
"DANGER VALLEY"
Produced and Directed by R. N. BRADBURY
Original Story by ROBERT EMMETT
RECORDED BY WESTERN ELECTRIC MIRROPHONIC SOUND
MONOGRAM MPC PICTURES

MONOGRAM PICTURES presents
Jack RANDALL
In
"MAN'S COUNTRY"
SUPERVISED By ROBERT TANSEY
DIRECTED by ROBERT HILL
SCREEN PLAY by ROBERT EMMETT
MONOGRAM MPC PICTURES

GUNS ON THEIR HIPS! SONGS ON THEIR LIPS!
CHARLES STARRETT
IN
RIDERS OF BLACK RIVER
WITH
IRIS MEREDITH
and
SONS OF THE PIONEERS
Famous Radio Stars
Screen play by BENNETT R. COHEN
Directed by NORMAN DEMING
a COLUMBIA PICTURE
COLUMBIA PICTURES

HOOFBEATS RINGIN'... COWBOYS SINGIN'!
SIX-GUNS BARKIN'... LOVERS LARKIN'!
The THUNDERING WEST
STARRING
CHARLES STARRETT
with
IRIS MEREDITH
and the
SONS OF THE PIONEERS
Famous Radio Stars
Screen play by BENNETT R. COHEN
Directed by SAM NELSON
A COLUMBIA PICTURE
COLUMBIA PICTURES

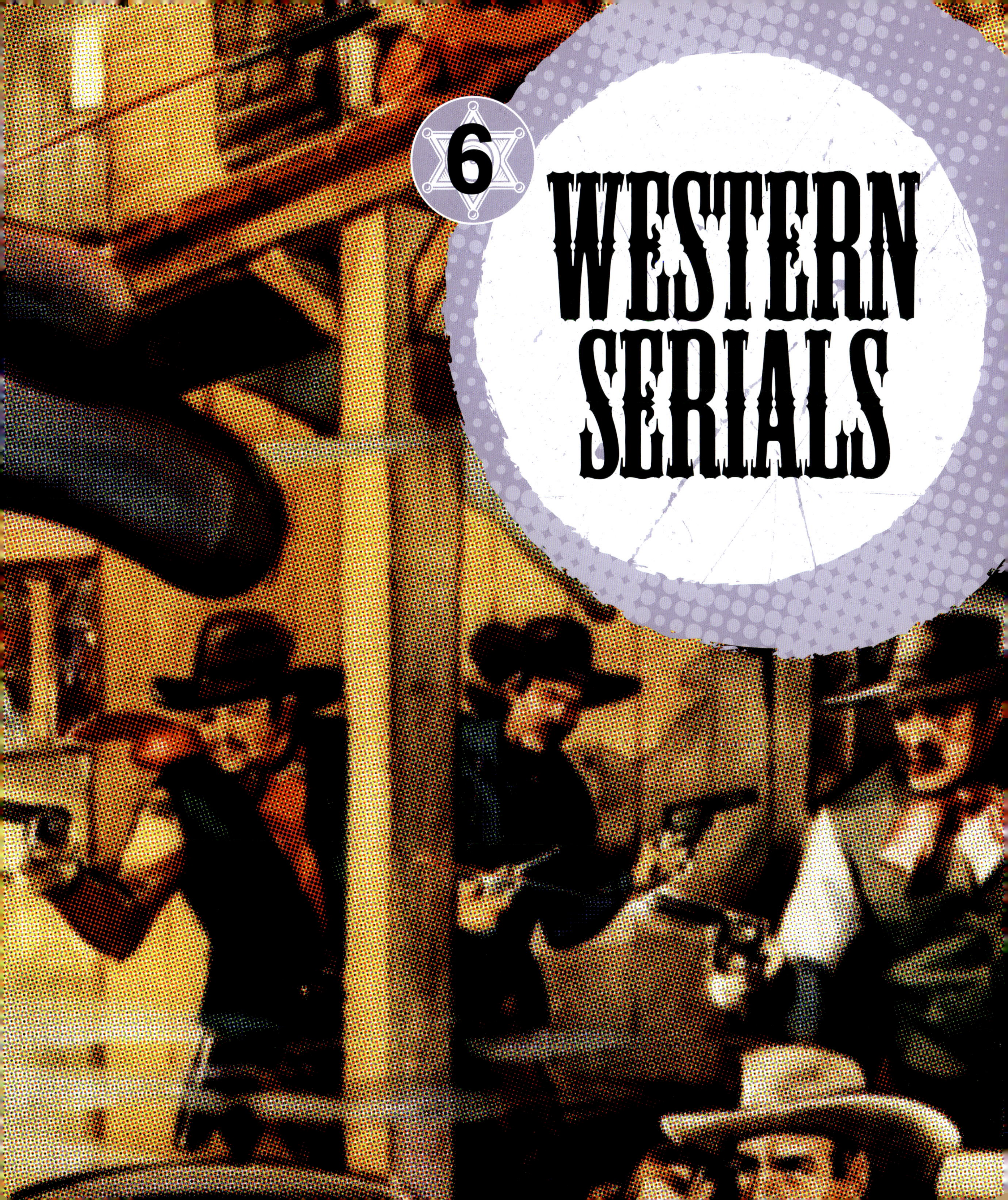
6
WESTERN
SERIALS

WINNING THE WEST WEEKLY

The "Continued in Our Next" style of storytelling was embraced by motion-picture producers in 1913, making weekly theater attendance a habit for millions of Americans. Movie serials revolve around melodramatic plots and pulse-pounding action that culminates in life-threatening situations for their protagonists. Western "chapter plays" enjoy tremendous popularity for the duration of the serial's tenure as a theatrical attraction . . .

BELOW: Ruggedly handsome William Desmond, a stage and vaudeville actor before breaking into films, became a top star at Universal and made nothing but Western chapter plays after *The Riddle Rider* (1924), one of the highest-grossing serials released during the twenties.

OPPOSITE: Oklahoma native Jack Hoxie, a former rodeo performer, had appeared in thirty-five films of various genres before securing the title role in *Lightning Bryce* (1919), which established him as a Western star. Quite popular during the silent era, he didn't fare as well in talkies.

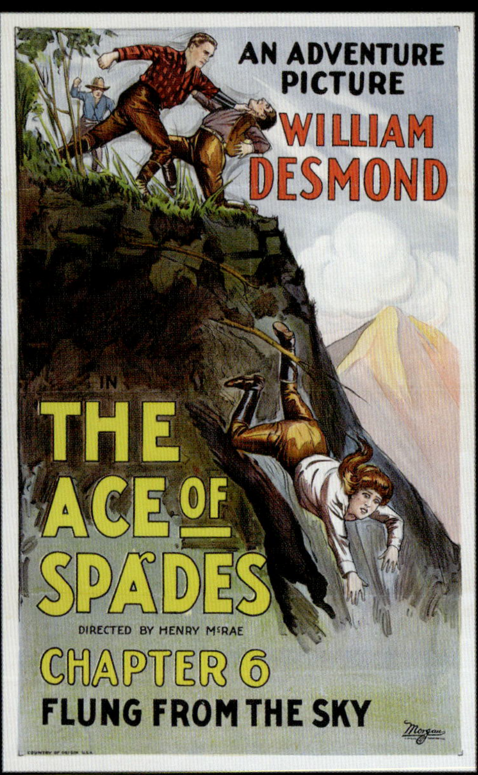

Serialized storytelling predated motion pictures by many decades, becoming especially popular in newspapers and magazines of the mid-nineteenth century. Novels were routinely published by installment in periodicals before being issued between hard covers. In the magazine business, serializing book-length works was considered a surefire way to build and maintain circulation: new readers coming upon early episodes of a particularly entertaining story invariably stayed with it through the final chapters. By that time, it was assumed, they were hooked on the magazine and would faithfully purchase future issues.

Eventually, the same approach to audience building was adopted by the motion-picture industry. The reasoning was that serialized films, with installments presented at weekly intervals on the same night, would help make theater attendance a habitual rather than occasional occurrence. And it did.

Although many studios produced series films, with the same leading characters appearing in self-contained short subjects, the first true serial was *The Adventures of Kathlyn* (1913), a melodramatic adventure yarn taking place mostly in India and chronicling the exploits of a plucky young woman (Kathlyn Williams) determined to find her long-lost father. To guarantee that thrill-hungry audiences would return week after week, each two-reel chapter ended with Kathlyn imperiled either by wild animals or human adversaries. Such endings came to be called "cliffhangers" by trade-journal reviewers because a fair number of them faded out with heroines dangling from rocky cliffs.

Given the popularity of Westerns, it was inevitable that producers of "chapter plays," as they were sometimes called, would turn to the genre. But the average horse-opera plot, while perfectly adequate for a five-reel feature, was woefully insufficient for a thirty-reel serial. Therefore, considerable

ARROW FILM CORPORATION
OFFERS
THE GREATEST SERIAL EVER MADE
LIGHTNING BRYCE
FEATURING
Ann Little AND Jack Hoxie
DIRECTED BY PAUL HURST
PRODUCED BY
NATIONAL FILM CORPORATION OF AMERICA, INC.
STORY BY JOE BRANDT
EPISODE FOUR
"THE NOOSE"

ABOVE LEFT: Based on the wildly popular radio show, *The Lone Ranger* was a box-office sensation, receiving more favorable reviews than most serials and playing major theaters in the nation's biggest cities. It was the highest earning of Republic Pictures' sixty-six serials.

ABOVE RIGHT: This candid photo was taken in December 1937, amid the picturesque Alabama Hills of Lone Pine, California, during the shooting of a scene for *The Lone Ranger*, with the masked rider (doubled by legendary Western stuntman Yakima Canutt) jumping off a boulder onto two uniformed troopers.

ingenuity was required from chapter-play scripters. Writers on the payroll of Carl Laemmle's Universal Pictures (originally called the Universal Film Manufacturing Company) took the easy way out, padding their plots with frequent and interminable Indian attacks on wagon trains. Such lazy scripting characterized Universal Western chapter plays made as late as the early 1940s, allowing producers to stretch their budgets by reusing action footage originally shot in the early twenties.

Other serial scribes transcended the genre's limitations by setting their Westerns in the present day, resulting in hybrids that found Stetson-wearing, six-shooting heroes flying planes, falling from skyscrapers, and negotiating waterways by speedboat. One such offering, *Lightning Bryce* (1919), extended its narrative by transferring hero and heroine from rolling plains to San Francisco's Chinatown for several chapters.

Marketing the serial called for inventive measures, with one of them eventually adopted for the promotion of *all* movies: plastering outsized posters on roadside billboards. In the nickelodeon era, theaters changed their short-subject programs on a daily basis; posters were displayed outside and in the lobby to attract the attention of passersby and, it was hoped, lure them into the venue on impulse. By the late teens, newly constructed picture palaces ran feature films with recognizable stars over several days—or, in rare cases, for a full week. Exhibitors therefore were justified in affixing posters to wooden fences or the sides of brick buildings. But mounting jumbo-sized posters on roadside billboards was too costly and time consuming to warrant the few days of exposure they would have.

A chapter play, however, would remain in theaters for up to twenty weeks (in the form's early years, when serials ran longer than they would later on), so exhibitors could more readily absorb the cost and effort of billboard advertising for four or five months of exposure. The first serial to utilize this concept was Pathé's legendary *The Perils of Pauline* (1914), with fifty-two billboards appearing in the New York metropolitan area. Just three years later, Vitagraph reported that it was promoting a chapter play entitled *The Fighting Trail* on twelve thousand billboards nationwide.

The advent of talking pictures temporarily slowed Western-serial proliferation while filmmakers grappled with the difficulty of recording sound outdoors. But this obstacle was overcome with relative speed, and the Depression years found each of the silent era's major cowboy stars—Tom Mix, Buck Jones, Tim McCoy, Hoot Gibson, Ken Maynard, Tom Tyler—toiling in episodic thrillers.

Republic Pictures supplied the industry's best Western serials, maintaining a high action quotient and feature-quality production values despite their limited budgets. The most profitable chapter play in the company's twenty-year history was *The Lone Ranger* (1938), which earned over $1.1 million—a significant feat inasmuch as most exhibitors rented episodes for as little as three dollars each.

Beginning in the thirties, serial posters differed from those for feature films, with a single design element accounting for the variance. During the teens and twenties, it had been common for chapter-play distributors to supply unique posters for each episode of each serial, but as the Depression tightened its grip on moviegoers and weekly theater admissions fell precipitously, the makers of episodic epics looked for ways to cut their costs. Budgets were trimmed and shooting schedules telescoped, but the austerity extended to the preparation of marketing materials as well.

Rather than commission illustrations for twelve or fifteen posters per serial, art directors settled for two: a full painting for the "chapter 1" paper and a partial painting for the succeeding installments. The latter were designed with a box in which could be inserted tinted versions of the black-and-white scene stills leased to theaters for lobby display. Each episode's poster had a different photograph. This proved an effective alternative to designing a dozen or more one-sheets per chapter play, each with its own painting. Universal was reluctant to adopt this format, but Republic and Columbia embraced it in the late thirties and continued to use it until theatrical serials ceased production in the mid-fifties.

By then, serials had lost their predominantly youthful viewers to television, which relied on old features and serials for programming in the years before major networks contracted with Hollywood studios to produce prime-time series. The kiddies were reluctant to spend their dimes and quarters to see Westerns and chapter plays in theaters when they could see them on TV for nothing. ✡

ABOVE: Columbia's *Tex Granger* (1948) was one of numerous Western serials adapted from popular comic strips and comic books. Licensing favorite characters from other media was a favorite tactic of Hollywood studios and gave them a leg up on advertising and promotional efforts.

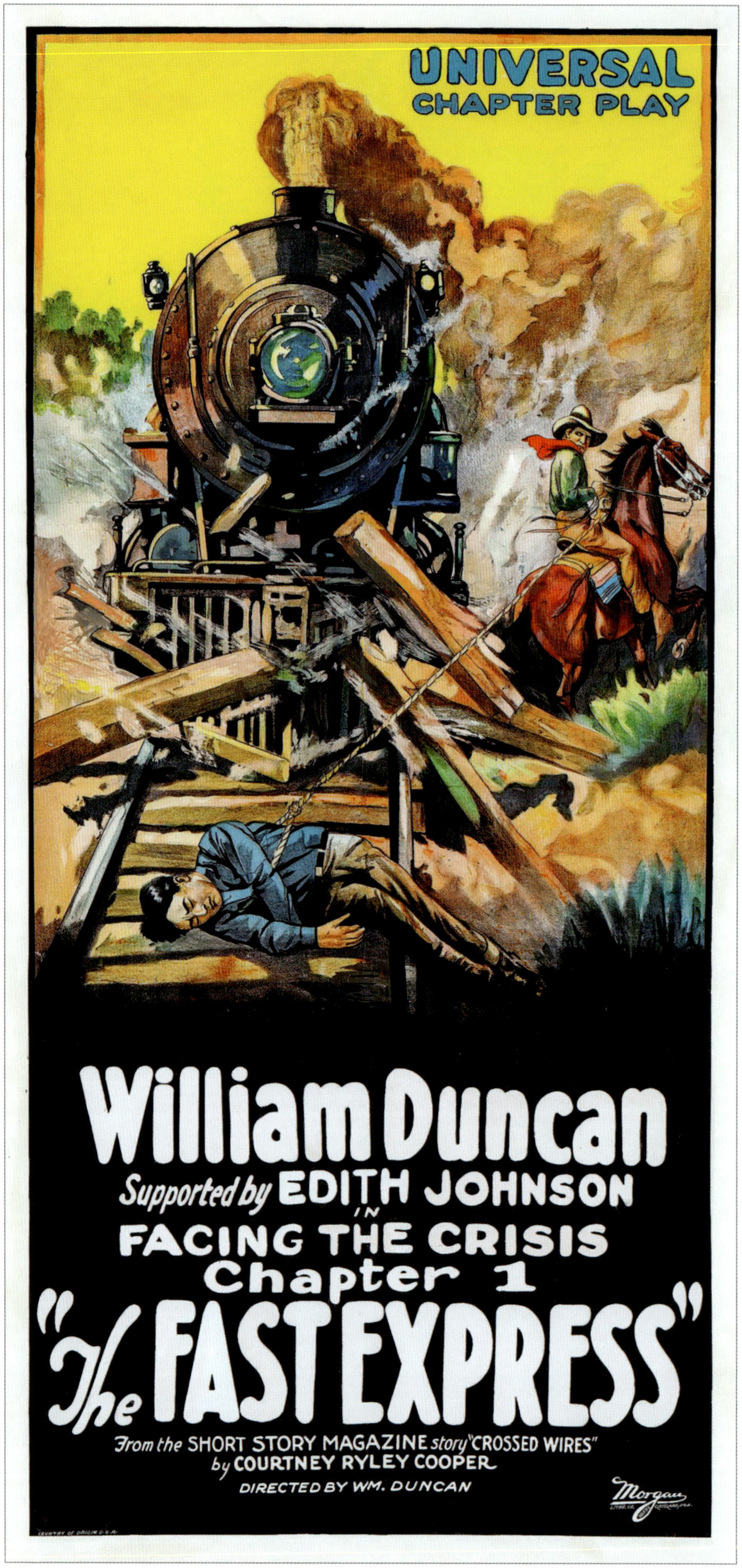

SILENT-ERA SERIALS

The earliest star of Western serials was Vitagraph Studios' William Duncan, a burly Scot who directed his starring vehicles, did his own stunts, and shot on location in rugged areas such as the Sierra Nevada mountain range. He later moved to Universal, which already had a sagebrush serial star in William "Riddle Rider" Desmond. By 1924, Duncan had worn out his welcome. Pathé was home to chapter-play queen Pearl White, but her episodic epics were urban-based affairs. Pearl's nearest rival, Ruth Roland, appeared in exciting Western serials with rousing action sequences and ingenious "cliffhanger" endings. Late in the silent era, demand for such serials was so strong that fly-by-night producers were able to market patchwork efforts such as *The Range Fighter* (1929), cobbled together from segments of six mid-twenties Ken Maynard feature films, with newly written intertitles that vainly attempted to fuse disparate plots into a unified narrative.

A PATHE' SERIAL
The open window was across the room—could she reach it?
RUTH ROLAND ..IN..
RUTH OF THE ROCKIES
From the novel "BROADWAY BAB" by Johnston McCulley
...... EPISODE 13 ......
"THE SURPRISE ATTACK"
Produced at ROBERT BRUNTON STUDIOS
By Ruth Roland Serial Productions, Inc.

A PATHÉ SERIAL
In the wake of the sinister shadow came Ruiz's hand.
Ruth Roland
..IN..
"The AVENGING ARROW"
by ARTHUR PRESTON HANKINS
..EPISODE 7..
"THE DOUBLE GAME"
Produced by Ruth Roland Serials, Inc.
...At The Robert Brunton Studios, Inc...

"Frenal double-crossed me—and you're going to pay!"
Dorothy Phillips
..IN..
THE BAR-C MYSTERY
WITH
Wallace MacDonald, Philo McCullough
and Ethel Clayton
PRODUCED BY C·W·PATTON
Pathépicture
TRADE MARK

EXHIBITORS' PICTURES CORPORATION presents
KEN MAYNARD
IN
"THE RANGE FIGHTER"
A Thrilling Serial in Ten Chapters
TALKING PROLOGUE
SOUND EFFECTS
MUSIC
EPISODE 8
"THE PIT OF DESPAIR"

MIGHTY MASCOT

Nat Levine incorporated Mascot Pictures in 1927 to take advantage of the burgeoning demand for serials. His philosophy: cram as much action as possible into each chapter and assume that Saturday-matinee audiences won't notice the lack of cohesive plotting and production niceties. Overall, Levine's chapter plays were among the cheapest ever produced, but he wasn't afraid to spend big money on marketable stars such as Tom Mix, Ken Maynard, and even Rin Tin Tin. Mascot's *The Lightning Warrior* (1931), one of its best chapter plays, was Rinty's final film; he died shortly after its completion. Nat's ace in the hole was stuntman Yakima Canutt, who devised and often performed the breathtaking sequences that distinguished Mascot serials from those of other small studios. His strangest episodic opus was *The Phantom Empire* (1934), a bizarre fusion of Western and science fiction that gave singing cowboy Gene Autry his first starring role.

MASCOT SERIALS
"BLAZING THE TRAIL"
1650 BROADWAY
NEW YORK N.Y.
ERIE
Nat Levine presents
JAMES FENIMORE COOPER'S
IMMORTAL CLASSIC
"The Last of the Mohicans"
with
HARRY CAREY
EDWINA BOOTH • HOBART BOSWORTH
JUNIOR COGHLAN
WALTER MILLER • LUCILE BROWNE • WALTER McGRAIL
NELSON McDOWELL • EDWARD HEARN & BOB KORTMAN
CHAPTER 3 "RIFLE OR TOMAHAWK"
DIRECTED BY
FORD BEEBE and
B.REEVES EASON
AN EPIC SERIAL IN 12 CHAPTERS

Nat Levine presents
REX and RIN-TIN-TIN, Jr.
KING of WILD HORSES
DOG HERO OF YOUNG AMERICA
(TOGETHER FOR THE FIRST TIME) in
"LAW OF THE WILD"
with BOB CUSTER
BEN TURPIN
LUCILE BROWNE
Directed by
ARMAND SCHAEFER and BREEZY EASON
Chapter 1.
"The MAN KILLER!"
a
MASCOT SUPER SERIAL in
12 Thrill-inspiring Chapters
"Blazing the Trail"
MASCOT SERIALS
1776 BROADWAY
NEW YORK, N.Y.

GREATEST WESTERN STAR IN HISTORY!
HIS FIRST SERIAL— HIS GREATEST PICTURE!
NAT LEVINE presents
TOM MIX
IDOL OF EVERY BOY IN THE WORLD
IN
"The MIRACLE RIDER"
with TONY, JR.
CHAPTER 1
"The VANISHING INDIAN"
SENSATIONAL 15 EPISODE SERIAL OF THE TEXAS RANGERS
"BLAZING THE TRAIL"
MASCOT SERIALS
1776 BROADWAY NEW YORK, N.Y.
A MASCOT MASTER SERIAL
DIRECTED BY B. REEVES EASON & ARMAND SCHAEFER
SUPERVISED BY VICTOR ZOBEL

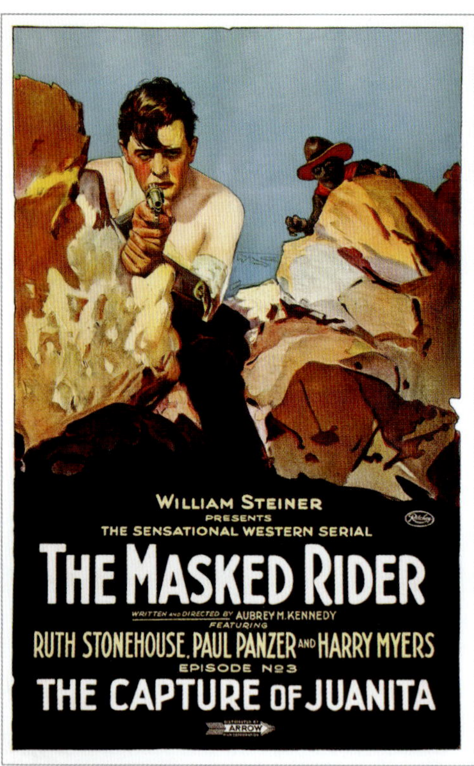

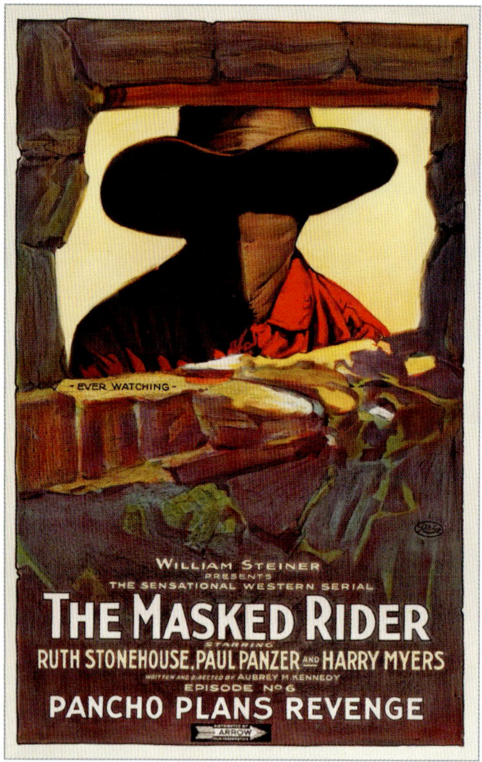

WHO *WERE* THOSE MASKED MEN?

Youthful fans of Western serials loved protagonists who wore facial coverings to obscure their identities. The first such character to headline a cowboy-themed chapter play was the eponymous mystery man of *The Masked Rider* (1919). Newly formed Republic Pictures got into the act in 1936 with *The Vigilantes Are Coming*, whose elaborately garbed hero was called "The Eagle," and the following year with *Zorro Rides Again*, the first of numerous serials featuring various incarnations of Johnston McCulley's famous pulp-fiction caballero. Top Western star Buck Jones wore a white mask and billowing white cloak to play *The Phantom Rider* in Universal's 1936 episodic epic. But by far the most beloved hero of this type was radio's legendary Masked Rider of the Plains, who reached the screen in *The Lone Ranger* (1938) and *The Lone Ranger Rides Again* (1939), two classic Republic serials directed by William Witney and John English.

Hi-yo Silver!
The LONE RANGER RIDES AGAIN
with
Robert LIVINGSTON
Chief THUNDER-CLOUD
SILVER CHIEF
DUNCAN RENALDO
Directed by WILLIAM WITNEY · JOHN ENGLISH
Associate Producer - ROBERT BECHE
Based on the Radio Serial.
"THE LONE RANGER" by FRAN STRIKER
Republic
SERIAL in
15 Whirlwind CHAPTERS
REPUBLIC SERIAL

ZORRO AND HIS PROGENY

The famous masked caballero of Old California, created by pulp fictioneer Johnston McCulley, first reached the screen in *The Mark of Zorro*, a 1920 feature film starring Douglas Fairbanks. But he was overlooked by serial producers until Republic Pictures decided to revitalize the character in 1937. *Zorro Rides Again* was a contemporary Western that starred John Carroll as a descendant of the original swashbuckling avenger. Its success inspired Republic to license McCulley's character several more times. *Zorro's Fighting Legion* (1939) reintroduced Don Diego Vega and pitted the dashing nineteenth-century caballero against power-hungry conspirators attempting to undermine the administration of Mexican president Benito Juarez. *Son of Zorro* (1947) and *Ghost of Zorro* (1949) featured more descendants and were typical Western serials. For *Zorro's Black Whip* (1944), Republic licensed the character just to use his name; the titular character was a female crusader who dressed in black (with a face-covering mask) and lashed miscreants with a bullwhip. Zorro himself neither appeared nor was mentioned. Stock footage from this chapter play was welded into two subsequent serials, *Don Daredevil Rides Again* (1951) and *Man with the Steel Whip* (1954).

Son of
ZORRO
GEORGE TURNER
PEGGY STEWART
ROY BARCROFT
EDWARD CASSIDY
Directed by SPENCER BENNET and FRED C. BRANNON
A REPUBLIC SERIAL IN 13 CHAPTERS

GHOST
OF ZORRO
CLAYTON MOORE
PAMELA BLAKE
ROY BARCROFT
GEORGE J. LEWIS
DIRECTED BY FRED BRANNON
A REPUBLIC SERIAL in 12 Chapters

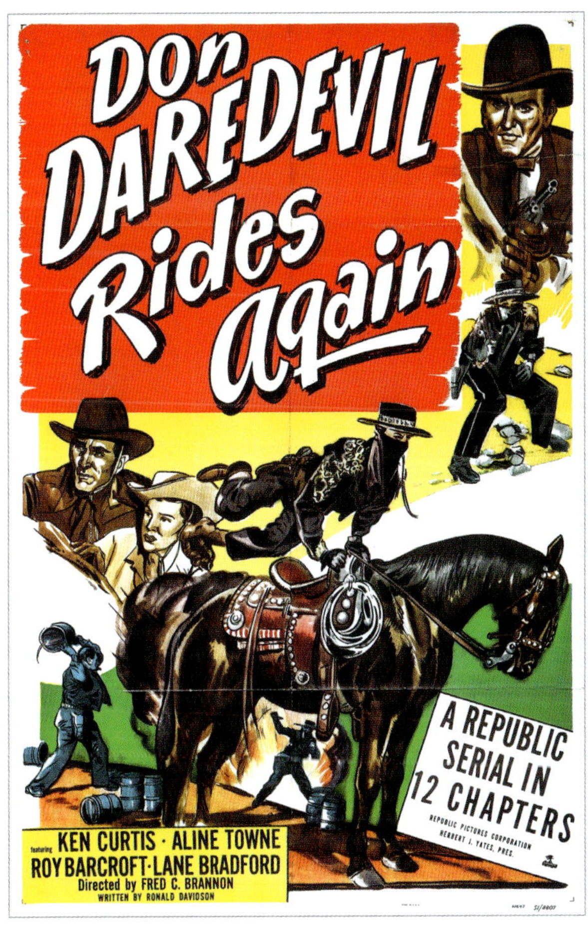
Don
DAREDEVIL
Rides
Again
A REPUBLIC
SERIAL IN
12 CHAPTERS
REPUBLIC PICTURES CORPORATION
HERBERT J. YATES, PRES.
featuring KEN CURTIS · ALINE TOWNE
ROY BARCROFT · LANE BRADFORD
Directed by FRED C. BRANNON
WRITTEN BY RONALD DAVIDSON

A
REPUBLIC
SERIAL IN
12 CHAPTERS
MAN WITH THE
STEEL WHIP
featuring
RICHARD SIMMONS · DALE VAN SICKEL
BARBARA BESTAR · MAURITZ HUGO
LANE BRADFORD
WRITTEN BY · RONALD DAVIDSON
ASSOCIATE PRODUCER and DIRECTOR
FRANKLIN ADREON

SERIAL HEROES FROM HISTORY

The idea of inserting historical figures into rip-roaring Western serials was an old one, dating back to Universal's 1921 smash-hit chapter play *Winners of the West*. The studio followed it up with such episodic thrillers as *In the Days of Buffalo Bill* (1922) and *The Oregon Trail* (1923). This practice continued in the sound era, most effectively in Columbia's *Great Adventures of Wild Bill Hickok* (1938), *Overland with Kit Carson* (1939), *Cody of the Pony Express* (1950), and *Son of Geronimo* (1953). It should go without saying that the scriptwriters greatly sanitized these old Westerners for juvenile consumption. A trio of Republic serials—*Jesse James Rides Again* (1947), *Adventures of Frank and Jesse James* (1948), and *The James Brothers of Missouri* (1950)—whitewashed those notorious outlaws beyond recognition. Equally unrecognizable were Davy Crockett, Jim Bowie, and an adolescent Kit Carson, all of whom appeared in Republic's *The Painted Stallion* (1937), an otherwise excellent chapter play.

SON OF GERONIMO
APACHE AVENGER
starring
CLAY MOORE
with
Rodd REDWING · Tommy FARRELL
Eileen ROWE · Bud OSBORNE
Story and Screen Play by
GEORGE H. PLYMPTON
ROYAL K. COLE and
ARTHUR HOERL
Produced by
SAM KATZMAN
Directed by
SPENCER G. BENNET
Chapter 15
PEACE TREATY
A COLUMBIA SUPER-SERIAL
Copyright 1952 Columbia Pictures Corp.
Country of Origin U.S.A.
43636
52/9805

UNIVERSAL SERIALS

Having been organized during the nickelodeon era, Universal made Westerns early and got into Western serial production in 1916. The company specialized in horse operas anyway, and with a 230-acre back lot on the southeastern edge of the San Fernando Valley, it had plenty of space to build Western ranch houses and town streets on which they could be shot. The lot's grassy, rolling hills and dirt roads made attractive backdrops for chase scenes and cattle drives. If Universal's Western serials had a generic fault, it was the overuse of stock footage—usually Indian attacks on wagon trains—originally shot for such episodic spectaculars as *Winners of the West*. The company released one Western chapter play each summer throughout much of the sound era, with Buck Jones and Johnny Mack Brown making four each during the thirties. Producer Henry MacRae supervised them all, never discouraging longtime scripters Basil Dickey and George Plympton from incorporating tried-and-true plot devices that had already been used dozens of times before. But the action was always fast and furious—and that, after all, is what the kiddies craved.

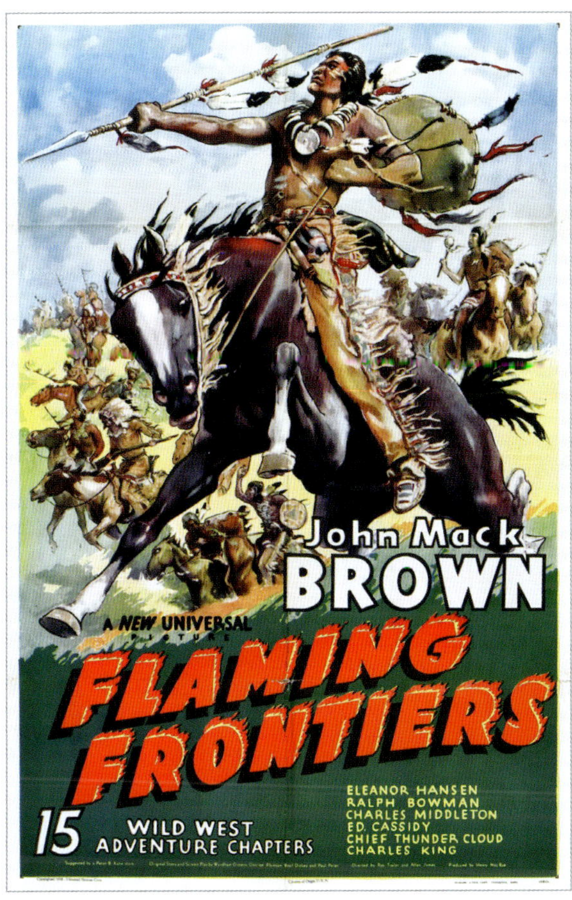
John Mack
BROWN
A NEW UNIVERSAL PICTURE
FLAMING FRONTIERS
15 WILD WEST ADVENTURE CHAPTERS
ELEANOR HANSEN
RALPH BOWMAN
CHARLES MIDDLETON
ED. CASSIDY
CHIEF THUNDER CLOUD
CHARLES KING

15 THRILL-PACKED CHAPTERS
THE New UNIVERSAL Presents
JOHN MACK BROWN
in
THE OREGON TRAIL
with
LOUISE STANLEY · FUZZY KNIGHT
BILL CODY, Jr. · ED LESAINT

"DESCENDING DOOM!"
Chapter 8 OF THE MILLION DOLLAR SERIAL!
DICK FORAN · LEO CARRILLO · BUCK JONES
and CHARLES BICKFORD
RIDERS OF DEATH VALLEY
with
LON CHANEY, Jr. NOAH BEERY, Jr.
"BIG BOY" WILLIAMS
JEANNE KELLY MONTE BLUE
Directed by FORD BEEBE and RAY TAYLOR · A UNIVERSAL SERIAL Associate Producer: HENRY MacRAE
Screen Play by SHERMAN LOWE, GEORGE PLYMPTON, BASIL DICKEY, JACK O'DONNELL · Original Story by Oliver Drake

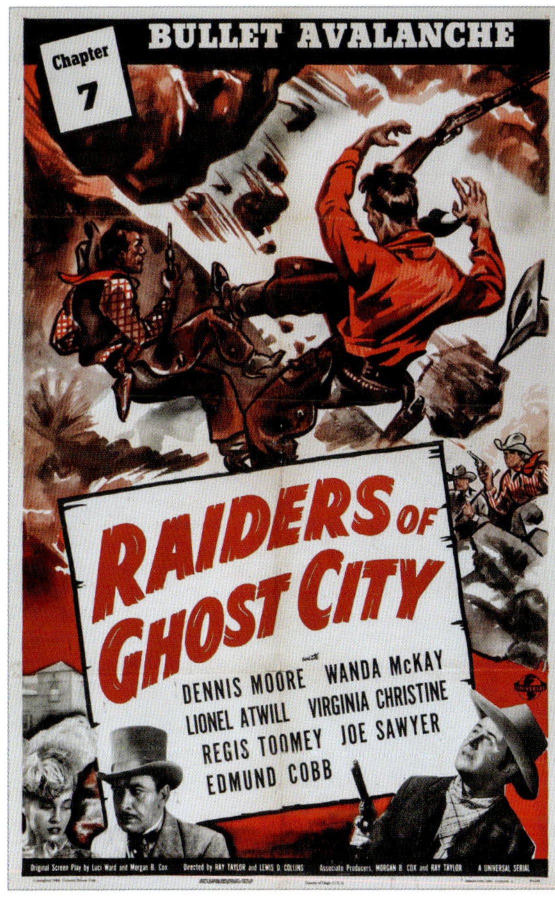
Chapter 7
BULLET AVALANCHE
RAIDERS OF GHOST CITY
with
DENNIS MOORE WANDA McKAY
LIONEL ATWILL VIRGINIA CHRISTINE
REGIS TOOMEY JOE SAWYER
EDMUND COBB
Original Screen Play by Luci Ward and Morgan B. Cox
Directed by RAY TAYLOR and LEWIS D. COLLINS
Associate Producers, MORGAN B. COX and RAY TAYLOR
A UNIVERSAL SERIAL

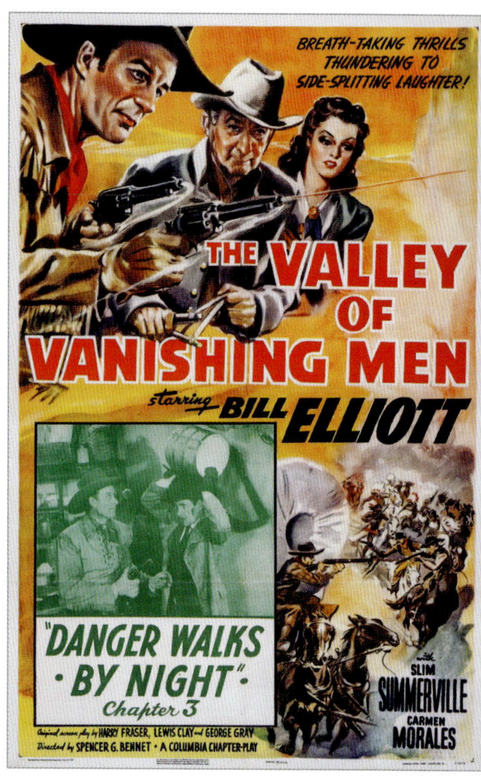

COLUMBIA SERIALS

Harry Cohn's Columbia Pictures was the last studio to enter the serial sweepstakes, and while the company rarely had a winner, it wasn't for lack of trying. Bill Elliott's *Great Adventures of Wild Bill Hickok* (1938), *Overland with Kit Carson* (1939), and *Valley of Vanishing Men* (1942) were pretty good, with loads of action. *Deadwood Dick* (1940) and *White Eagle* (1941) had loyal adherents among the moppet brigade. But thereafter, Columbia lost interest in Western serials, cutting their budgets and demonstrating a steadily increasing reliance on stock footage from the earlier, more extravagant productions. When legendarily parsimonious producer Sam Katzman took control of the studio's serial unit in 1945, he began a corner-cutting regime that lasted until Columbia terminated chapter-play production some eleven years later. By that time, unit director Spencer Bennet was being forced to shoot a fifteen-episode, five-hour serial in less than three weeks. It was hardly worth the effort.

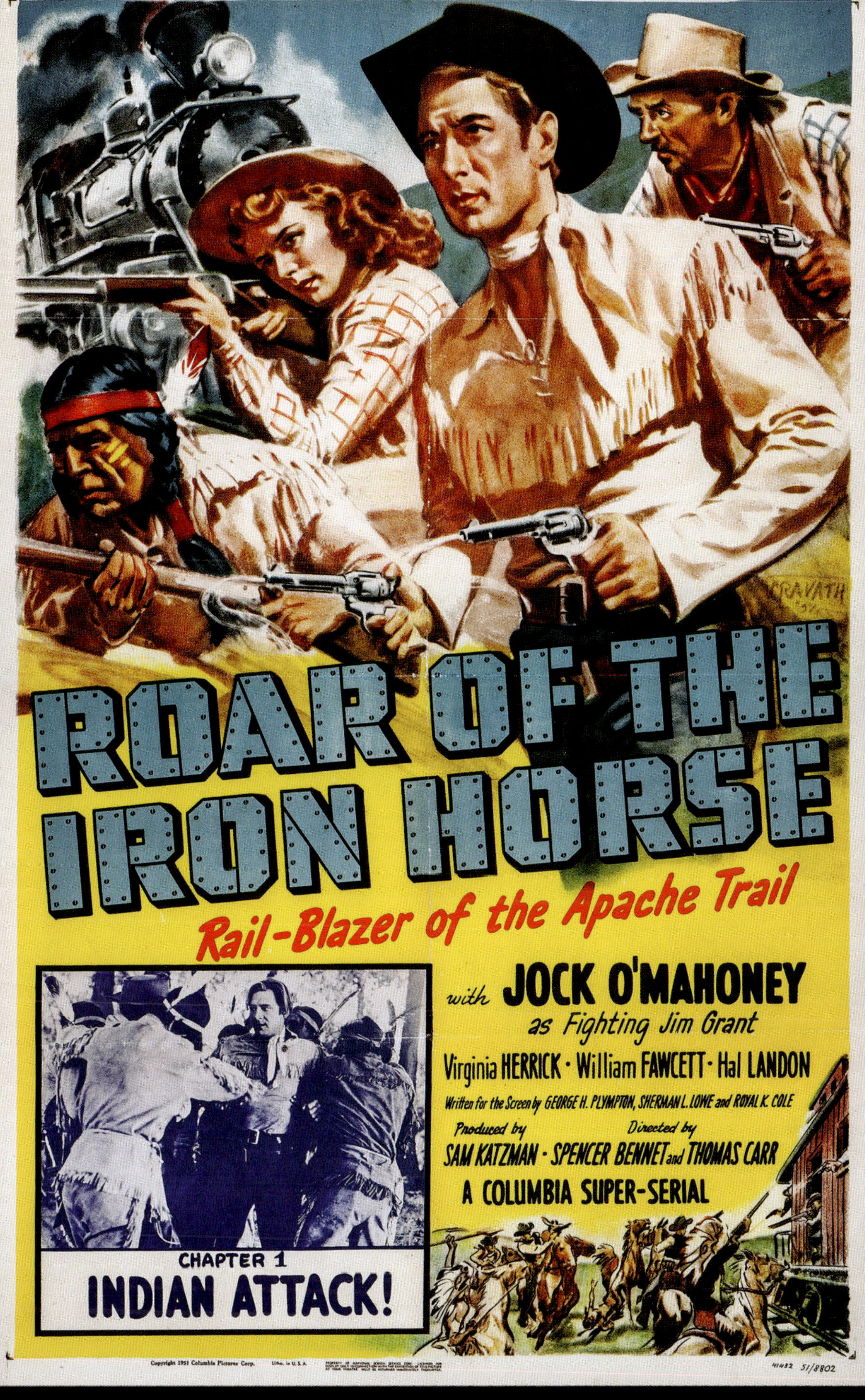
ROAR OF THE IRON HORSE
Rail-Blazer of the Apache Trail
with JOCK O'MAHONEY
as Fighting Jim Grant
Virginia HERRICK · William FAWCETT · Hal LANDON
Written for the Screen by GEORGE H. PLYMPTON, SHERMAN L. LOWE and ROYAL K. COLE
Produced by
SAM KATZMAN
Directed by
SPENCER BENNET and THOMAS CARR
A COLUMBIA SUPER-SERIAL
CHAPTER 1
INDIAN ATTACK!
Copyright 1951 Columbia Pictures Corp.
Litho. in U.S.A.
41432 51/8802

REPUBLIC SERIALS

Chapter-play aficionados most highly value Republic's serials—sixty-six made over a twenty-year span—and with good reason. The early ones, supervised by Mascot's Nat Levine, had the rough edges associated with the Poverty Row period of the mid-thirties. But by the time the *Lone Ranger* and the early *Zorro* serials were made, Republic product had become extremely slick, despite the low budgets. Technically—in terms of cinematography, sound recording, editing, and musical scoring—the studio's chapter plays were of a very high order, meeting major-studio standards. As the industry's preeminent supplier of B-grade horse operas, Republic had perfected outdoor action filmmaking to the *n*th degree. Directors worked in absolute harmony with handpicked crews; carefully planned action sequences were skillfully executed by the top stuntmen in the business. In addition to the *Lone Ranger* and *Zorro* serials, Republic's finest Western chapter plays included *Adventures of Red Ryder* (1940), *King of the Texas Rangers* (1941), and the most action-packed of them all, *Daredevils of the West* (1943).

A REPUBLIC
Serial in 12 Chapters

GHOST RIDERS OF THE WEST

FORMERLY ENTITLED "THE PHANTOM RIDER"

featuring

ROBERT KENT · PEGGY STEWART

and

LeROY MASON · GEORGE J. LEWIS · KENNE DUNCAN · HAL TALIAFERRO

CHIEF THUNDERCLOUD · MONTE HALE

Original Screen Play by ALBERT DeMOND · BASIL DICKEY · JESSE DUFFY · LYNN PERKINS · BARNEY SARECKY

Directed by SPENCER BENNET and FRED BRANNON

7
THE
MAN FROM
BAR-20

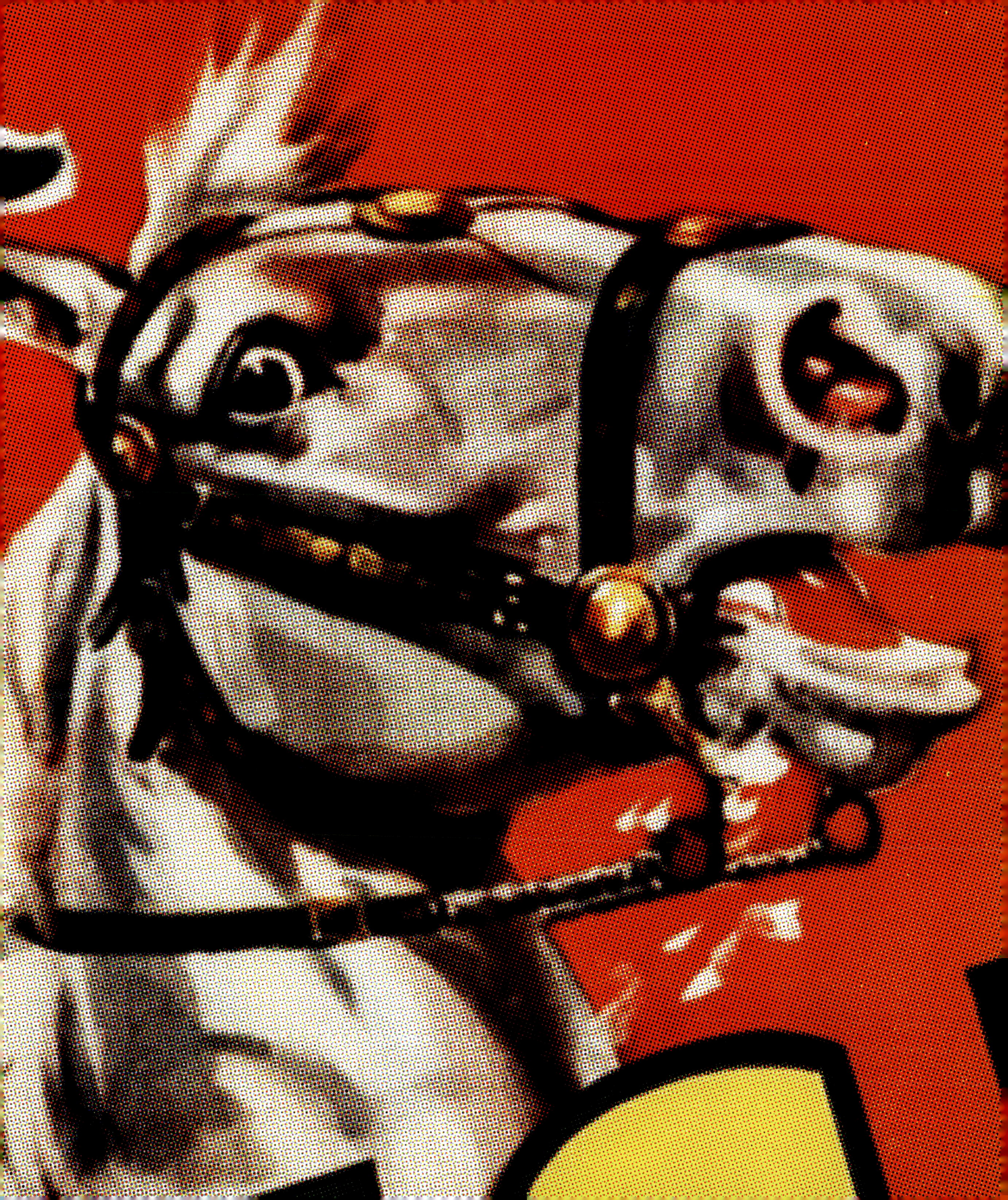

HOPALONG CASSIDY RIDES!

Paramount's release of *Hop-a-long Cassidy* (1935) introduces moviegoers to pulp fiction's most beloved Western hero. On screen, as played by the silent-era matinee idol William Boyd, he is the Sir Galahad of a frontier Camelot known as the Bar-20 Ranch. Under the auspices of producer Harry Sherman, this wildly profitable series manages to maintain an unusually high average over the following thirteen years, eventually running to sixty-six feature films . . .

Born on February 3, 1883, in Streator, Illinois, Clarence Edward Mulford grew up in a solidly middle-class household. Small of frame, quiet, and introverted, he was an indifferent student with limited social skills and a disdain for athletics. His principal interest was the Wild West—or, at least, the Wild West depicted in the lurid dime novels of that era. Clarence read in prodigious quantities the almost wholly fictitious exploits of Buffalo Bill, Wild Bill Hickok, and Kit Carson, living vicariously through their adventures. After graduating from high school, he toiled in several humdrum jobs before finding steady work as a local-government employee, dispensing marriage licenses in Brooklyn.

As a young man, Mulford was animated by two passions: physical fitness and writing. Weight training and roadwork developed his undersized body, while putting pen to paper developed his mind. "The Fight at Buckskin" wasn't the first story he wrote, but it was the first he sold. This 6,250-word yarn introduced readers of *Outing Magazine* to the scrappy cowpunchers of the Bar-20, a Texas cattle ranch managed for an eastern syndicate by foreman Buck Peters. His loyal "waddies" included Red Connors, Johnny Nelson (also known as "the Kid"), Lanky Smith, Skinny Thompson, Pete Wilson, Billy Williams, and a particularly colorful gent known as Hopalong Cassidy.

The Cassidy of Mulford's early stories is a raucous cowboy whose habits certainly wouldn't make him welcome in polite society. He's an inveterate tobacco chewer (and spitter) prone to swearing and fond of concocting creative insults good-naturedly directed at his fellow punchers. Described in an early story as "passably good-looking," Hopalong sports a thatch of unruly red hair and typically wears the faded denims, chaps, and broad-brimmed sombreros

common to working cattlemen. He can be volatile, but for the most part he is a cool character with a keen mind and a general's grasp of battlefield strategy.

Mulford's tales were accurate with regard to history, location, and the minutiae of ranch life, but the principal characters in the Bar-20 saga bore little resemblance to real working cowhands in the late nineteenth century. From the first, Hoppy, Buck, and the others were mythical figures comparable to Odysseus and his adventurers, or to the knights of Arthurian legend. Hardly perfect men, they nonetheless adhered to a rigid moral code, using violence primarily to achieve rough justice in a region of the country not yet bound by the rule of law.

ABOVE: William Boyd reviews the script with director Nate Watt on location for *North of the Rio Grande* (1937). By this time, Paramount had taken over the funding of the series, which was previously underwritten by a trio of private investors doing business as Western Pictures Corporation.

OPPOSITE: A poster for the 1935 series opener, *Hop-a-long Cassidy*. Advertising and promotional material for this entry—and this one only—hyphenated "Hopalong," which was never done in Clarence E. Mulford's stories. Oddly, the film's main title card repeated this punctuation error.

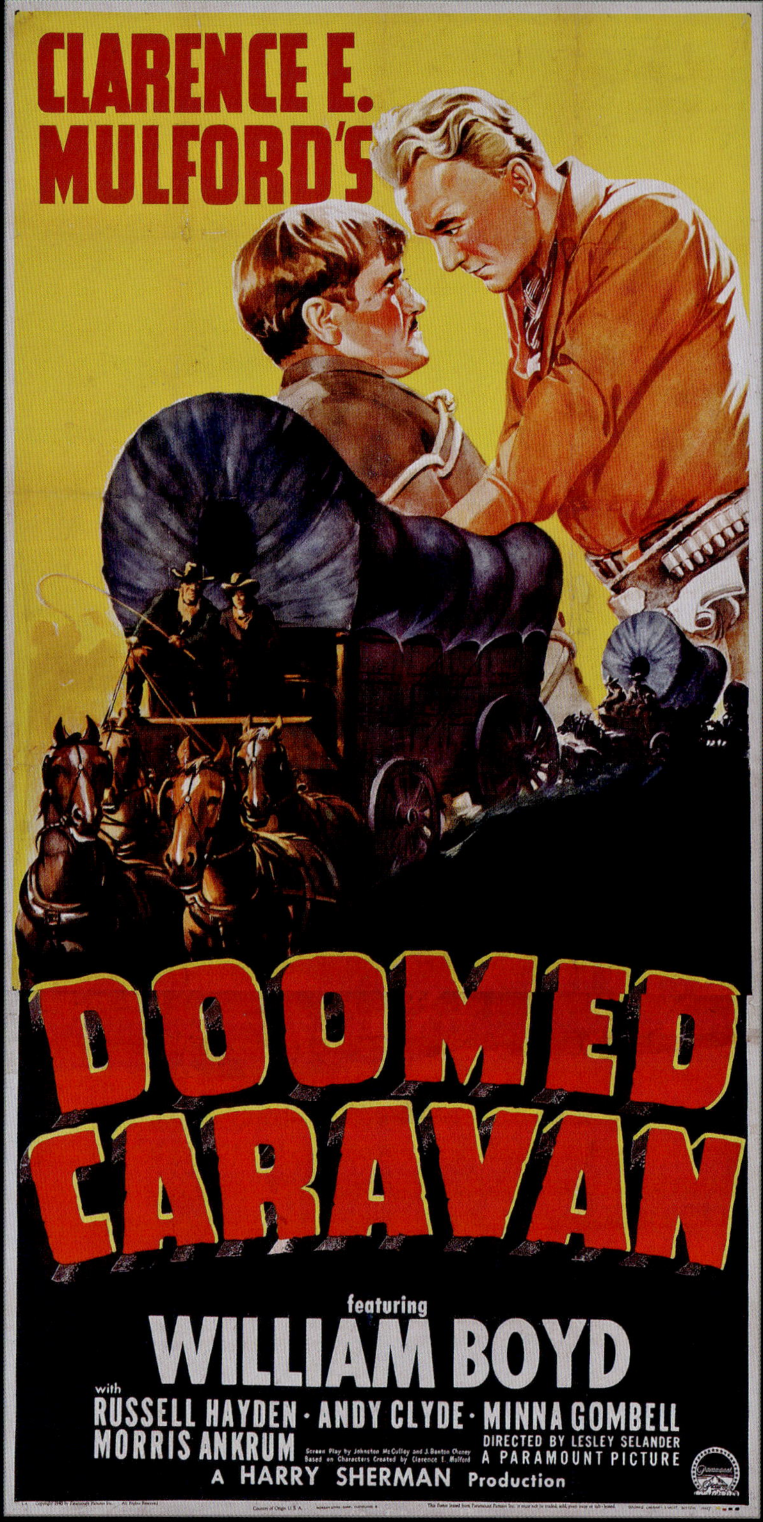

ABOVE LEFT: *Renegade Trail* (1939), among the best Hoppys of the year, reinforced the character's appeal to adolescent males by stressing Cassidy's friendship with a fatherless young boy (Sonny Bupp) whose admiration for the Bar-20 foreman bordered on hero worship.

ABOVE RIGHT: *Doomed Caravan* (1941) revolves around the efforts of Hoppy and his pals to smash an outlaw gang raiding shipments made by a freighting company run by a woman. Completion of filming was delayed when Boyd's horse ran into a tree, breaking the star's leg.

Over the next thirty years, Hopalong and his friends galloped through numerous novels and short stories, most of them published first in pulp magazines. The men from Bar-20 had millions of fans when, in 1935, movie producer Harry A. Sherman licensed the film rights to Mulford's entire oeuvre. Sherman had learned that Paramount, eager to cash in on the B-Western boom, was willing to distribute a series of low-budget horse operas, provided the entries maintained a level of quality commensurate with the studio's lofty standards.

According to the contract dated February 27, 1935, Prudential Studios Corporation—the company formed by Sherman and his partner, Jack Trop—was to pay Mulford $2,500 for each book of his that they adapted to film. Ten percent of the initial $2,500 was paid upon signing, with the remainder to be remitted when the first movie went before the cameras.

Initially, Sherman cast well-known character actor James Gleason in the role of Hopalong. Then, when Gleason dropped out a matter of days before principal photography was to commence, Sherman contacted several "at liberty" actors with sufficient gravitas to do Hoppy justice. He settled on William Boyd, a former protégé of the legendary director Cecil B. DeMille, who'd given the Ohio native supporting parts in some of his best-remembered films of the twenties, including *Manslaughter* (1922), *Road to Yesterday* (1925), and *King of Kings* (1927). In recent years, Boyd had achieved some little prominence as a dependable leading man of moderate-budgeted action films. Top-lining a series of B Westerns represented a comedown for him, but his career momentum had slowed to a standstill. He accepted Sherman's offer of $5,000 per film for six Hopalong Cassidy oaters. If those met with audience favor, Paramount would keep the series going.

Shot in three weeks for a meager $63,000 (a fortune by Poverty Row standards but a pittance to major studios), *Hop-a-long Cassidy*—the hyphenation was quickly dropped—elicited favorable reviews and did surprisingly good business. Picture patrons enthusiastically welcomed the series opener, and the next five series installments in the series enjoyed the same degree of success.

Between 1935 and 1948, William Boyd starred in sixty-six Hoppy feature films. In the early fifties, he gambled every cent he had to buy out Harry Sherman and take control of the property. He then cut a deal with the NBC network to broadcast the older films. Hoppy mania swept the country. In addition to producing a series of fifty-two half hour episodes for TV, Boyd made a fortune licensing Hopalong Cassidy for dozens of consumer products. He died in 1973, leaving his widow, Grace, a phenomenally wealthy woman, though in true cowboy-hero fashion, he left a significant chunk of his fortune to children's hospitals.

Paramount marketed the Hopalong Cassidy Westerns shrewdly and skillfully, earning gobs of money from the series until 1942, when the studio transferred distribution of it to United Artists, at that time badly in need of product. Paramount's art department never employed a consistent approach to poster design. Certain eccentricities in visual style popped up now and again: for example, one artist displayed a weakness for silhouettes, grouped in threes and filled in with primary colors. The "style A" one-sheet for *Pirates on Horseback* shows three riders; the *Border Vigilantes* poster depicts Hoppy holding a trio of desperadoes at gunpoint, their hands raised skyward.

This puzzling quirk in layout was imitated by UA's art department, which upped the ante for the *Leather Burners* one-sheet by showing a half-dozen silhouetted, differently colored riders that overshadow the rendering of Hoppy, with guns drawn, in the bottom right-hand corner. For the most part, though, the Hopalong Cassidy posters were extremely handsome. ✡

ABOVE: Boyd with his longtime producer, Harry "Pop" Sherman, on the set of *Heart of Arizona* (1938), one of the very best entries in the Hopalong series. During their nine-year working relationship, Boyd and Sherman frequently locked horns over the star's salary, but they remained friends.

THE EARLY YEARS

The first dozen Hopalong Cassidy films were adapted from Clarence E. Mulford's novels, although their fidelity to the original works varied considerably from picture to picture. They established a formula that would be used throughout the series, with Hoppy invariably supported by two sidekicks: a handsome young cowboy (initially Johnny Nelson, played by Jimmy Ellison) and a grizzled, garrulous old-timer (Windy Halliday, played by the bewhiskered George Hayes). They all worked at the fabled Bar-20 Ranch, managed by Buck Peters (played in the first film by Charles Middleton, but most effectively by William Duncan in several succeeding entries). Hoppy's closest friend, Red Connors, was a fixture in Mulford's books yet was curiously written out of the movies after two appearances. The 1935–36 sextet was later sold to Sherman S. Krellberg's Goodwill Productions, which reissued them to theaters in the late forties.

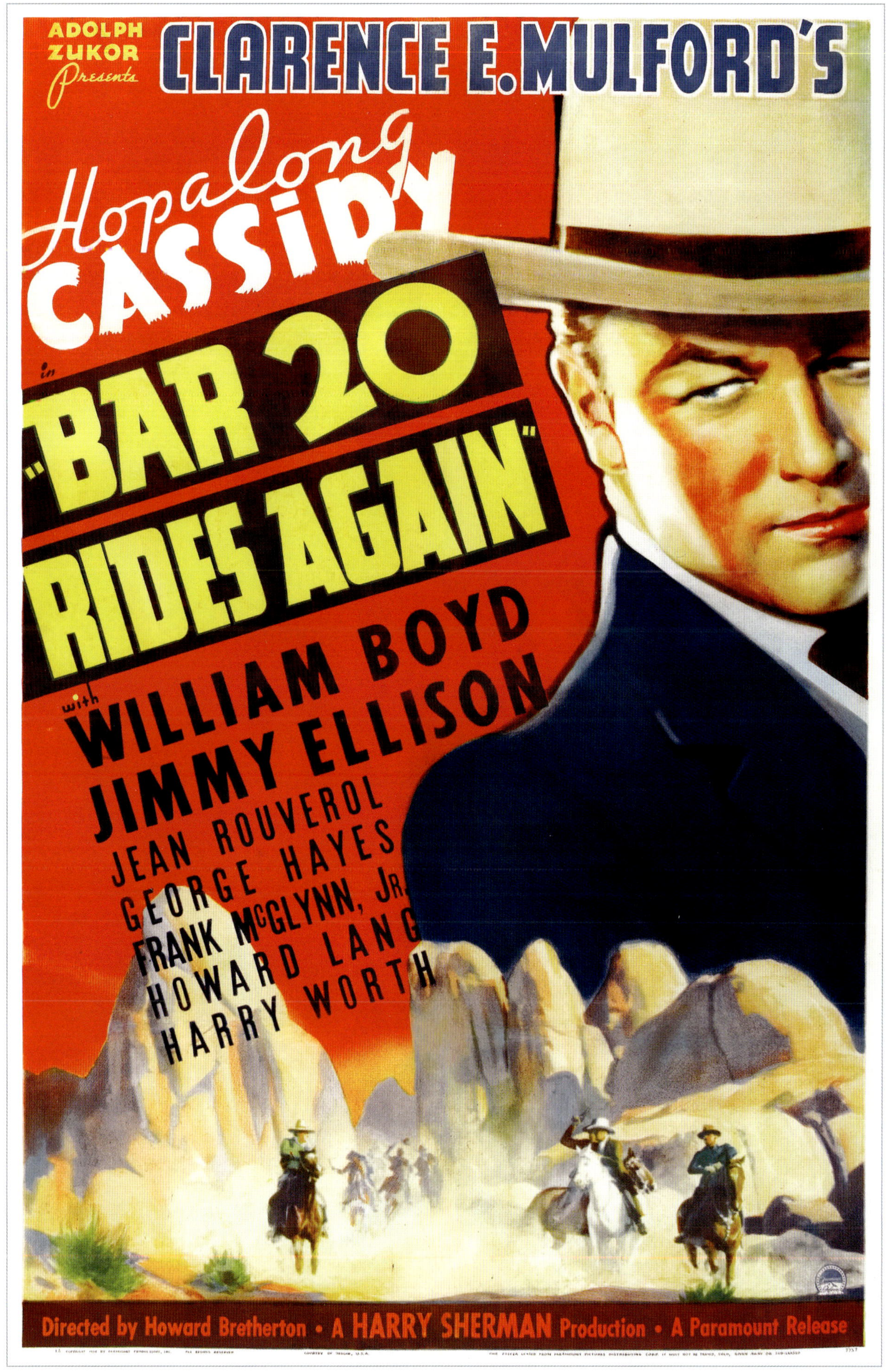
ADOLPH ZUKOR Presents
CLARENCE E. MULFORD'S
Hopalong CASSIDY
in
"BAR 20 RIDES AGAIN"
with
WILLIAM BOYD
JIMMY ELLISON
JEAN ROUVEROL
GEORGE HAYES
FRANK McGLYNN, JR.
HOWARD LANG
HARRY WORTH
Directed by Howard Bretherton • A HARRY SHERMAN Production • A Paramount Release

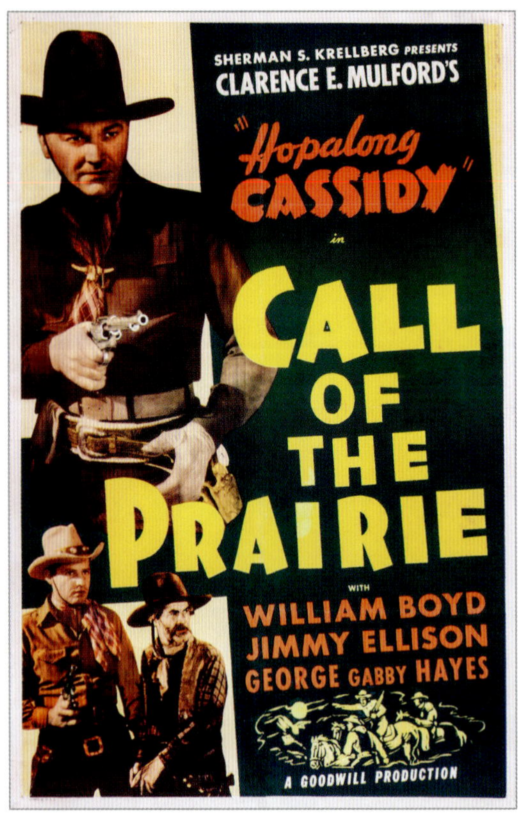
SHERMAN S. KRELLBERG PRESENTS
CLARENCE E. MULFORD'S
"Hopalong CASSIDY"
in
CALL OF THE PRAIRIE
WITH
WILLIAM BOYD
JIMMY ELLISON
GEORGE GABBY HAYES
A GOODWILL PRODUCTION

SHERMAN S. KRELLBERG PRESENTS
CLARENCE E. MULFORD'S
Hopalong CASSIDY
3 ON THE TRAIL
WILLIAM BOYD
JIMMY ELLISON
GEORGE GABBY HAYES
A GOODWILL PRODUCTION

SHERMAN S. KRELLBERG PRESENTS
CLARENCE E. MULFORD'S
Hopalong CASSIDY
HEART OF THE WEST
WITH
WILLIAM BOYD
JIMMY ELLISON
GEORGE GABBY HAYES
A GOODWILL PRODUCTION

CLARENCE E. MULFORD'S
"HOPALONG CASSIDY RETURNS"
with
WILLIAM BOYD
GEORGE HAYES
GAIL SHERIDAN
EVELYN BRENT
Directed by Nate Watt · a HARRY SHERMAN Production · A Paramount Release

WESTERN CLASSICS
presents
CLARENCE E. MULFORD'S
BORDERLAND
WITH
WILLIAM
BOYD
GEORGE "GABBY"
HAYES
Distributed through
SCREEN GUILD
PRODUCTIONS, INC.

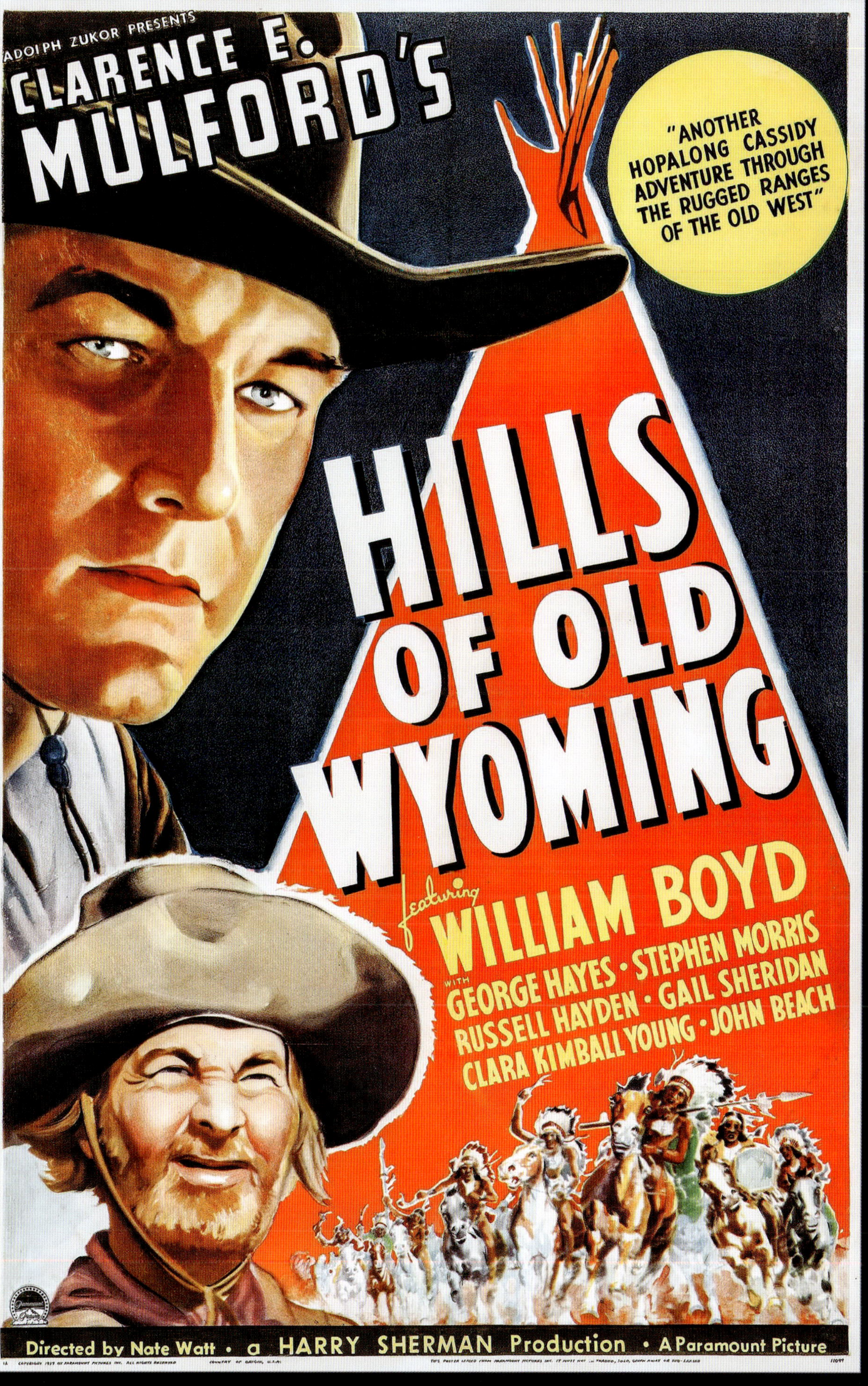
ADOLPH ZUKOR PRESENTS
CLARENCE E. MULFORD'S
"ANOTHER HOPALONG CASSIDY ADVENTURE THROUGH THE RUGGED RANGES OF THE OLD WEST"
HILLS OF OLD WYOMING
featuring
WILLIAM BOYD
WITH
GEORGE HAYES · STEPHEN MORRIS
RUSSELL HAYDEN · GAIL SHERIDAN
CLARA KIMBALL YOUNG · JOHN BEACH
Directed by Nate Watt · a HARRY SHERMAN Production · A Paramount Picture

HOPPY HITS HIS STRIDE

Encouraged by the favorable reaction to the series, Paramount assumed the burden of financing the films and increased Harry Sherman's budgets, even allowing Pop to reuse background music originally written for the studio's epic Westerns, including *The Plainsman*, *The Texas Rangers*, and *Trail of the Lonesome Pine*. Working with the same technical crew and many of the same actors in picture after picture, Sherman turned the Hopalong Cassidy series into a crowd-pleasing, reliably profitable enterprise. In annual exhibitor lists of the top ten cowboy stars, William Boyd consistently ranked number two, his popularity surpassed only by that of Gene Autry (and, after 1942, Roy Rogers). The loss of George Hayes to Republic in 1939 dealt a serious but not crippling blow to the franchise and, in the long run, didn't affect Hoppy's box-office standing.

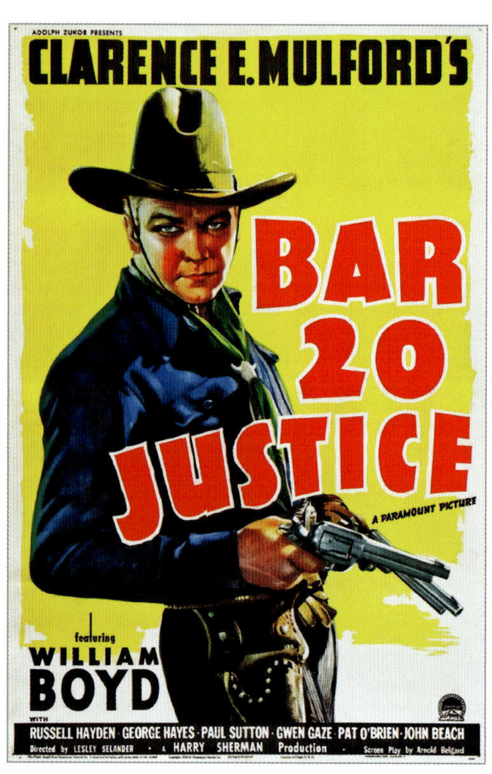

Adolph Zukor presents
CLARENCE E. MULFORD'S
IN OLD MEXICO
featuring
WILLIAM BOYD
with
GEORGE HAYES · RUSSELL HAYDEN · PAUL SUTTON
BETTY AMANN · JANE CLAYTON
Directed by EDWARD D. VENTURINI
Screen Play by Harrison Jacobs
a HARRY SHERMAN Production · A PARAMOUNT PICTURE

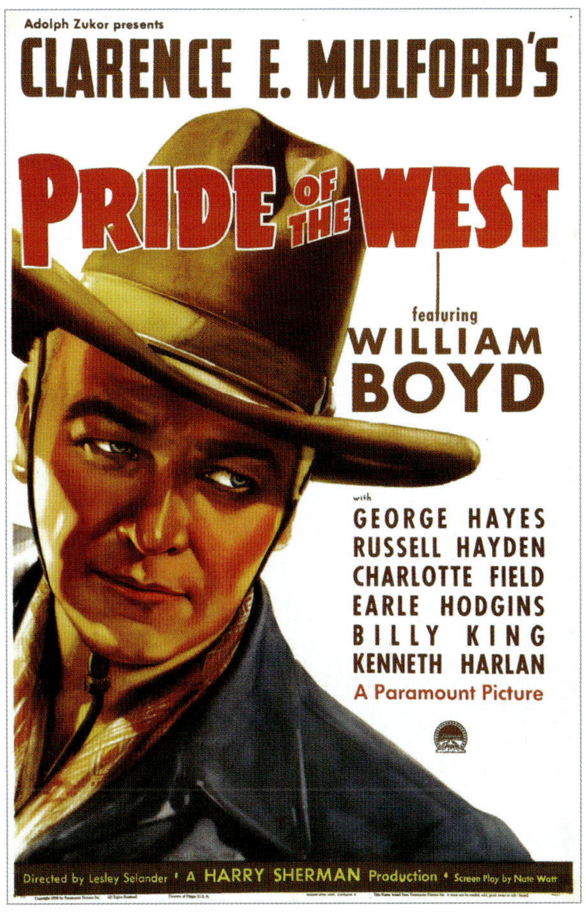
Adolph Zukor presents
CLARENCE E. MULFORD'S
PRIDE OF THE WEST
featuring
WILLIAM BOYD
with
GEORGE HAYES
RUSSELL HAYDEN
CHARLOTTE FIELD
EARLE HODGINS
BILLY KING
KENNETH HARLAN
A Paramount Picture
Directed by Lesley Selander · A HARRY SHERMAN Production · Screen Play by Nate Watt

CLARENCE E. MULFORD'S
RANGE WAR
featuring
WILLIAM BOYD
with
RUSSELL HAYDEN · WILLARD ROBERTSON · MATT MOORE
PEDRO DE CORDOBA · BETTY MORAN · BRITT WOOD
Directed by Lesley Selander
A Harry Sherman Production
A PARAMOUNT PICTURE

Paramount presents
CLARENCE E. MULFORD'S
RENEGADE TRAIL
featuring
WILLIAM BOYD
GEORGE HAYES
RUSSELL HAYDEN
CHARLOTTE WYNTERS
SONNY BUPP and
THE KING'S MEN
Directed by Lesley Selander
A HARRY SHERMAN Production
A Paramount Picture

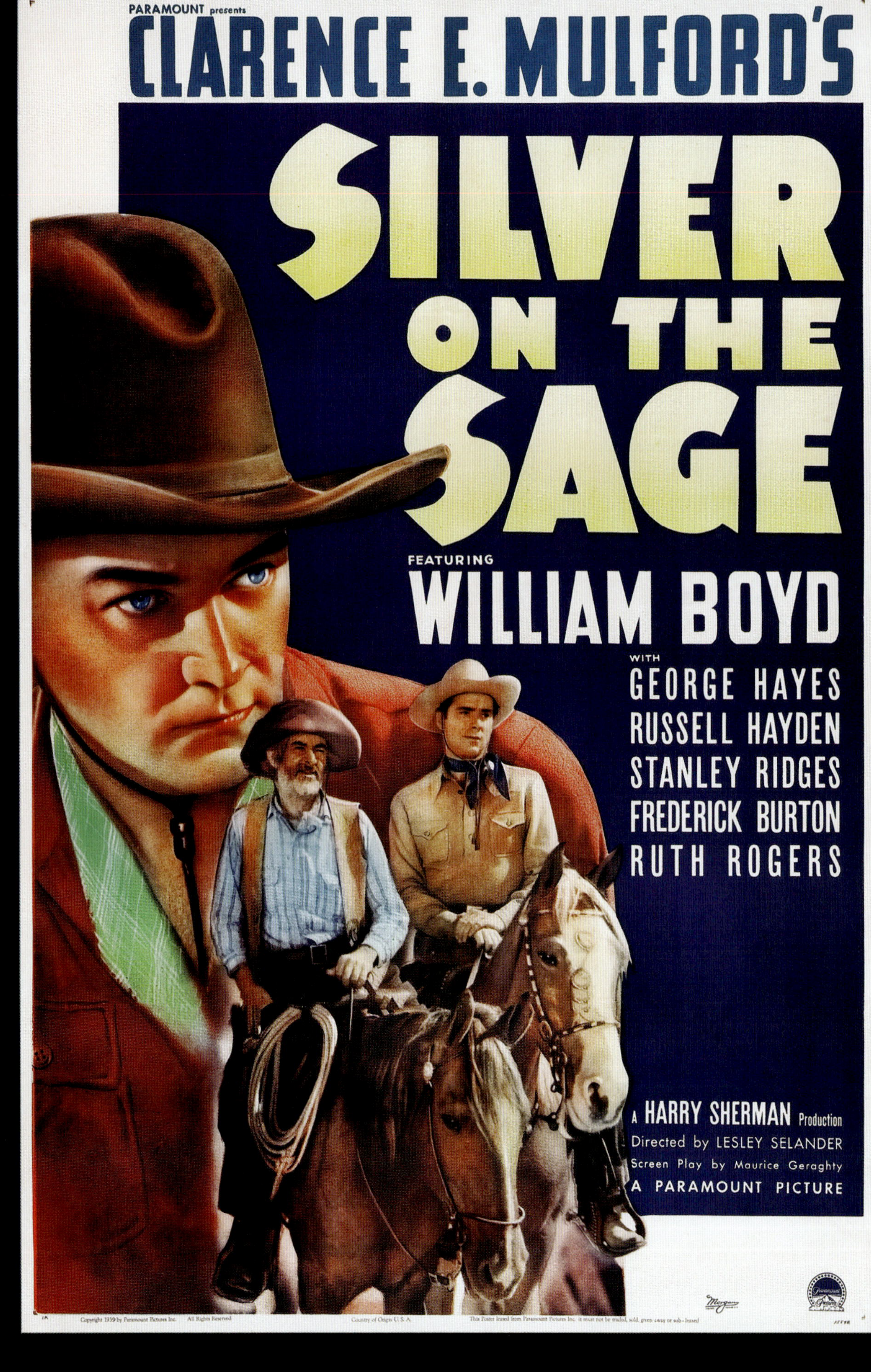

PARAMOUNT presents
CLARENCE E. MULFORD'S
SILVER ON THE SAGE
FEATURING
WILLIAM BOYD
WITH
GEORGE HAYES
RUSSELL HAYDEN
STANLEY RIDGES
FREDERICK BURTON
RUTH ROGERS
A HARRY SHERMAN Production
Directed by LESLEY SELANDER
Screen Play by Maurice Geraghty
A PARAMOUNT PICTURE
Copyright 1939 by Paramount Pictures Inc. All Rights Reserved
Country of Origin U.S.A.
This Poster leased from Paramount Pictures Inc. it must not be traded, sold, given away or sub-leased

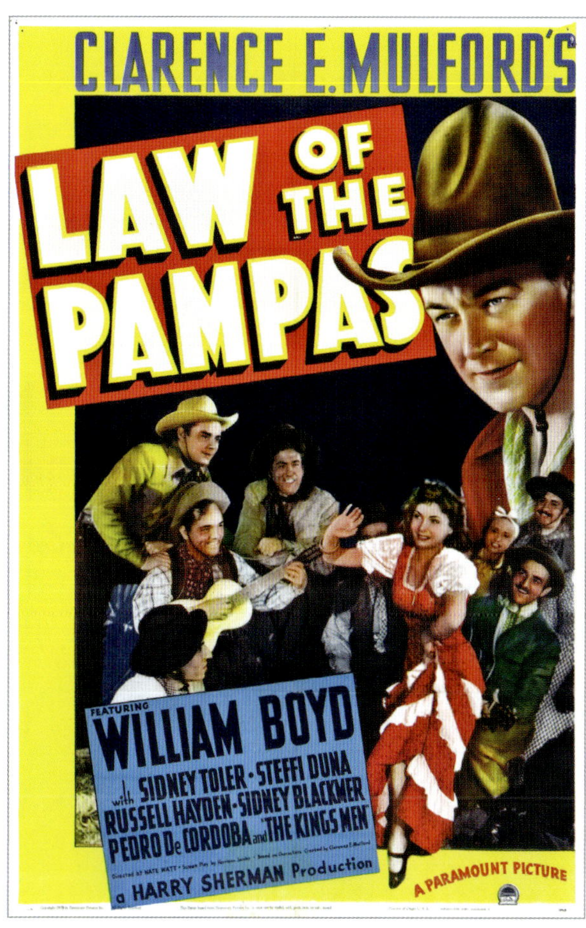

CLARENCE E. MULFORD'S
LAW OF THE PAMPAS
featuring
WILLIAM BOYD
with SIDNEY TOLER · STEFFI DUNA
RUSSELL HAYDEN · SIDNEY BLACKMER
PEDRO De CORDOBA and THE KINGS MEN
a HARRY SHERMAN Production
A PARAMOUNT PICTURE

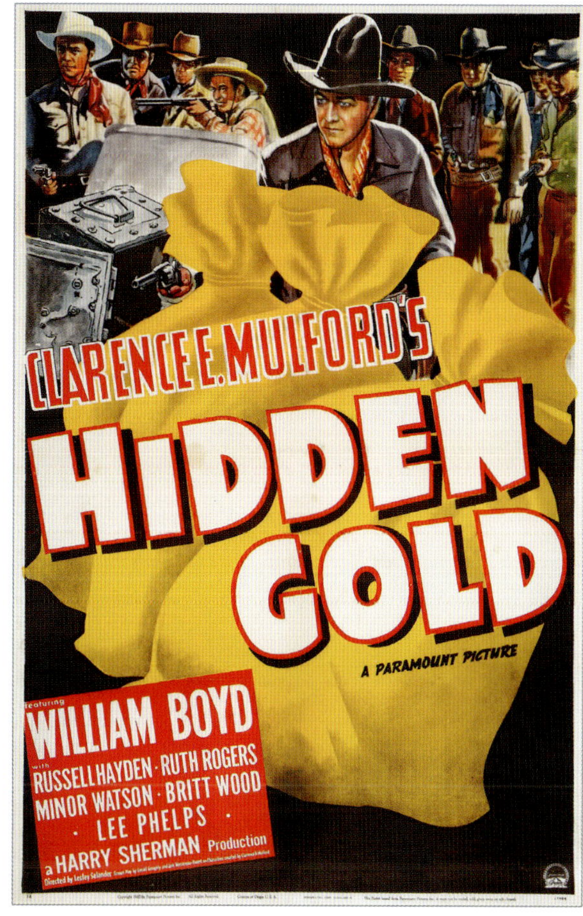

CLARENCE E. MULFORD'S
HIDDEN GOLD
A PARAMOUNT PICTURE
featuring
WILLIAM BOYD
with
RUSSELL HAYDEN · RUTH ROGERS
MINOR WATSON · BRITT WOOD
· LEE PHELPS ·
a HARRY SHERMAN Production

CLARENCE E. MULFORD'S
Stagecoach War
featuring WILLIAM BOYD
RUSSELL HAYDEN BRITT WOOD JULIE CARTER
HARVEY STEPHENS J. FARRELL MacDONALD
and "THE KING'S MEN" a HARRY SHERMAN Production
DIRECTED BY LESLEY SELANDER
A PARAMOUNT PICTURE

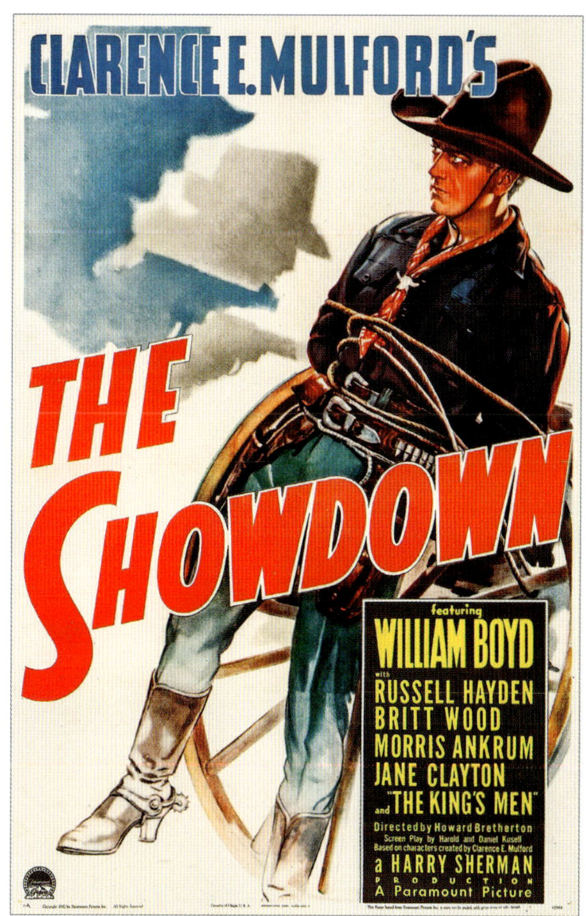

CLARENCE E. MULFORD'S
THE SHOWDOWN
featuring
WILLIAM BOYD
with
RUSSELL HAYDEN
BRITT WOOD
MORRIS ANKRUM
JANE CLAYTON
and "THE KING'S MEN"
Directed by Howard Bretherton
Screen Play by Harold and Daniel Kusell
Based on characters created by Clarence E. Mulford
a HARRY SHERMAN
PRODUCTION
A Paramount Picture

HOPPY'S NEW SIDEKICKS

Johnny Nelson was written out of the series in 1937, when Jimmy Ellison left the Hoppy unit for better opportunities (which, it turned out, were slow to materialize). He was replaced by Lucky Jenkins, another handsome young hothead with an eye for the ladies. Russell Hayden played the part until 1941 and was a huge asset to the team. Although he and Boyd didn't get along offscreen, on camera they worked harmoniously. *Three Men from Texas* (1940) introduced Scottish comedian Andy Clyde as California Carlson, replacing George Hayes as the humorous sidekick. Clyde's humor was broader than Hayes's; he relied heavily on mugging and pratfalls to get laughs. Fortunately, he and Boyd clicked. Hayden's replacement, Brad King, played a revived Johnny Nelson but proved a bland substitute, utterly lacking in charisma and never effectively establishing an onscreen rapport with Boyd and Clyde. He left the series after just five films.

CLARENCE E.
MULFORD'S
DOOMED
CARAVAN
featuring
WILLIAM
BOYD
with
RUSSELL HAYDEN
· ANDY CLYDE ·
MINNA GOMBELL
MORRIS ANKRUM
DIRECTED BY LESLEY SELANDER
a HARRY SHERMAN Production
A PARAMOUNT PICTURE

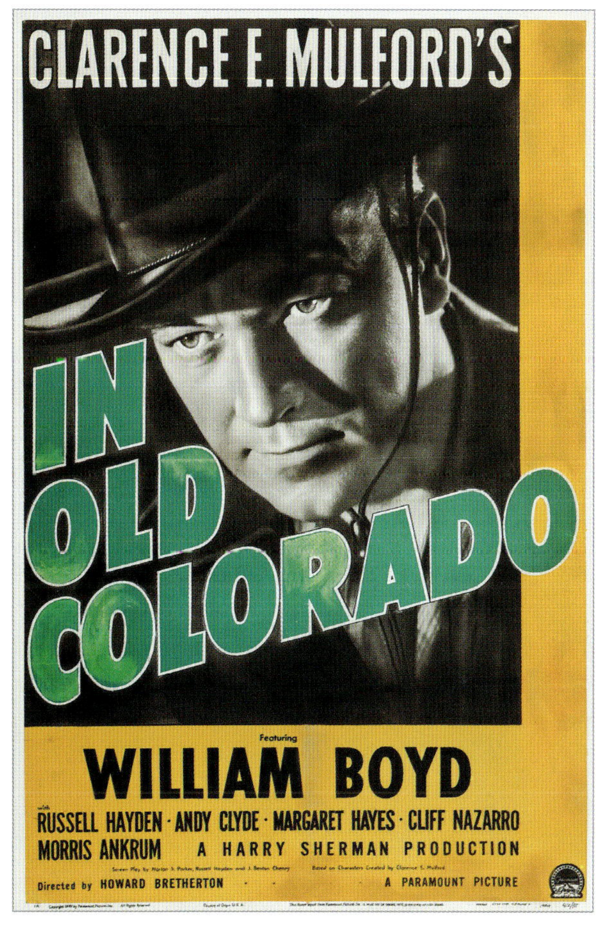
CLARENCE E. MULFORD'S
IN
OLD
COLORADO
featuring
WILLIAM BOYD
with
RUSSELL HAYDEN · ANDY CLYDE · MARGARET HAYES · CLIFF NAZARRO
MORRIS ANKRUM A HARRY SHERMAN PRODUCTION
Directed by HOWARD BRETHERTON A PARAMOUNT PICTURE

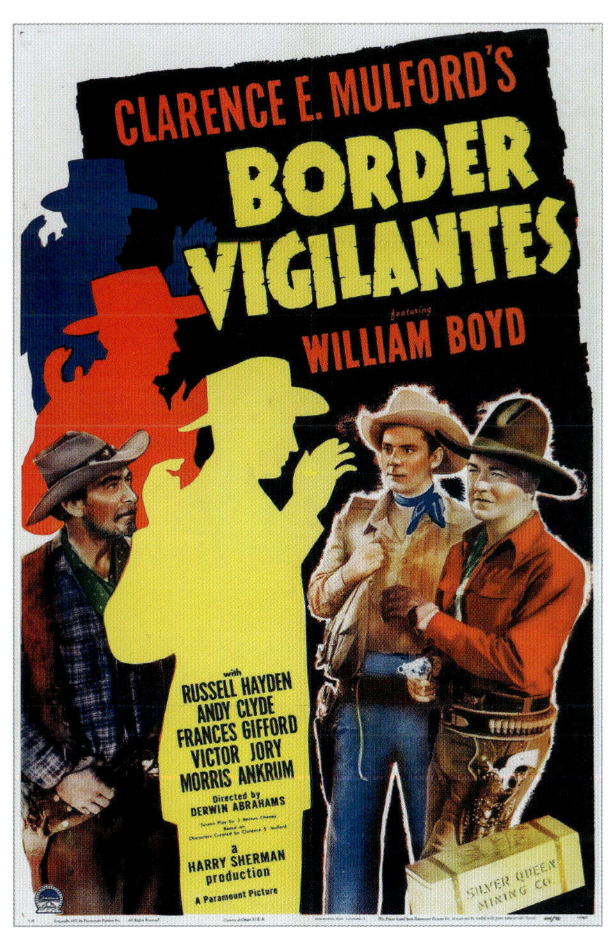
CLARENCE E. MULFORD'S
BORDER
VIGILANTES
featuring
WILLIAM BOYD
with
RUSSELL HAYDEN
ANDY CLYDE
FRANCES GIFFORD
VICTOR JORY
MORRIS ANKRUM
Directed by
DERWIN ABRAHAMS
a
HARRY SHERMAN
production
A Paramount Picture
SILVER QUEEN
MINING CO.

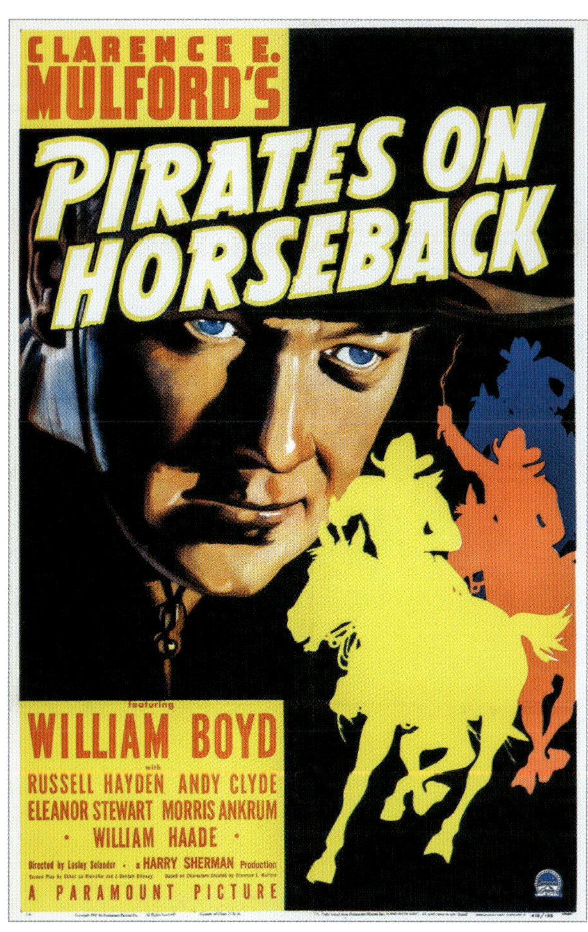
CLARENCE E.
MULFORD'S
PIRATES ON
HORSEBACK
featuring
WILLIAM BOYD
with
RUSSELL HAYDEN ANDY CLYDE
ELEANOR STEWART MORRIS ANKRUM
· WILLIAM HAADE ·
Directed by Lesley Selander · a HARRY SHERMAN Production
A PARAMOUNT PICTURE

CLARENCE E. MULFORD'S
WIDE OPEN TOWN
WILLIAM BOYD
RUSSELL HAYDEN · ANDY CLYDE · EVELYN BRENT
VICTOR JORY · MORRIS ANKRUM · BERNICE KAY
DIRECTED BY LESLEY SELANDER
A HARRY SHERMAN Production
A PARAMOUNT PICTURE

CLARENCE E. MULFORD'S
WIDE OPEN TOWN
featuring
WILLIAM BOYD
RUSSELL HAYDEN
ANDY CLYDE
EVELYN BRENT
VICTOR JORY
MORRIS ANKRUM
BERNICE KAY
DIRECTED BY LESLEY SELANDER
a HARRY SHERMAN Production
A PARAMOUNT PICTURE

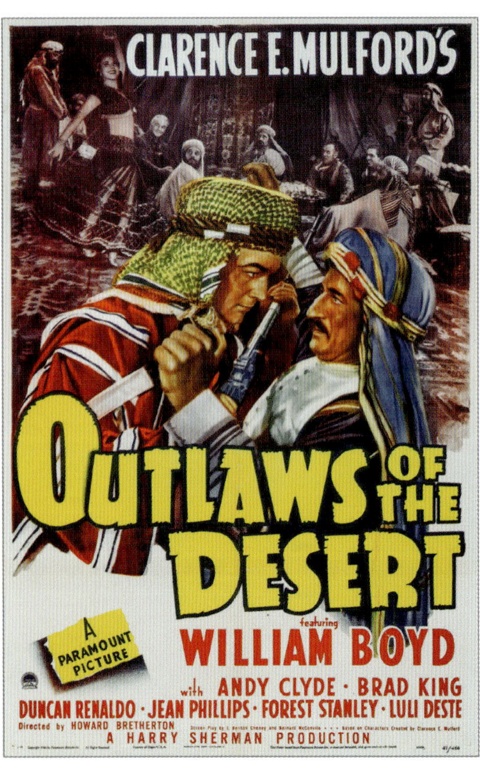
CLARENCE E. MULFORD'S
OUTLAWS OF THE DESERT
A PARAMOUNT PICTURE
featuring
WILLIAM BOYD
with ANDY CLYDE · BRAD KING
DUNCAN RENALDO · JEAN PHILLIPS · FOREST STANLEY · LULI DESTE
Directed by HOWARD BRETHERTON
A HARRY SHERMAN PRODUCTION

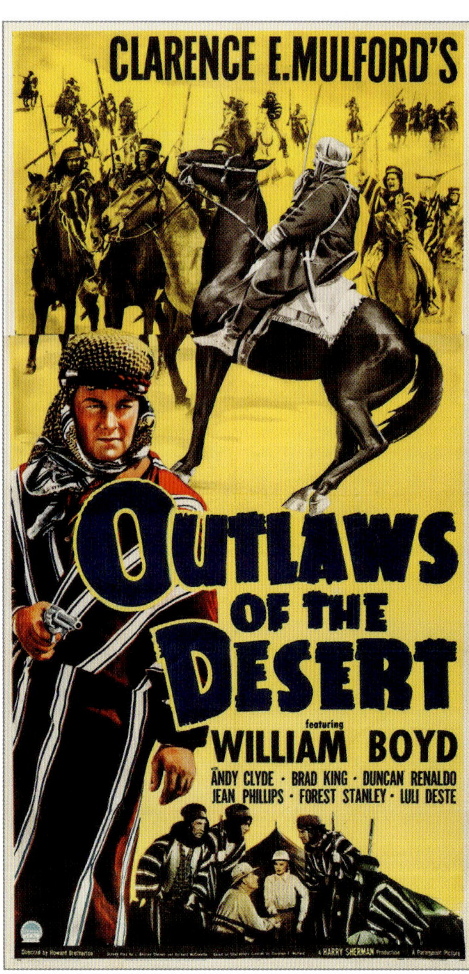
CLARENCE E. MULFORD'S
OUTLAWS OF THE DESERT
featuring
WILLIAM BOYD
ANDY CLYDE · BRAD KING · DUNCAN RENALDO
JEAN PHILLIPS · FOREST STANLEY · LULI DESTE

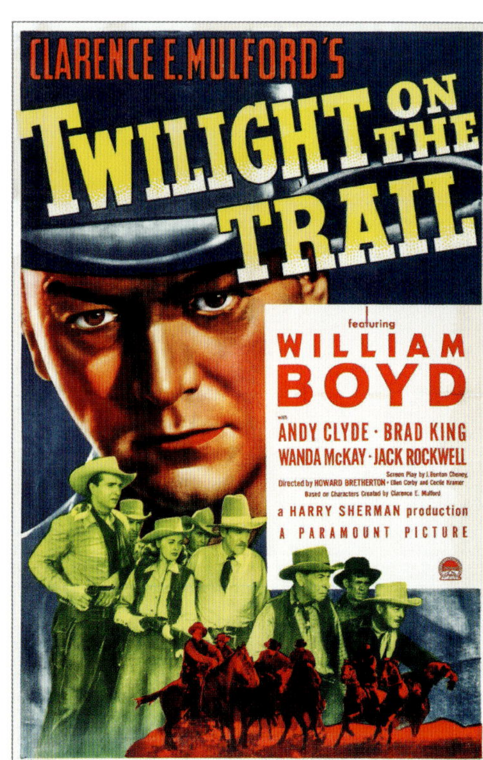
CLARENCE E. MULFORD'S
TWILIGHT ON THE TRAIL
featuring
WILLIAM BOYD
ANDY CLYDE · BRAD KING
WANDA McKAY · JACK ROCKWELL
Directed by HOWARD BRETHERTON
a HARRY SHERMAN production
A PARAMOUNT PICTURE

CLARENCE E. MULFORD'S
Stick to Your Guns
Featuring
WILLIAM . BOYD
with
ANDY CLYDE · BRAD KING · JACQUELINE HOLT
DICK CURTIS · WELDON HEYBURN
Based on Characters Created by Clarence E. Mulford
Screen Play by J. Benton Cheney
Directed by LESLEY SELANDER · A HARRY SHERMAN Production · A Paramount Picture
Copyright 1941 by Paramount Pictures Inc.
All Rights Reserved
Country of Origin U.S.A.
41/489

HOPPY AT UNITED ARTISTS

With production costs steadily rising (thanks to Boyd's yearly salary hikes, wartime material shortages, and increased unionization in Hollywood), the Hopalong Cassidy films gradually became less profitable. So, in 1942, Paramount sold the series to United Artists, which at the time desperately needed films to fulfill its distribution contracts. Harry Sherman instituted economizing measures—such as shooting installments back to back with the same casts—and ramped up the Hoppys' action quotient. Jay Kirby and Jimmy Rogers (son of humorist Will Rogers) filled the youthful-sidekick slot, and Andy Clyde remained as California Carlson. Having finally exhausted the supply of Mulford books to adapt, Pop Sherman bought the rights to other Western novels and had his scripters shoehorn Hoppy and his pals into their narratives. Future superstar Robert Mitchum had supporting roles in a handful of the UA Hoppys, as did George Reeves, later to become famous as TV's Superman. But profits continued to fall, and Sherman quit producing the series in 1944.

HARRY SHERMAN PRODUCTIONS presents
CLARENCE E. MULFORD'S
Hoppy Serves a Writ
featuring
WILLIAM BOYD
as Hopalong Cassidy
with
ANDY CLYDE
JAY KIRBY
VICTOR JORY
GEORGE REEVES
JAN CHRISTY
Directed by GEORGE ARCHAINBAUD
Released thru UNITED ARTISTS
A HARRY SHERMAN Production

HARRY SHERMAN PRODUCTIONS presents
CLARENCE E. MULFORD'S
Hoppy Serves a Writ
featuring
WILLIAM BOYD
as Hopalong Cassidy
ANDY CLYDE · JAY KIRBY · VICTOR JORY · GEORGE REEVES · JAN CHRISTY
Directed by GEORGE ARCHAINBAUD
A HARRY SHERMAN Production
Released thru UNITED ARTISTS

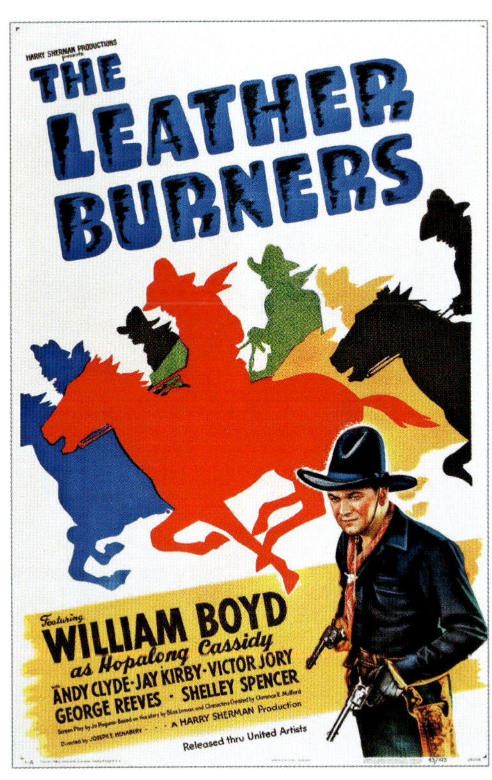
HARRY SHERMAN PRODUCTIONS presents
THE LEATHER BURNERS
Featuring
WILLIAM BOYD
as Hopalong Cassidy
with
ANDY CLYDE · JAY KIRBY · VICTOR JORY
GEORGE REEVES · SHELLEY SPENCER
A HARRY SHERMAN Production
Released thru United Artists

He Met the Best of the West!
HARRY SHERMAN PRODUCTIONS presents
COLT COMRADES
Featuring WILLIAM BOYD
as Hopalong Cassidy
with
ANDY CLYDE · JAY KIRBY · LOIS SHERMAN
VICTOR JORY · GEORGE REEVES · DOUGLAS FOWLEY
Directed by LESLEY SELANDER
A HARRY SHERMAN Production
Released thru UNITED ARTISTS

'Hoppy' at his best!
HARRY SHERMAN PRODUCTIONS presents
FALSE COLORS
featuring
WILLIAM BOYD
as Hopalong Cassidy
with
ANDY CLYDE · JIMMY ROGERS · DOUGLASS DUMBRILLE
CLAUDIA DRAKE · TOM SEIDEL · BOB MITCHUM
Directed by GEORGE ARCHAINBAUD
A HARRY SHERMAN Production
Released thru UNITED ARTISTS

HARRY SHERMAN PRODUCTIONS presents
CLARENCE E. MULFORD'S
BORDER PATROL
featuring
WILLIAM BOYD
as Hopalong Cassidy
with ANDY CLYDE · JAY KIRBY
RUSSELL SIMPSON · CLAUDIA DRAKE
GEORGE REEVES · DUNCAN RENALDO
A HARRY SHERMAN Production
Directed by LESLEY SELANDER
Released thru UNITED ARTISTS

HARRY SHERMAN PRODUCTIONS presents
CLARENCE E. MULFORD'S
BAR 20
Released thru UNITED ARTISTS
featuring
WILLIAM BOYD
as Hopalong Cassidy
with
ANDY CLYDE · GEORGE REEVES · DUSTINE FARNUM · VICTOR JORY
DOUGLAS FOWLEY · BETTY BLYTHE · FRANCIS McDONALD
Directed by LESLEY SELANDER
Screen Play by Morton Grant, Norman Houston, Michael Wilson
Based on Characters Created by Clarence E. Mulford
A HARRY SHERMAN Production

HARRY A. SHERMAN PRODUCTIONS presents
LUMBERJACK
featuring
WILLIAM BOYD
with ANDY CLYDE · JIMMY ROGERS
DOUGLASS DUMBRILLE · ELLEN HALL
FRANCIS McDONALD
DIRECTED BY LESLEY SELANDER
Screenplay by Norman Houston and Barry Shipman Based on Characters created by Clarence E. Mulford
A HARRY A. SHERMAN PRODUCTION
Released thru United Artists

HARRY A. SHERMAN PRODUCTIONS presents
LUMBERJACK
featuring
WILLIAM BOYD
with ANDY CLYDE
JIMMY ROGERS
DOUGLASS DUMBRILLE
ELLEN HALL
FRANCIS McDONALD
Screenplay by NORMAN HOUSTON and BARRY SHIPMAN
Based on Characters created by CLARENCE E. MULFORD
Directed by LESLEY SELANDER · A HARRY A. SHERMAN Production · Released thru United Artists

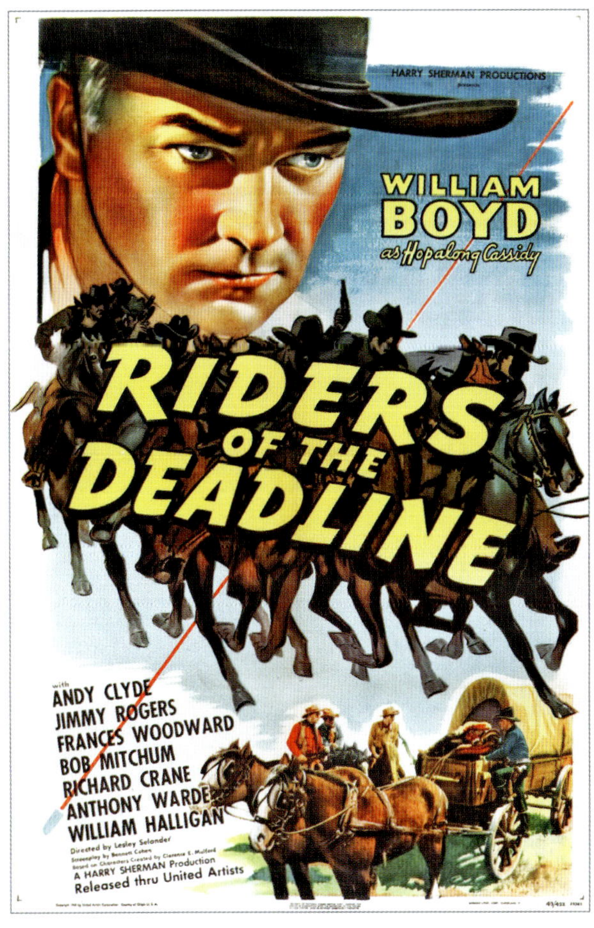
HARRY SHERMAN PRODUCTIONS
WILLIAM
BOYD
as Hopalong Cassidy
RIDERS OF THE DEADLINE
with
ANDY CLYDE
JIMMY ROGERS
FRANCES WOODWARD
BOB MITCHUM
RICHARD CRANE
ANTHONY WARDE
WILLIAM HALLIGAN
Directed by Lesley Selander
A HARRY SHERMAN Production
Released thru United Artists

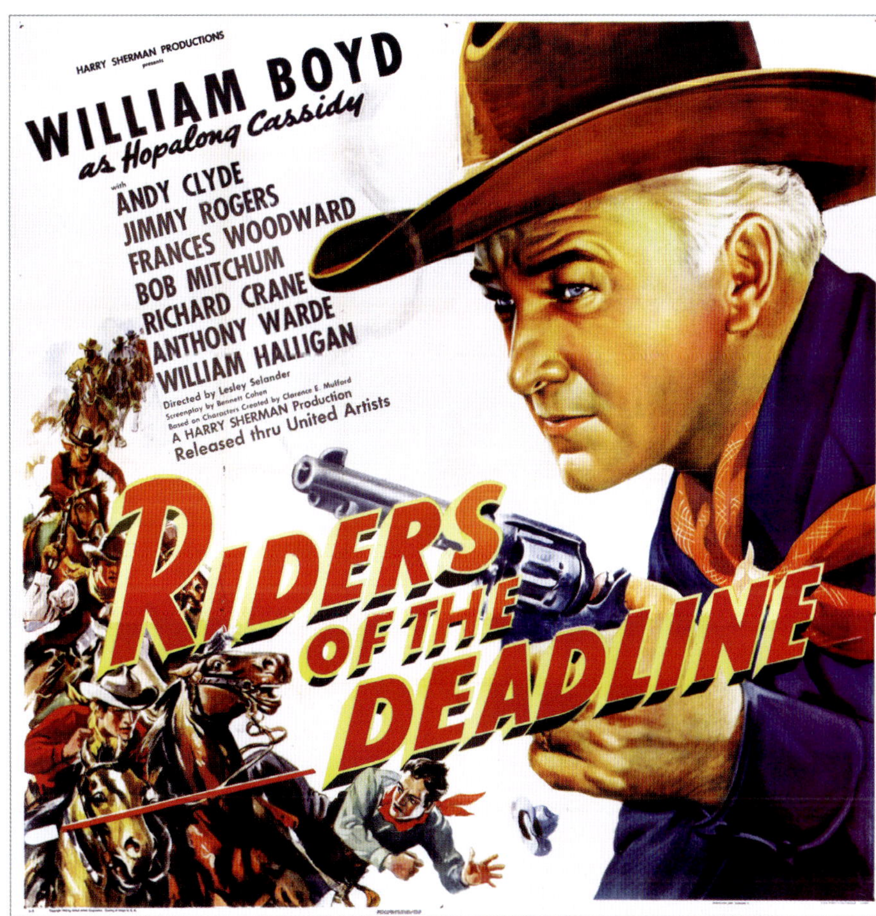
HARRY SHERMAN PRODUCTIONS
presents
WILLIAM BOYD
as Hopalong Cassidy
with
ANDY CLYDE
JIMMY ROGERS
FRANCES WOODWARD
BOB MITCHUM
RICHARD CRANE
ANTHONY WARDE
WILLIAM HALLIGAN
Directed by Lesley Selander
Screenplay by Bennett Cohen
Based on Characters Created by Clarence E. Mulford
A HARRY SHERMAN Production
Released thru United Artists
RIDERS OF THE DEADLINE

HARRY SHERMAN PRODUCTIONS presents
MYSTERY MAN
EXCHANGE BANK
featuring
WILLIAM BOYD
with
ANDY CLYDE · JIMMY ROGERS · DON COSTELLO
ELEANOR STEWART · FRANCIS McDONALD
DIRECTED BY GEORGE ARCHAINBAUD
A HARRY SHERMAN PRODUCTION
RELEASED THRU VARIETY FILM, DISTRIBUTORS, INC.
COUNTRY OF ORIGIN, U.S.A.

HARRY SHERMAN PRODUCTIONS
presents
FORTY THIEVES
featuring
WILLIAM BOYD
with
ANDY CLYDE · JIMMY ROGERS · DOUGLASS DUMBRILLE · LOUISE CURRIE · KIRK ALYN
Directed by LESLEY SELANDER · Screenplay by Michael Wilson and Bernie Kamins Based on Characters created by Clarence E. Mulford · A HARRY SHERMAN PRODUCTION · Released thru UNITED ARTISTS

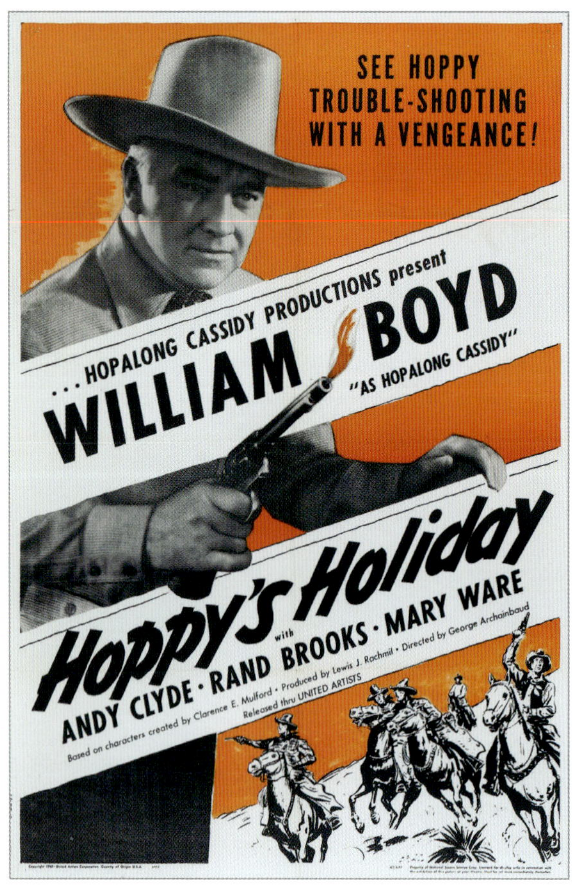

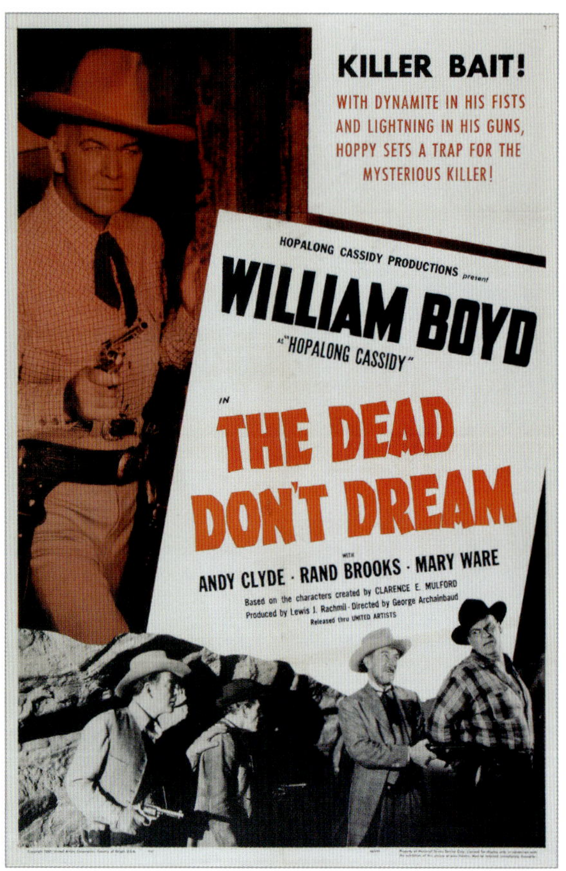

THE TWILIGHT YEARS

The Hopalong Cassidy character remained dormant for two years until, in early 1946, William Boyd—typecast in the part and finding it impossible to get roles in other films—scraped together enough money to buy the property from Harry Sherman, who was now producing "A" Westerns. Boyd got financing for a new group of Hoppy films and secured a distribution deal with United Artists. He produced twelve series entries over the next two years, retaining Andy Clyde as California and casting personable Rand Brooks as a revived Lucky Jenkins. He jettisoned the old familiar Hoppy costume and adopted a more contemporary look. Boyd also eschewed horse-opera clichés, instead showing a predilection for stage-bound whodunits. By 1948, the concept was played out, but the following year he was able to sell the older films to the NBC television network, which played them in prime time, introducing the character to a new generation of young viewers and making Boyd fabulously wealthy.

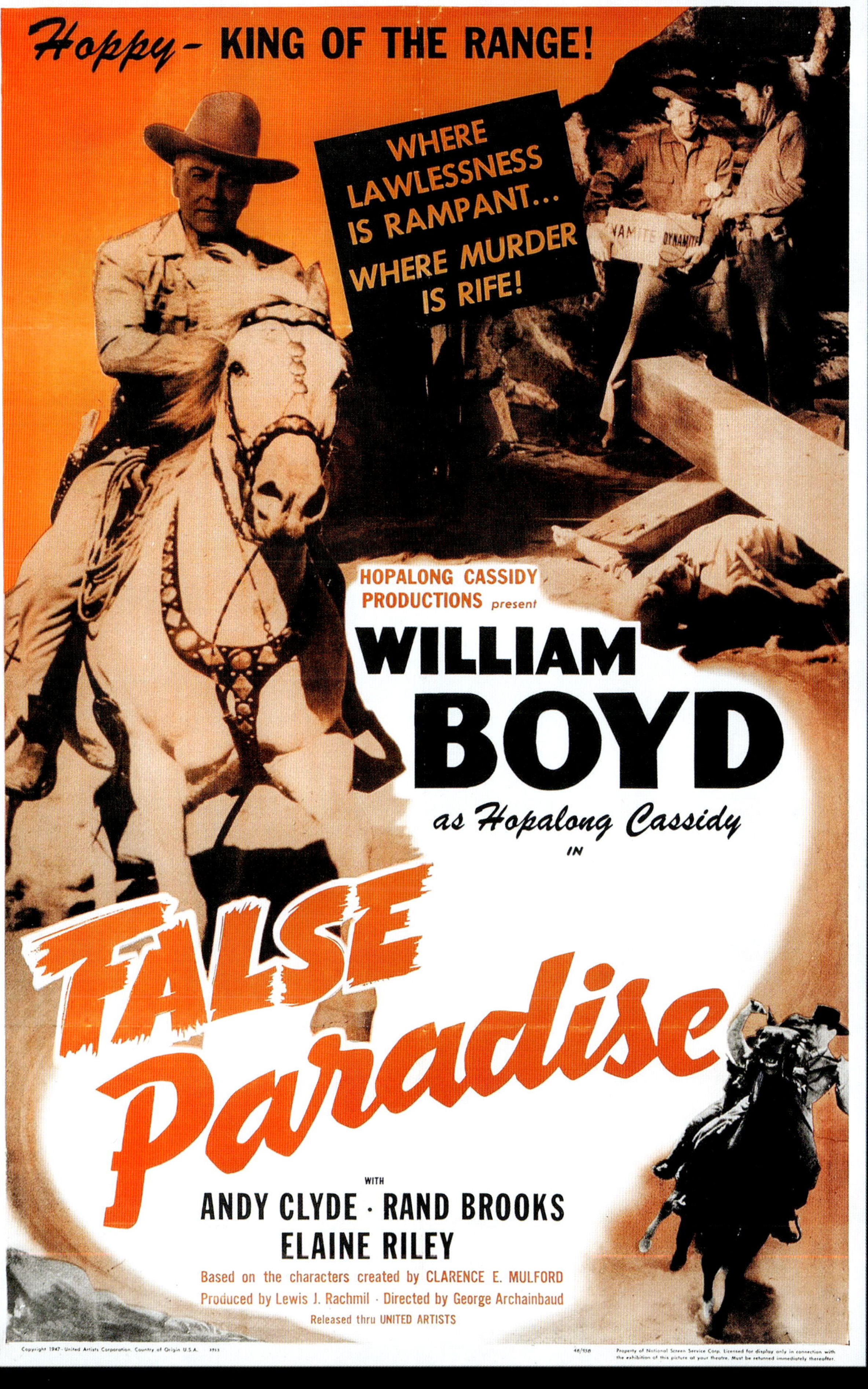
Hoppy - KING OF THE RANGE!
WHERE LAWLESSNESS IS RAMPANT... WHERE MURDER IS RIFE!
DYNAMITE DYNAMITE
HOPALONG CASSIDY PRODUCTIONS present
WILLIAM BOYD
as Hopalong Cassidy
IN
FALSE Paradise
WITH
ANDY CLYDE · RAND BROOKS
ELAINE RILEY
Based on the characters created by CLARENCE E. MULFORD
Produced by Lewis J. Rachmil · Directed by George Archainbaud
Released thru UNITED ARTISTS
Copyright 1947 - United Artists Corporation. Country of Origin U.S.A.
48/558
Property of National Screen Service Corp. Licensed for display only in connection with the exhibition of this picture at your theatre. Must be returned immediately thereafter.

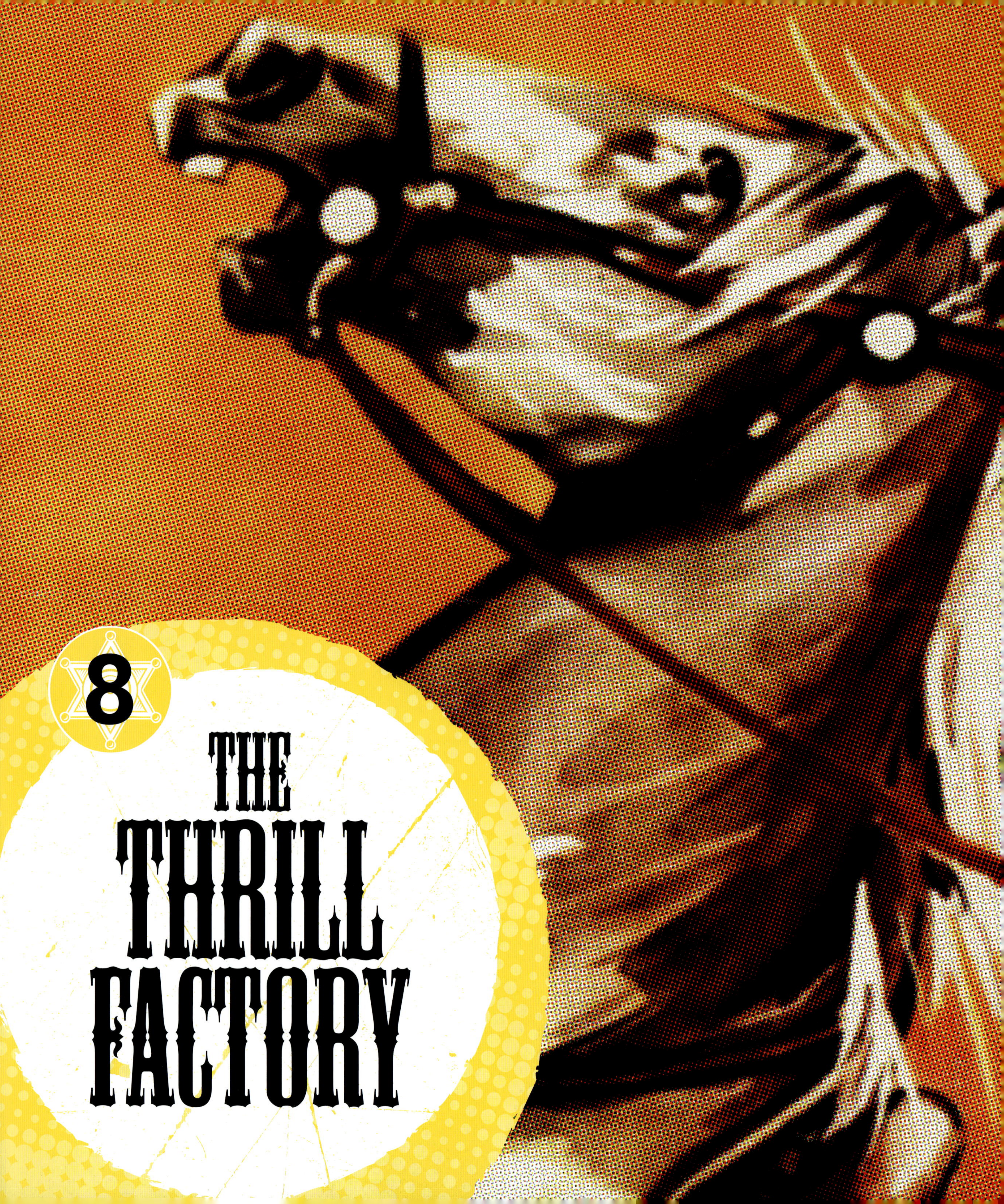
8
THE
THRILL
FACTORY

WHERE WESTERNS WERE KING

Taking over the former Mack Sennett studio in the San Fernando Valley north of Hollywood, Republic Pictures in 1935 begins cranking out low-budget movies for Saturday matinees and the bottom half of double bills in rural, suburban, and small-town venues. By customizing production methods to specialize in such fare, Republic is successful almost immediately, particularly with the fast-action B Westerns that will become its staple for two decades . . .

BELOW: The first entry in Republic's Three Mesquiteers series introduced Bob Livingston and Ray Corrigan, then largely unknown, as Stony Brooke and Tucson Smith, respectively. Veteran character actor Syd Saylor, playing Lullaby Joslin, believed himself too prominent to be stuck in a series with relative newcomers; he quit after completing this film.

Herbert J. Yates, a former executive of the American Tobacco Company and the American Record Corporation, used his Consolidated Film Industries—the laboratory that provided processing services and struck release prints for numerous Poverty Row companies—to force himself into motion-picture production and distribution. In 1935, most of Consolidated's clients were in arrears, battered by the Depression and requiring help from Yates to stay in business. Yates decided to foreclose on several of these corporate entities (chiefly Mascot, Liberty, and Monogram) and merge them into a new entity, Republic Pictures Corporation.

From the first, Yates aimed to become the preeminent supplier of Saturday-matinee B Westerns. Previously we mentioned how the instantaneous success of Gene Autry put the company on the Hollywood map. By 1936—its second year in business—Republic was distributing twenty-four low-budget horse operas annually. And by concentrating on this particular area of filmmaking, which demanded performers and technicians with highly specialized skill sets, the newly formed studio quickly established itself as nonpareil in productions of this genre.

The studio's first-year output of Westerns consisted of eight Autrys and eight John Waynes, before the latter left Republic to pursue other opportunities. He was replaced by a series featuring the Three Mesquiteers, characters created by author William Colt MacDonald for pulp magazine stories. The trio consisted of Tucson Smith (played by Ray Corrigan), Stony Brooke (Bob Livingston), and Lullaby Joslin (Syd Saylor in the series opener, Max Terhune thereafter). Eight Autrys and eight Mesquiteers weren't enough, though, and Yates contracted with

independent producer A. W. Hackel for eight films starring Bob Steele, which gave Republic the twenty-four oaters it had promised exhibitors.

This marked the beginning of what would become a Western-movie dynasty. In short order, Republic corralled the best writers, directors, and stunt performers the genre had to offer. Experienced crews, accustomed to working on tight schedules for little money, honed their skills so they could complete a six-reel feature film—running approximately fifty-five minutes, give or take—in a six-day workweek. They knew all the shortcuts but developed a few more to further streamline the process. Republic became a veritable B-Western factory, grinding out standardized product while maintaining a remarkably high level of technical quality. And for peanuts, too: during the late thirties, their horse operas seldom cost more than $40,000 to make, with many brought in for significantly less.

The Mesquiteers series, which lasted seven years, saw the first of many casting changes in 1938, when Bob Livingston was promoted to non-Western feature films and John Wayne returned to assume the role of Stony Brooke. The Duke had fared badly in a series of straight adventure films produced at Universal, and now he needed work. Even though the scripts were tailored to keep the focus on Wayne, he chafed at having to share the spotlight with Corrigan and Terhune. But that wouldn't last long.

ABOVE LEFT: John Wayne replaced Livingston for the eight installments released during 1938–39 and—since he was an already-established Western star—dominated the poster art and got larger billing than his two costars, even though their names were all supposed to be the same size.

ABOVE RIGHT: Corrigan was reportedly furious that Wayne's image alone dominated the *Pals of the Saddle* one-sheet. This apparent slight threatened his resolve to quit the series, which he did following the completion of the eighth film. The following year, he and Max Terhune formed two-thirds of a Mesquiteers imitation trio, the Range Busters.

ABOVE LEFT: Wild Bill Elliott didn't particularly resemble the comic-strip cowboy Red Ryder, but he did a bang-up job in the sixteen films he made in two years (1944–46). The Red Ryders were slick and action-packed, just as Republic Western fans had come to expect.

ABOVE RIGHT: This cast-and-crew shot was taken after shooting wrapped on the last day of *Sheriff of Las Vegas* (1944). Bill Elliott stands to the right, next to a white-haired crew member. His double, Tom Steele, stands to the left, next to fellow stuntman Duke Green.

With four of the year's eight entries in the can, Wayne took a sabbatical to appear in an A Western for his mentor, director John Ford. The film was *Stagecoach*. After completing his scenes, Duke trudged back to Republic and toiled in the second quartet of Mesquiteers oaters scheduled for distribution during the 1938–39 season. *Stagecoach* hit theater screens in March '39 and scored decisively with critics and moviegoers alike. John Wayne was locked into a long-term contract with Republic, but he would never appear in one of their B Westerns again. The Three Mesquiteers series was overhauled again, with Bob Livingston returning as Stony and Duncan Renaldo and Raymond Hatton replacing Corrigan and Terhune.

The casting changes didn't stop there. Over the years, Republic's expertise in horse-opera production made stars of several actors with little or no previous experience in Westerns. Among these were Don "Red" Barry, Allan Lane, Eddie Dew, Sunset Carson, and Monte Hale. Only Dew failed to make the grade, his highly touted "John Paul Revere" series meeting with audience apathy. The studio poached only one established Western star, Columbia's Wild Bill Elliott. He made a series of eight starring as himself, then sixteen as comic-strip cowboy Red Ryder, before being promoted to higher-budget genre offerings. Allan Lane succeeded him as Red, playing the role for just one year. In 1947 he was rechristened "Rocky" Lane and became wildly popular, with his eponymous series lasting until 1953.

The responsibility for creating Republic's posters fell to the company's advertising and publicity department. Initially, that office operated out of the

company's New York office under the direction of Edward F. Finney, who left Republic after one year to join the fledgling Grand National studio upon being promised he would be able to produce Westerns in addition to running the advertising and promotion shop. Finney's departure heralded years of constant turmoil, with no fewer than a dozen people running the department prior to Republic's cessation of film production in 1959.

Notwithstanding the managerial uncertainty, the company's posters were remarkably consistent for Republic's first decade of existence. It seems likely that for the first year or so, art chores were farmed out to various freelancers, but as early as 1936 the posters were displaying a uniform look, with paintings appearing to be the work of one man and the hand-lettered copy the work of another. The artist's portraiture was uneven—especially in the early and mid-forties, as his workload increased—and occasionally a star's facial features were all but unrecognizable. There was a respite in the 1938–39 release year, when a new man temporarily joined the overworked staff and rendered some extremely handsome portraits of Autry, the Mesquiteers, and newcomer Roy Rogers. The paintings in this group are among the best ever employed in Republic posters.

Beginning in 1939–40, there was a brief push to economize in poster production, resulting in the frequent use of two-color designs and the employment of monochromatic photos in boxes to cut down on the amount of space the artist needed to fill. These changes didn't last long, although in the years following World War II there was a partial shift from hand-lettered to typeset copy. ★

ABOVE: Cast and crew take a break during filming of *Riders of the Black Hills* (1938) at the historic Vasquez Rocks in Southern California. To the left is Bob Livingston's stunt double, Duke Taylor, holding Starlight's reins. Director George Sherman sits on the camera trick's top platform, checking his script; bit player Art Dillard and Max Terhune are seated on the camera truck's bottom platform. Corrigan stands, munching a snack; an unidentified script girl and Livingston are seated to his right.

THE THREE MESQUITEERS

Prolific pulp-fictioneer William Colt MacDonald created the Mesquiteers in a 1929 magazine serial, "Law of the Forty-Fives," which was adapted to the screen under that title in 1934. A second Mesquiteers movie, *Powdersmoke Range*, appeared the following year and was an all-star production featuring Harry Carey, Hoot Gibson, and Guinn "Big Boy" Williams as Tucson, Stony, and Lullaby. In early 1936, Nat Levine licensed exclusive screen rights to the characters for Republic Pictures, which that September released the first of fifty-one Mesquiteers oaters made during a seven-year period. The trio's composition changed numerous times, with John Wayne, Raymond Hatton, Duncan Renaldo, Bob Steele, Tom Tyler, Rufe Davis, and Jimmie Dodd replacing Livingston, Corrigan, and Terhune. Screenwriters couldn't agree on a specific time frame for the series, whose stories took place as early as the Civil War and as late as World War II. The one constant was action, always staged and shot in the polished Republic manner.

REPUBLIC PICTURES
Presents
THE THREE MESQUITEERS
in
"HEART OF THE ROCKIES"
Starring
BOB LIVINGSTON
RAY CORRIGAN
MAX TERHUNE
A Republic PICTURE
REPUBLIC PICTURES
Directed by JOSEPH KANE
Screen Play by JACK NATTEFORD · OLIVER DRAKE
Original Story by BERNARD McCONVILLE
Based on characters created by WILLIAM COLT MacDONALD
Associate Producer SOL C. SIEGEL

REPUBLIC PICTURES
presents
THE THREE MESQUITEERS
in "THE TRIGGER TRIO"
with
RAY CORRIGAN
MAX TERHUNE
RALPH BYRD
Directed by WILLIAM WITNEY
Associate Producer SOL C. SIEGEL
REPUBLIC PICTURES
a REPUBLIC picture

Republic PICTURES presents
The 3 MESQUITEERS
Outlaws of SONORA
Bob LIVINGSTON
Ray CORRIGAN
Max TERHUNE
Directed by GEORGE SHERMAN
Associate Producer WILLIAM BERKE
Based on characters created by WILLIAM COLT MacDONALD
A Republic PICTURE

THE 3 MESQUITEERS
in
HEROES OF THE HILLS
with
BOB LIVINGSTON
RAY CORRIGAN
MAX TERHUNE
Directed by GEORGE SHERMAN
Based on characters created by WILLIAM COLT MacDONALD
Associate Producer – WILLIAM BERKE
A Republic PICTURE

COVERED WAGON DAYS
featuring
THE 3 MESQUITEERS
ROBERT LIVINGSTON
RAYMOND HATTON · DUNCAN RENALDO
WITH
KAY GRIFFITH
GEORGE DOUGLAS
Directed by GEORGE SHERMAN
BASED ON CHARACTERS CREATED BY
WILLIAM COLT MacDONALD
A Republic PICTURE
REPUBLIC PICTURES
Country of Origin U.S.A.
MORGAN LITHO CORP. CLEVELAND O.

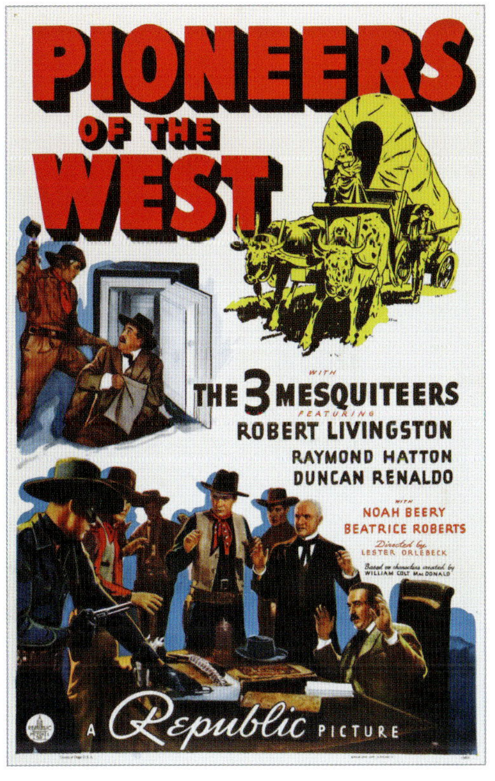
PIONEERS OF THE WEST
WITH
THE 3 MESQUITEERS
FEATURING
ROBERT LIVINGSTON
RAYMOND HATTON
DUNCAN RENALDO
WITH
NOAH BEERY
BEATRICE ROBERTS
Directed by LESTER ORLEBECK
A Republic PICTURE

THE 3 MESQUITEERS IN
OKLAHOMA RENEGADES
WITH
ROBERT LIVINGSTON
RAYMOND HATTON · DUNCAN RENALDO
FLORINE McKINNEY · AL HERMAN · LASSES WHITE
A Republic PICTURE

THE 3 MESQUITEERS
SADDLEMATES
A REPUBLIC PICTURE
ROBERT LIVINGSTON
BOB STEELE · RUFE DAVIS
with GALE STORM · LES ORLEBECK - Director
Based on characters created by WILLIAM COLT MacDONALD

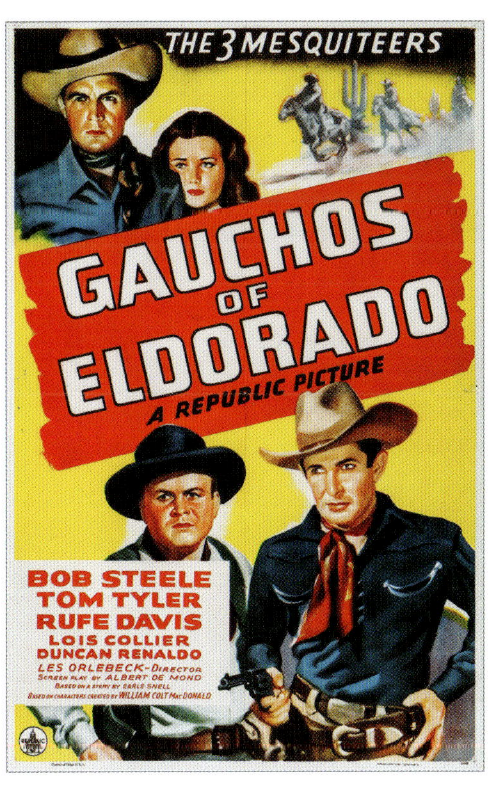
THE 3 MESQUITEERS
GAUCHOS OF ELDORADO
A REPUBLIC PICTURE
BOB STEELE
TOM TYLER
RUFE DAVIS
LOIS COLLIER
DUNCAN RENALDO
LES ORLEBECK-Director
SCREEN PLAY BY ALBERT DE MOND
BASED ON CHARACTERS CREATED BY WILLIAM COLT MacDONALD

WEST OF CIMARRON
A REPUBLIC PICTURE
THE 3 MESQUITEERS
FEATURING
BOB STEELE · TOM TYLER
RUFE DAVIS WITH LOIS COLLIER JAMES BUSH
LES ORLEBECK— DIRECTOR
BASED ON CHARACTERS CREATED BY WILLIAM COLT MacDONALD

THE 3 MESQUITEERS
OUTLAWS OF CHEROKEE TRAIL
A REPUBLIC PICTURE
FEATURING
BOB STEELE
TOM TYLER
RUFE DAVIS
WITH
LOIS COLLIER
TOM CHATTERTON
LES ORLEBECK—DIRECTOR
ORIGINAL SCREEN PLAY BY ALBERT DEMOND
BASED ON CHARACTERS CREATED BY WILLIAM COLT McDONALD
ASSOCIATE PRODUCER—LOUIS GRAY

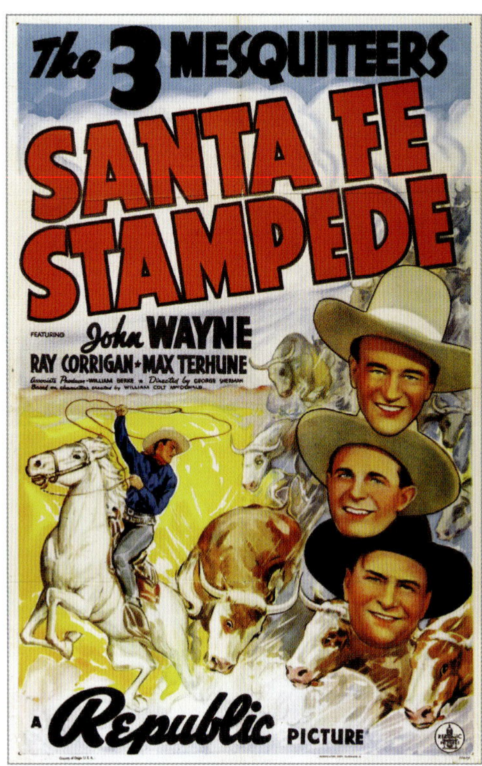

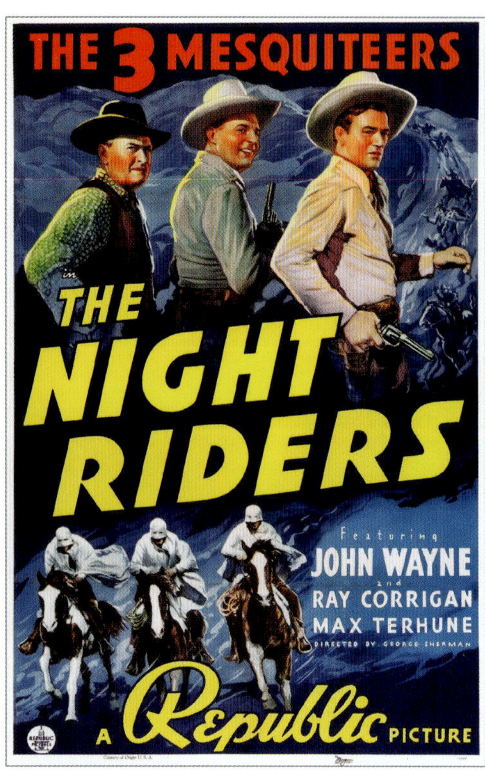

THE WAYNE MESQUITEERS

When Bob Livingston was "promoted" to Republic non-Westerns, the role of Stony Brooke was assigned to John Wayne, who at the time was still working in B movies but was a bigger box-office attraction than any of the original Mesquiteers. Already ambitious, Wayne collaborated on script rewrites with unit director George Sherman; of course, his input resulted in more screen time for Stony, effectively reducing Tucson and Lullaby to mere sidekicks. Actors Corrigan and Terhune seethed and vowed to leave Republic when their yearly contracts came up for renewal. Ironically, despite the behind-the-scenes tension, the Wayne Mesquiteers films were among the best Westerns that Republic had produced to date. With four of the contractual eight installments done, the Duke took a sabbatical to film *Stagecoach* for John Ford before returning to Republic to make the other four Mesquiteers pictures. By that time, *Stagecoach* was playing in major theaters across the country, and John Wayne's decade-long tenure as a B-Western star had finally come to an end.

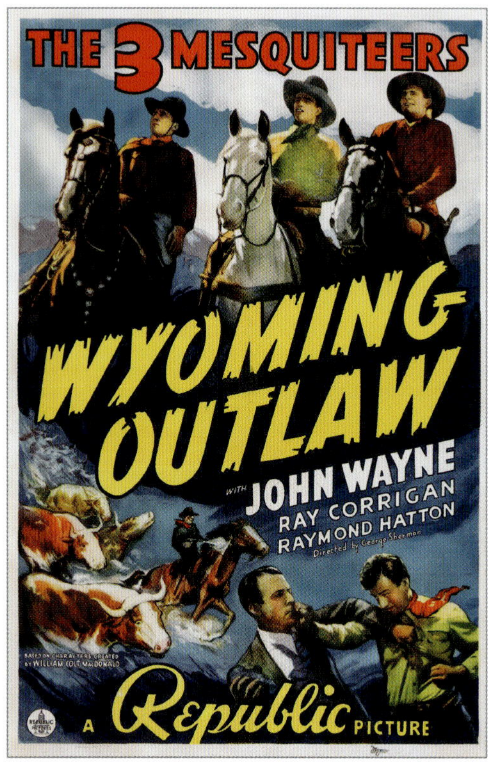

THE 3 MESQUITEERS
IN
NEW FRONTIER
FEATURING
JOHN WAYNE · RAY CORRIGAN
RAYMOND HATTON
with PHYLIS ISLEY
Directed by GEORGE SHERMAN
BASED ON CHARACTERS CREATED BY WILLIAM COLT MacDONALD
A Republic PICTURE
REPUBLIC PICTURES
Country of Origin U.S.A.

DON "RED" BARRY

Entering films in 1933, Donald M. Barry bounced from studio to studio, mostly essaying unbilled bit parts until he wound up at Republic Pictures. He had meaty supporting roles in several 1939 films, including a Three Mesquiteers opus and two Roy Rogers musical Westerns. Small of stature but with plenty of talent (and an ego to match), Barry attracted the attention of Republic president Herbert J. Yates, who saw him as a potential cowboy star and cast him in the title role of a 1940 serial, *Adventures of Red Ryder*. Although the pugnacious, pint-sized performer was all wrong for tall and lanky Red, Barry acquitted himself well in the part and earned his own Western series. His starring vehicles were inexpensively made, but they usually had excellent scripts that allowed Don to show off his acting chops. Between 1940 and 1944, he top-lined twenty-nine B Westerns for Republic, many of them among the studio's best.

ARIZONA TERRORS
A REPUBLIC PICTURE
DON "Red" BARRY
LYNN MERRICK
AL. ST. JOHN
REED HADLEY
SCREEN PLAY BY DORIS SCHROEDER — TAYLOR CAVEN
GEORGE SHERMAN — DIRECTOR
REPUBLIC PICTURES
Country of Origin U.S.A.
MORGAN LITHO. CORP. CLEVELAND, O.

SUNDOWN KID
A REPUBLIC PICTURE
DON "Red" BARRY
IAN KEITH
HELEN MACKELLAR
LINDA JOHNSON
EMMETT LYNN
ELMER CLIFTON – DIRECTOR
SCREEN PLAY BY NORMAN S. HALL
ORIGINAL STORY BY EDDY WHITE
REPUBLIC PICTURES

DON "Red" BARRY
DAYS OF OLD CHEYENNE
A REPUBLIC PICTURE
LYNN MERRICK
WILLIAM HAADE
EMMETT "PAPPY" LYNN
HERBERT RAWLINSON
ELMER CLIFTON – DIRECTOR

DON (Red) BARRY
DEAD MAN'S GULCH
A REPUBLIC PICTURE
LYNN MERRICK
CLANCY COOPER
EMMETT "PAPPY" LYNN
JOHN ENGLISH – DIRECTOR

DON "RED" BARRY
CALIFORNIA JOE
A REPUBLIC PICTURE
REPUBLIC PICTURES
WALLY VERNON
HELEN TALBOT
TWINKLE WATTS
SPENCER BENNET—DIRECTOR
ORIGINAL SCREENPLAY BY NORMAN S. HALL
Country of Origin U.S.A.
MORGAN LITHO. CORP. CLEVELAND, O.

SMILEY BURNETTE AND SUNSET CARSON

When Gene Autry entered military service in 1942, Republic was left with his rotund sidekick, Smiley Burnette. The studio used him to anchor a highly touted series featuring a newly created character, John Paul Revere, played first by the charismatically challenged Eddie Dew and then by a disinterested Bob Livingston. The pictures made no impression on audiences, and Revere faded away, unloved and unmissed. Smiley was then given his own series, with top billing and a boyish giant named Sunset Carson to handle the action and flirt with the leading ladies. Carson's acting ability was negligible, but the six-foot-six former rodeo rider made up for that as soon as he hopped into a saddle. After four pictures, Smiley was given the boot and Sunset was boosted to star billing. He quickly became a top box-office draw—and just as quickly became difficult to handle. Republic dropped him in 1946 after eleven solo outings.

CALL OF
THE ROCKIES
starring
SMILEY BURNETTE
with
SONNY "SUNSET" CARSON
HARRY WOODS ★ KIRK ALYN
ELLEN HALL
LESLEY SELANDER—Director
ORIGINAL SCREENPLAY BY BOB WILLIAMS
A Republic PICTURE

FIREBRANDS
OF ARIZONA
A REPUBLIC PICTURE
starring
SMILEY BURNETTE
with SUNSET CARSON
PEGGY STEWART
EARLE HODGINS
ROY BARCROFT
LESLEY SELANDER — Director
REPUBLIC PICTURES

SHERIFF OF
CIMARRON
A REPUBLIC PICTURE
starring
SUNSET CARSON
with LINDA STIRLING
OLIN HOWLIN
and RIELY HILL · JACK INGRAM
Directed by YAKIMA CANUTT
ORIGINAL SCREEN PLAY BY BENNETT COHEN

SANTA FE
SADDLEMATES
A REPUBLIC PICTURE
starring
SUNSET CARSON
with Linda STIRLING
Olin HOWLIN
Roy BARCROFT
Directed by THOMAS CARR
ORIGINAL SCREEN PLAY BY BENNETT COHEN
REPUBLIC PICTURES

The CHEROKEE FLASH
starring
SUNSET CARSON
with LINDA STIRLING
TOM LONDON
ROY BARCROFT
Directed by THOMAS CARR
ORIGINAL SCREEN PLAY BY BETTY BURBRIDGE
A Republic Picture

Sunset
CARSON
in
BANDITS OF THE BADLANDS
A REPUBLIC PICTURE
with
PEGGY STEWART
SI "RAWHIDE" JENKS
and JOHN MERTON
DIRECTED BY THOMAS CARR
ORIGINAL SCREEN PLAY BY DORIS SCHROEDER

ALIAS BILLY THE KID
SUNSET CARSON
PEGGY STEWART
TOM LONDON
ROY BARCROFT
Directed by THOMAS CARR
SCREEN PLAY BY EARLE SNELL AND BETTY BURBRIDGE
ORIGINAL STORY BY NORMAN SHELDON
A
REPUBLIC
PICTURE
REPUBLIC PICTURES
Country of Origin U. S. A.
MORGAN LITHO. CORP. CLEVELAND O.

RIO GRANDE
Raiders
starring
SUNSET CARSON
LINDA STIRLING
BOB STEELE
DIRECTED BY THOMAS CARR
SCREEN PLAY BY NORTON S. PARKER
BASED ON A STORY BY NORMAN S. HALL
A REPUBLIC PICTURE
REPUBLIC PICTURES
Country of Origin U.S.A.

WILD BILL ELLIOTT AND RED RYDER

Upon joining Republic's roster of B-Western stars in 1943 after four years with Columbia, Wild Bill Elliott brought along his memorable tagline, "Folks call me 'wild,' but I'm really a peaceable man"—uttered in every film but belied by the ridin', fightin', and shootin' he did in practically every reel. Elliott's first eight vehicles had him playing himself, but in 1944 he assumed the role of Fred Harman's comic-strip cowpoke Red Ryder. Elliott was only marginally more suited for the part than Don Barry had been four years earlier, but his performance was so earnest—and the films themselves so well made—that Saturday-matinee audiences readily accepted him. Wild Bill shot and slugged his way through sixteen installments of the series in two years before yielding the character to Allan Lane. At that point, he was promoted to relatively mature Westerns intended primarily for adult audiences, some of them made in Republic's Trucolor process, which was reserved for more expensive productions.

WILD BILL ELLIOTT
GEORGE "Gabby" HAYES
WAGON TRACKS WEST
A REPUBLIC PICTURE
TOM TYLER
ANNE JEFFREYS
HOWARD BRETHERTON-DIRECTOR
ORIGINAL SCREEN PLAY BY WILLIAM LIVELY

WILD BILL ELLIOTT as
RED RYDER
VIGILANTES OF DODGE CITY
A REPUBLIC PICTURE
BOBBY BLAKE
ALICE FLEMING
LINDA STIRLING
WALLACE GRISSELL, Director

WILD BILL ELLIOTT
as RED RYDER
CHEYENNE WILDCAT
with BOBBY BLAKE
ALICE FLEMING
PEGGY STEWART • FRANCIS McDONALD
LESLEY SELANDER, Director
A REPUBLIC PICTURE

STARRING
WILD BILL ELLIOTT as
RED RYDER
MARSHAL OF LAREDO
A REPUBLIC PICTURE
with BOBBY BLAKE
ALICE FLEMING
Peggy STEWART • Don COSTELLO
Directed by R. G. SPRINGSTEEN
ORIGINAL SCREEN PLAY BY BOB WILLIAMS

Starring
WILD BILL ELLIOTT as
RED RYDER
TEXAS MANHUNT
Bobby BLAKE
Alice FLEMING
IAN KEITH
WILLIAM HAADE
VIRGINIA CHRISTINE
REPUBLIC PICTURES
A REPUBLIC PICTURE
DIRECTED BY LESLIE SELANDER
ORIGINAL SCREEN PLAY BY EARLE SNELL and CHARLES KENYON

WILD BILL ELLIOTT as
RED RYDER
CALIFORNIA
GOLD RUSH
BOBBY BLAKE
ALICE FLEMING
PEGGY STEWART
RUSSELL SIMPSON
Directed by R. G. SPRINGSTEEN
ORIGINAL SCREEN PLAY BY BOB WILLIAMS
A REPUBLIC PICTURE
REPUBLIC PICTURES

ALLAN LANE AND MONTE HALE

Handsome but wooden Lane, a former RKO contract player, moved to Republic in 1944 and inherited what had been the Don "Red" Barry series, which he bought to a conclusion after six pleasant but nondescript installments. In 1946, he inherited the Red Ryder series from Bill Elliott, playing the role in seven good entries. Lane built a loyal fan following, and Republic decided to save the cost of licensing Red Ryder by instead starting a brand-new series and calling the star Rocky Lane. In this incarnation, Lane lasted until 1953, making unpretentious, fast-action films with solid, relatively mature plots and situations. Monte Hale, an affable Oklahoman who staged musical acts at rodeos and vaudeville shows all over the Southwest, joined Republic in 1946 as a second-string singing cowboy. His first four starring vehicles were Trucolor musical Westerns, but he quickly transitioned to straight action. Both he and Lane kept making pictures until TV usurped the market for B Westerns in the early fifties.

ALLAN LANE as
RED RYDER
Stagecoach to
DENVER
with BOBBY BLAKE
MARTHA WENTWORTH
PEGGY BARCROFT
ROY BARCROFT
PEGGY STEWART
Directed by R. G. SPRINGSTEEN
ORIGINAL SCREEN PLAY BY EARLE SNELL
REPUBLIC PICTURES
A REPUBLIC PICTURE
Country of Origin U.S.A.
31842

ALLAN LANE as
RED RYDER
OREGON TRAIL SCOUTS
BOBBY BLAKE
MARTHA WENTWORTH
Directed by R. G. SPRINGSTEEN
A
REPUBLIC
PICTURE

Oklahoma Badlands
starring
ALLAN "ROCKY" LANE
And His Stallion
BLACK JACK
with
EDDY WALLER
MILDRED COLES
Directed by YAKIMA CANUTT
ORIGINAL SCREEN PLAY BY BOB WILLIAMS
A REPUBLIC PICTURE

MAN FROM RAINBOW VALLEY
A MAGNACOLOR PRODUCTION
starring
Monte HALE and Adrian BOOTH
with
SAGEBRUSH SERENADERS
DIRECTED BY ROBERT SPRINGSTEEN
ORIGINAL SCREEN PLAY BY BETTY BURBRIDGE
A REPUBLIC PICTURE

All the Action and
Color of the West Now
in TRUCOLOR
LAST FRONTIER
Uprising
in TRUCOLOR
starring MONTE HALE • ADRIAN BOOTH
with FOY WILLING and The Riders of the Purple Sage
Directed by LESLEY SELANDER
SCREEN PLAY BY HARVEY GATES • • • • BASED ON AN ORIGINAL STORY BY JEROME ODLUM
A REPUBLIC PRODUCTION
REPUBLIC PICTURES
Country of Origin U.S.A.
31302

9
THE REST OF
THE RANGE
RIDERS

FADING STARS AND NEW FACES

The thirties draw to a close with the films of Gene Autry, William Boyd, and George O'Brien capturing the lion's share of Saturday-matinee revenues, while such A-movie productions as *Stagecoach*, *Jesse James*, and *Dodge City* earn big bucks at prestige theaters in the major cities. At the same time, old favorites Buck Jones, Tim McCoy, Ken Maynard, and Harry Carey see their popularity waning as studios reshuffle their Western stars and series . . .

The period immediately preceding America's entrance into World War II was a time of transition for B Westerns. Poverty Row oaters gradually faded from view, replaced by those from Republic, the recently reconstituted Monogram, and a small new studio called PRC (Producers Releasing Corporation). These outfits dominated the low end of the business, leaving major studios RKO, Universal, and Columbia to supply a somewhat higher-class product. During this period, Paramount and 20th Century-Fox released their last B Westerns, leaving the market to less prestigious companies.

RKO produced the most polished low-budget horse operas, beginning in 1938 with a fast-action series starring George O'Brien—still popular nearly fifteen years after achieving stardom in John Ford's 1924 epic *The Iron Horse*. O'Brien had gained weight but continued to perform his own stunts, and he remained credible as the love interest for ingenues nearly half his age. His breezy, devil-may-care attitude endeared the barrel-chested Irishman to adults as well as children, and the RKO O'Briens secured bookings in theaters that normally eschewed B Westerns. Manufactured on budgets occasionally reaching $100,000, they boasted solid production values and devoted more resources to scripting—an area habitually stinted on by the smaller studios.

Ironically, maintaining a high level of quality made O'Brien's films less profitable, so in 1940 RKO replaced him with up-and-coming Tim Holt. The son of silent-era Western hero Jack Holt, Tim was barely twenty-one years old when he won his own series and became RKO's chief cowboy star. He had already appeared in a number of non-Western films and taken meaty supporting roles in O'Brien's *Renegade Ranger* and Harry Carey's *The Law West of Tombstone* (the latter being Carey's final starring oater). But young Holt caught on with action-

BELOW: In the mid-thirties, George O'Brien ranked number two (after Buck Jones) in annual lists of the top ten Western stars. By 1938, when *Renegade Ranger* was made, he had been overtaken by Gene Autry and William Boyd, but he still enjoyed great popularity with adults and children alike.

hungry audiences in a hurry, and the fact that he commanded a much smaller salary than his predecessor made his series more profitable for the studio. He had a string of modestly appointed but expertly made Westerns to his credit when he entered military service in 1942.

Columbia made a stab at turning former male model Bob Allen into a horse-opera star, but the native New Yorker never passed muster with Saturday-matinee moppets. His successor, Jack Luden, fared even more poorly, with his proposed six-film series curtailed after four installments. But in Charles Starrett, the studio had an established favorite whose late-thirties and early forties Westerns maintained a consistency that became almost legendary. During this period he solidified his standing as a top box-office attraction. Another favorite was Gordon Elliott, who was promoted to features after playing the title role in a 1938 Columbia serial, *The Great Adventures of Wild Bill Hickok*. That success found him billed thereafter as "Wild Bill" Elliott.

In 1939, singing cowboy Bob Baker surrendered his position as Universal's resident Western star and suffered the indignity of playing second fiddle to newly hired Johnny Mack Brown, whose own career had faltered. After making

ABOVE: Western film notables attended a ceremony honoring George Marshall on his twenty-fifth anniversary as a director, on August 5, 1940. The ceremony was restaged for photographers backstage at the Pantages Theatre on Hollywood Boulevard. *Standing from left*: Eddie Polo, a female friend of hugger William Desmond, Lane Chandler, John Wayne, Leo Carrillo, Marshall, Johnny Mack Brown, Tim McCoy, Yakima Canutt, Noll O'Day, Montie Montana, and Kermit Maynard. *Front row, from left*: Glenn Tryon, Buck Jones, Bill Elliott, Russell Hayden, Jimmy Rogers, Guinn Williams, and Will James. Brown has on the outfit and holster he wore that day while shooting scenes for *Pony Post*.

ABOVE: Noah Beery Jr. (*at right, in black hat and light shirt*) prepares to shoot a scene for *Forbidden Valley* (Universal, 1938), a "B-plus" Western based on Stuart Hardy's then-popular novel *The Mountains Are My Home.* From the look of things, it was a chilly morning on location.

six films in that role, Baker quit the series. He never found a permanent berth at any other studio and by 1942 was playing unbilled bit roles. Mack Brown, meanwhile, entered the 1940s with singer-sidekick Fuzzy Knight providing musical support and comedy relief in slick, fast-paced Westerns that often matched the best being produced by Republic.

After an ill-advised attempt to launch Jack Randall as a singing cowboy, Monogram kept him on in straight action Westerns through 1940. The studio also recruited former RKO Western star Tom Keene, who top-lined four so-so 1938 pictures and brought him back for a lamentable 1941 series produced on a shoestring. Awful in almost every way, they failed miserably at the nation's box offices and snuffed out Keene's starring career as if it were a flickering candle.

The period 1938–41 also saw the genre's formerly biggest stars either flailing about in substandard offerings or absent from the screen altogether. Tom Mix had retired following his 1935 serial *The Miracle Rider*. Hoot Gibson disappeared after taking a supporting role in *The Painted Stallion*, a 1937 Republic chapter play. Buck Jones left Universal in 1937 and signed with independent producers L. G. Leonard and Monroe Shaff, for whom he starred in six mediocre oaters distributed by Columbia. They were received with indifference, and Buck's solo career ended. Tim McCoy, whose early thirties movies had been among the best B Westerns on the market, drifted to Monogram for a series of four, then to Sam Katzman's Victory Pictures for eight, and finally to newly formed PRC for six. With each move, the quality of Tim's oaters declined, and after a year at PRC he was unable to continue as a star.

Ken Maynard suffered a similar fate, toiling in four weak Westerns for Grand National and then scraping the barrel's bottom with eight truly execrable films for Colony Pictures. He too was washed up as a cowboy star by the time World War

II got underway. Likewise, Tom Tyler and Bob Steele—both of whom had risen to prominence in the late 1920s for FBO—finished the '30s in subpar vehicles that severely eroded their standing. Clearly, it was the end of an era. But with the exception of Tom Mix, who died in an automobile accident in 1940, the old timers would return during the war years—greatly diminished in stature, perhaps, but ready for their last hurrahs. Only now they would appear in teams . . .

It's impossible to gauge the quality of the abovementioned films by their posters, most of which were significantly more appealing than the Westerns they promoted. In keeping with the general excellence of RKO's Westerns, that studio's paintings were rendered with great care. But some of the cheapest oaters had striking one-sheets too. Monogram showed particular interest in stone lithography, the printing process explained in this book's introduction. Stone lithos by this point were somewhat archaic, yet they accounted for a sizable percentage of movie posters through the forties, after which they all but disappeared. ✸

ABOVE LEFT: *Forbidden Valley* was the last in a handful of starring vehicles for young Beery, who was much better suited to playing supporting roles. He eventually became a distinguished and much-in-demand character actor in films and TV, finishing his lengthy career as James Garner's father on *The Rockford Files*.

ABOVE RIGHT: Columbia's top B-Western star, Charles Starrett, played a frontier doctor called "The Medico" in a 1941 series. It didn't catch on and was terminated after just three entries. Starrett kept grinding out pedestrian horse operas until 1944, when he struck pay dirt with the Durango Kid character, which he continued to play for the duration of his career.

GEORGE O'BRIEN AT RKO

In his four years at Hollywood's smallest major studio from 1936 to 1940, O'Brien didn't have the advantages he had enjoyed at Fox earlier in the decade. RKO didn't purchase screen rights to novels by Zane Grey or Max Brand for him to adapt (although it did license some Grey yarns years later). Nor did he take lengthy excursions to beautiful locations outside California, as he had done previously. And the budgets for his RKOs were only half that of his Fox pictures. But the breezy, barrel-chested Irishman didn't let it bother him: George was his same devil-may-care self, adding clever touches to the traditional plots he was given. Action scenes were plentiful but never gratuitous, and he did practically all his own stunts, such as transferring from his galloping horse to speeding trains and runaway stagecoaches. O'Brien's films also were graced with charming and beautiful ingenues such as Rita Hayworth, Laraine Day, Marjorie Reynolds, Cecilia Parker, and Virginia Vale. On balance, his RKOs were among the best B Westerns of the late thirties.

GEORGE O'BRIEN
in
"TROUBLE IN SUNDOWN"
with
ROSALIND KEITH · RAY WHITLEY · CHILL WILLS
DIRECTED BY DAVID HOWARD · PRODUCED BY BERT GILROY
SCREEN PLAY BY OLIVER DRAKE · DORRELL McGOWAN · STUART McGOWAN

GEORGE O'BRIEN
THE MARSHAL OF MESA CITY
VIRGINIA VALE
PRODUCED BY BERT GILROY
DIRECTED BY DAVID HOWARD

GEORGE O'BRIEN
in
BULLET CODE
WITH
VIRGINIA VALE
PRODUCED by BERT GILROY
DIRECTED by DAVID HOWARD
SCREEN PLAY by DORIS SCHROEDER

GEORGE O'BRIEN
in
LEGION OF THE LAWLESS
VIRGINIA VALE
DIRECTED BY DAVID HOWARD
PRODUCED BY BERT GILROY
Screen play by DORIS SCHROEDER

GEORGE O'BRIEN
STAGE TO CHINO
VIRGINIA VALE and "PALS of the GOLDEN WEST"
Produced by BERT GILROY · Directed by EDWARD KILLY
Screen play by MORTON GRANT and ARTHUR V. JONES

GEORGE O'BRIEN
in
TRIPLE JUSTICE
WITH
VIRGINIA VALE
PRODUCED by BERT GILROY
DIRECTED by DAVID HOWARD

THE RISE OF TIM HOLT

In 1940, George O'Brien was the second-highest-salaried actor in B Westerns, his RKO oaters no longer as profitable as they had been just a couple of years earlier. The studio replaced O'Brien with twenty-one-year-old contract player Tim Holt, whose father Jack had been a Western star in the twenties. Young Holt was paid a fraction of his predecessor's wages, and the budgets on his pictures were not as generous, but he inherited the O'Brien production unit, which turned out first-rate B product, and audiences found him appealing. His films were full of action and slickly crafted. For his part, Tim was tickled to death to be a cowboy star, even after earning recognition for his showy roles in "civilian" pictures such as 1942's *The Magnificent Ambersons* and *Hitler's Children*. Drafted the following year, he served with distinction in the Army Air Corps before resuming his Western career after returning home in 1946.

TIM
HOLT
IN
THE FARGO KID
RAY WHITLEY · EMMETT LYNN
JANE DRUMMOND
PRODUCED BY BERT GILROY · DIRECTED BY EDWARD KILLY
SCREEN PLAY BY MORTON GRANT and ARTHUR V. JONES

TIM
HOLT
IN
ALONG THE RIO GRANDE
WITH
RAY WHITLEY
BETTY JANE RHODES
EMMETT LYNN
EXECUTIVE PRODUCER LEE MARCUS
PRODUCED BY BERT GILROY • DIRECTED BY EDWARD KILLY

TIM HOLT IN
SIX-GUN GOLD
with
RAY WHITLEY
JAN CLAYTON
LEE (LASSES) WHITE
PRODUCED BY
BERT GILROY
DIRECTED BY
DAVID HOWARD
SCREEN PLAY BY NORTON S. PARKER
RKO RADIO PICTURES

TIM
HOLT
IN
CYCLONE ON HORSEBACK
with
MARJORIE REYNOLDS
RAY WHITLEY
LEE [LASSES] WHITE
Produced by
BERT GILROY
Directed by
EDWARD KILLY
SCREEN PLAY BY NORTON S. PARKER

TIM HOLT
IN
DUDE COWBOY
WITH
MARJORIE REYNOLDS ★ RAY WHITLEY
LEE (LASSES) WHITE ★ LOUISE CURRIE
Produced by BERT GILROY Directed by DAVID HOWARD
STORY AND SCREEN PLAY BY MORTON GRANT
RKO RADIO PICTURES
41/308

TIM
HOLT
IN
RIDING THE
WIND
with
RAY
WHITLEY • MARY
DOUGLAS
LEE (LASSES) WHITE
PRODUCED BY BERT GILROY
DIRECTED BY EDWARD KILLY
SCREEN PLAY BY MORTON GRANT AND EARLE SNELL

TIM
HOLT
IN
BANDIT RANGER
with
CLIFF "Ukulele Ike" EDWARDS
PRODUCED BY
BERT GILROY
DIRECTED BY
LESLEY SELANDER

TIM HOLT
IN
The
AVENGING
RIDER
with
CLIFF "UKULELE IKE" EDWARDS
ANN SUMMERS
PRODUCED BY
BERT GILROY
DIRECTED BY
SAM NELSON
SCREEN PLAY BY HARRY O. HOYT & MORTON GRANT

TIM
HOLT
in
RED RIVER
ROBIN HOOD
with
CLIFF "Ukulele Ike" EDWARDS
BARBARA MOFFETT
PRODUCED BY BERT GILROY
DIRECTED BY LESLEY SELANDER
SCREEN PLAY BY BENNETT R. COHEN

MONOGRAM COWBOYS

Impoverished but scrappy little Monogram Pictures, earnestly attempting to compete with the classier and better-capitalized Republic, offered several series of B Westerns to small independent exhibitors in the late thirties and early forties. They were produced quickly and cheaply, embracing every cliché in the genre to avoid disappointing unsophisticated small-town audiences. Tom Keene, who at the dawn of the talkie era was RKO's top cowboy star, ambled through two series: a 1937–38 quartet that was not half bad and a 1941–42 group of eight, one more execrable than another. Jack Randall failed spectacularly as a singing cowboy in his earliest Monograms and didn't fare much better in his straight action pictures of 1938–40. Occasional experiments such as Ed Finney's *Silver Stallion*—an effort to make a leading man of stuntman Dave Sharpe—were indifferently received. Yet, the demand for Westerns was such that the studio eked out enough profit to remain solvent.

TOM
Keene
IN
"LONE STAR LAW MEN"
WITH
SUGAR DAWN
BETTY MILES
Produced and Directed by
ROBERT TANSEY
Original Story by
ROBERT EMMETT and
FRANCES KAVANAUGH
MONOGRAM PICTURES
A Monogram PICTURE

Tom KEENE

IN

"DYNAMITE CANYON"

WITH

★SUGAR DAWN★

SLIM ANDREWS

"RUSTY"

THE WONDER HORSE

PRODUCED · DIRECTED by
ROBERT TANSEY

ORIGINAL STORY · SCREENPLAY by
ROBERT EMMETT
FRANCES KAVANAUGH

A MONOGRAM PICTURE

MADE IN U.S.A.

MONOGRAM
PICTURES
PRESENTS
Jack RANDALL in
"WILD HORSE
CANYON"
with
DOROTHY SHORT
RUSTY The WONDER HORSE
SUPERVISED BY
ROBERT TANSEY
Directed by ROBERT HILL
Screenplay by ROBERT EMMETT

MONOGRAM PICTURES
PRESENTS
Jack RANDALL
WITH
"RUSTY"
THE
WONDER
HORSE
IN
"OVERLAND MAIL"
Directed by ROBERT HILL
Supervised by ROBERT TANSEY
Screenplay by ROBERT EMMETT

MONOGRAM
PICTURES
PRESENTS
Jack RANDALL IN
"COVERED
WAGON
TRAILS"
PRODUCED BY
HARRY S. WEBB
DIRECTED BY
RAYMOND K. JOHNSON
STORY & SCREENPLAY BY TOM GIBSON

"SILVER STALLION"
DAVID SHARPE
CHIEF "TONTO" THUNDERCLOUD
LEROY MASON
"THUNDER" The Wonder Horse
"CAPTAIN BOOTS" Famous Police Dog
Produced and Directed
by EDWARD FINNEY
Supervised by AL HERMAN
Screenplay by ROBERT EMMET
A MONOGRAM PICTURE

THE OLD GUARD IN DECLINE

The years immediately before World War II were pretty dismal ones for the generation of silent-era Western stars who had weathered the tumultuous transition to sound. Tom Mix had retired for good after making a Mascot serial, *The Miracle Rider* (1935), and died five years later in a car accident. Hoot Gibson's starring career petered out in 1937, following a lackluster series of Poverty Row cheapies. Tim McCoy's 1935 departure from Columbia heralded the beginning of a precipitous decline that bottomed out with an embarrassing stint at PRC, the runt of Hollywood's litter, in 1940. Tom Tyler fizzled out in 1937 after years of substandard pictures. Even the mighty Buck Jones couldn't sustain his top-dog status in the face of competition from singing cowboys and changing tastes. His independently produced 1937–38 series flopped despite being distributed by Columbia, and no further offers were forthcoming. Bob Steele lasted longer than the others, albeit in increasingly shoddy productions.

MONOGRAM PICTURES presents
Tim McCOY
in
"WEST OF RAINBOW'S END"
Directed by ALAN JAMES
Screenplay by STANLEY ROBERTS
and GENNARO REA
Original Story by ROBERT EMMETT
PRODUCED by
CONCORD PRODUCTIONS Inc.
SUPERVISED by
MAURICE CONN
MONOGRAM MPC PICTURES

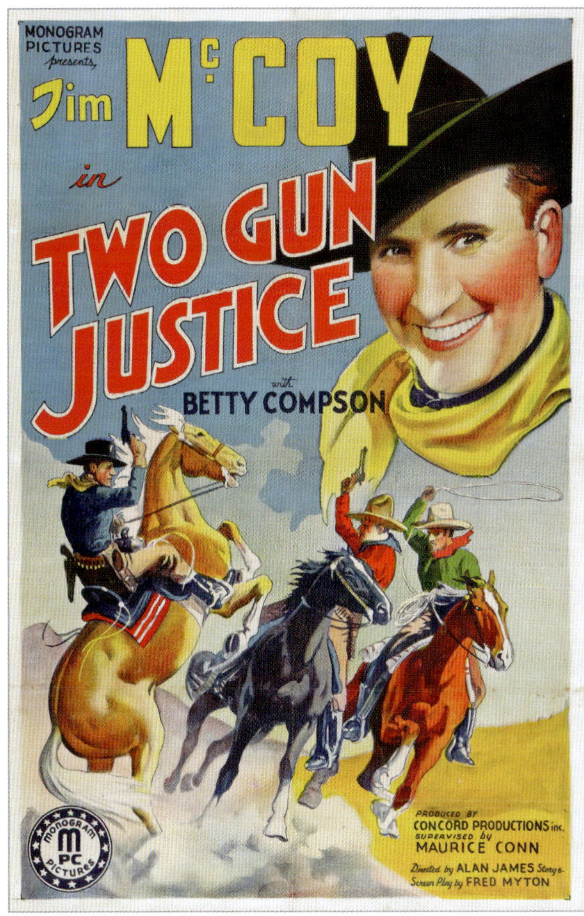
MONOGRAM PICTURES presents,
Tim McCOY
in
TWO GUN JUSTICE
with BETTY COMPSON
PRODUCED BY
CONCORD PRODUCTIONS inc.
SUPERVISED by
MAURICE CONN
Directed by ALAN JAMES Story & Screen Play by FRED MYTON
MONOGRAM MPC PICTURES

MONOGRAM PICTURES PRESENTS
TIM McCOY
in
"PHANTOM RANGER"
WITH
SUZANNE KAAREN
PRODUCED BY
CONCORD PRODUCTIONS inc
SUPERVISED by MAURICE CONN
Directed by SAM NEWFIELD
Screenplay by JOSEPH O'DONNELL
Original Story by JOSEPH O'DONNELL
and STANLEY ROBERTS
MONOGRAM MPC PICTURES

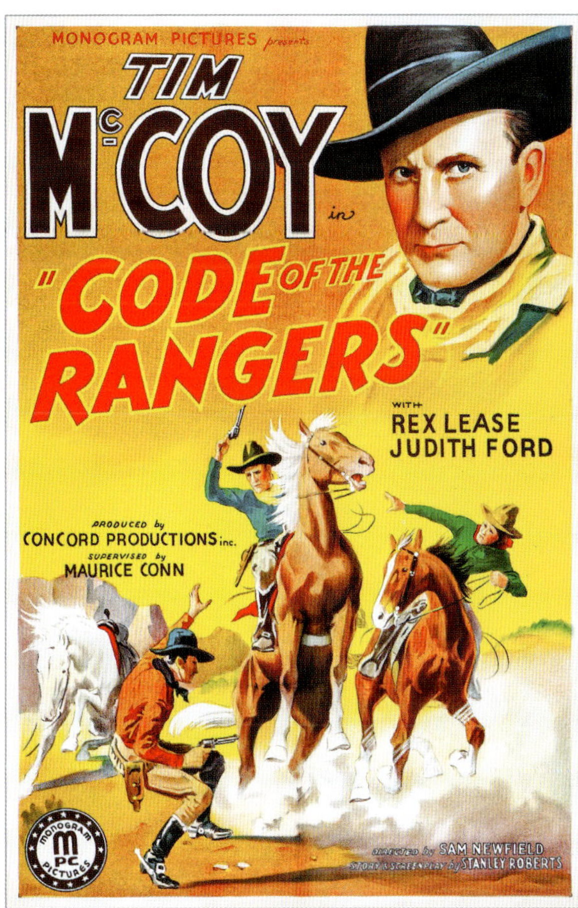
MONOGRAM PICTURES presents
TIM McCOY
in
"CODE OF THE RANGERS"
WITH
REX LEASE
JUDITH FORD
PRODUCED by
CONCORD PRODUCTIONS inc.
SUPERVISED by
MAURICE CONN
DIRECTED by SAM NEWFIELD
STORY & SCREENPLAY by STANLEY ROBERTS
MONOGRAM MPC PICTURES

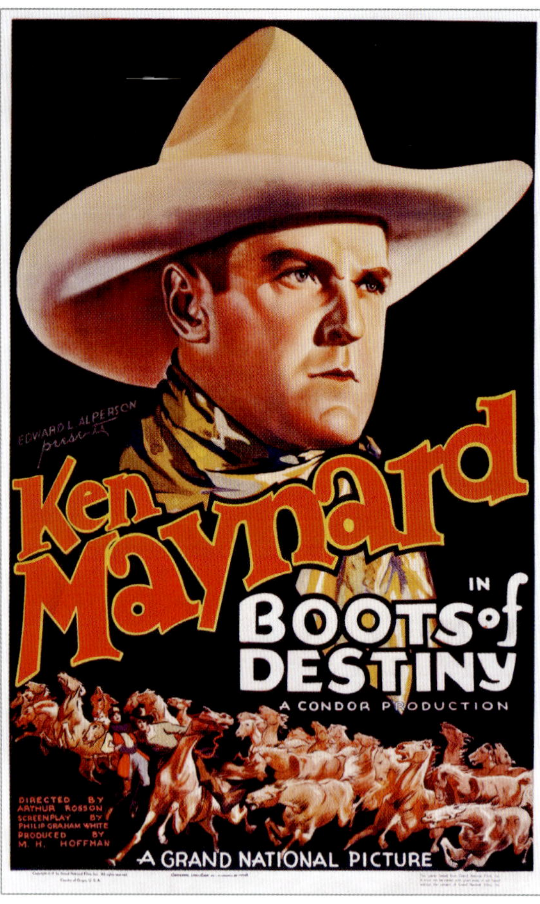
EDWARD L. ALPERSON presents
Ken Maynard
IN
BOOTS of DESTINY
A CONDOR PRODUCTION
DIRECTED BY ARTHUR ROSSON
SCREENPLAY BY PHILIP GRAHAM WHITE
PRODUCED BY M. H. HOFFMAN
A GRAND NATIONAL PICTURE

EDWARD L. ALPERSON PRESENTS
Ken MAYNARD
"Whirlwind" Horseman
PRODUCED BY MAX and ARTHUR ALEXANDER
DIRECTED BY BOB HILL SCREEN PLAY BY GEORGE PLYMPTON
A GRAND NATIONAL PICTURE

HARRY S. WEBB
METROPOLITAN PICTURES CORP
presents
BOB STEELE
IN
Smoky Trails
with
Joan CARMEN
Murdock MacQUARRIE
Directed by BERNARD B. RAY

METROPOLITAN PICTURES CORP.
HARRY S. WEBB
presents
Bob STEELE
IN
PINTO CANYON
WITH
Louise Kenneth Ted
STANLEY · DUNCAN · ADAMS
Produced by
HARRY S. WEBB
Directed by
RAYMOND K. JOHNSON
LITHO. IN USA

JOHNNY MACK AND CO.

The gentleman from Alabama, Johnny Mack Brown, made twenty-four Westerns for independent producer A. W. Hackel between 1935 and 1938. They were cheapies, and Brown rightly felt he deserved better. In 1939, he signed with Universal Pictures, which immediately teamed him with singing cowboy Bob Baker and comedy sidekick Fuzzy Knight. Unhappy about being a second banana, Baker left after six pictures, leaving Johnny Mack to continue with Fuzzy. A formula-busting innovation gave him a female sidekick in the person of comely Nell O'Day, who appeared in supporting roles and never once was an object of romantic interest. But how that girl could ride! Brown's Universal Westerns were among the fastest-moving ever made, and he was reported to throw the most realistic punch in Hollywood. With solid production values and terrific musical scores, his oaters competed favorably with those of Republic, then considered to be making the best B Westerns in the business.

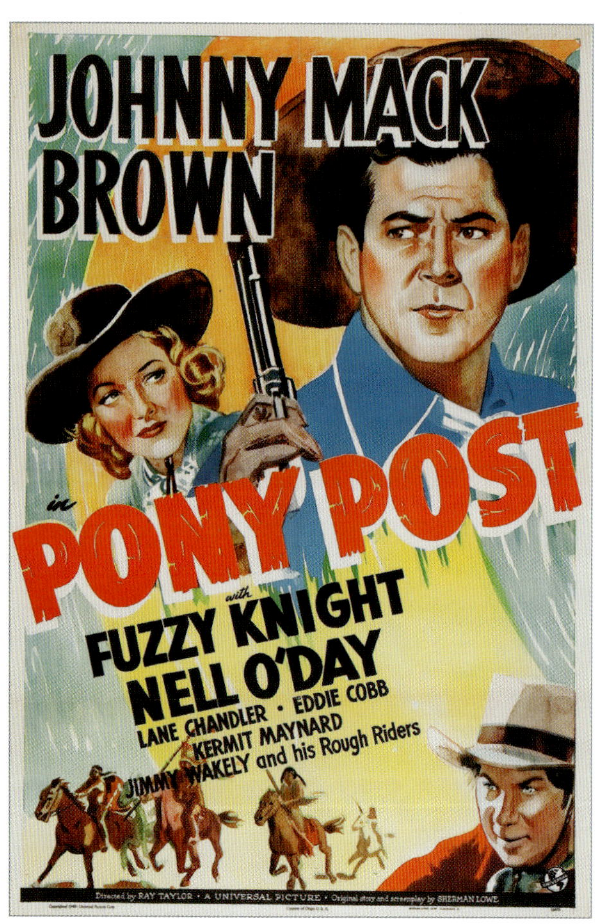

JOHNNY MACK BROWN
IN
RAGTIME COWBOY JOE
with
FUZZY KNIGHT
NELL O'DAY
THE TEXAS RANGERS
UNIVERSAL
A UNIVERSAL PICTURE
ORIGINAL SCREENPLAY BY SHERMAN LOWE
DIRECTED BY RAY TAYLOR
Copyrighted 1940 Universal Pictures Corp.
Country of Origin U.S.A.

JOHNNY MACK BROWN
in
The
MASKED RIDER
with
FUZZY KNIGHT
Grant WITHERS · Carmela CANSINO
The JOSE CANSINO DANCERS
The GUADALAJARA TRIO
and NELL O'DAY
A UNIVERSAL PICTURE
SCREEN PLAY BY SHERMAN LOWE AND VICTOR I. McLEOD
ORIGINAL STORY BY SAM ROBINS
DIRECTED BY FORD BEEBE
ASSOCIATE PRODUCER: WILL COWAN

JOHNNY MACK BROWN
in
STAGECOACH BUCKAROO
with
FUZZY KNIGHT
Anne NAGEL • Herbert RAWLINSON
GUARDSMEN QUARTETTE
and NELL O'DAY
Play, AL Martin • Based on an Original Story "Shotgun Messenger" by ARTHUR ST. CLAIRE • Directed by RAY TAYLOR • Associate Producer, WILL COWAN • A UNIVERSAL PICTURE
Country of Origin U.S.A.
21623

COLUMBIA COWBOYS AND OTHER NEWCOMERS

In the mid-to-late 1930s, Columbia turned over its B Westerns to independent producer Larry Darmour. There were cheaper producers in town, but not many, and not by much. Darmour's first batch included eight starring Ken Maynard, whose best days were behind him. Once his commitment had been fulfilled, Darmour was happy to dump him in favor of Columbia contract player Bob Allen, a former male model. Though a good actor, Allen made a spectacularly inauthentic cowboy, and his "Ranger" series was canceled after six 1936–37 installments. Next was Jack Luden, who had briefly shown promise in later silent oaters for Paramount. But he too flopped. Darmour finally had a winner in Bill Elliott, but the studio elected to take the production of his Westerns in-house after the 1938–39 season. Meanwhile, Cesar Romero made a sufficiently suave Cisco Kid in six well-mounted Westerns made and released by 20th Century-Fox in 1939–40. Buster Crabbe, the screen's original Flash Gordon, went from space opera to horse opera in 1940, starring as Billy the Kid (later Billy Carson) in a lengthy string for PRC. He was the last major cowboy star to begin a series before World War II.

SMASHING ACTION!
PHANTOM GOLD
with
JACK LUDEN
BETH MARION ★ "TUFFY"
Screen play by NATE GATZERT
Directed by JOSEPH LEVERING
A COLUMBIA PICTURE

BOTH BARRELS BLAZIN'! ALL HANDS SINGIN'!
CHARLES STARRETT
THE DURANGO KID
WITH
LUANA WALTERS
AND THE
SONS OF THE PIONEERS
FAMOUS RADIO STARS
ORIGINAL SCREEN PLAY by PAUL FRANKLIN
DIRECTED BY LAMBERT HILLYER
A COLUMBIA PICTURE

THE CISCO KID AND THE LADY
Cesar ROMERO
Marjorie WEAVER
Chris-Pin MARTIN
George MONTGOMERY
Robert BARRAT
Virginia FIELD
Harry GREEN
Directed by HERBERT I. LEEDS
Associate Producer John Stone
A 20th CENTURY-FOX PICTURE

VIVA CISCO KID
WITH
CESAR ROMERO
Jean ROGERS
Chris-Pin MARTIN
Minor WATSON
Stanley FIELDS
SOL M. WURTZEL
Norman Foster
A 20th CENTURY-FOX PICTURE

Producers Releasing Corporation presents
Buster CRABBE
Billy the Kid
IN
Sheriff OF SAGE VALLEY
WITH
AL (Fuzzy) ST. JOHN
TEX O'BRIEN
P.R.C.
Produced by SIGMUND NEUFELD
Directed by SHERMAN SCOTT

A P.R.C. PICTURE
Buster CRABBE
as
Billy the Kid
IN
FUGITIVE OF THE PLAINS
WITH
AL (Fuzzy) ST. JOHN
Produced by SIGMUND NEUFELD
Directed by SAM NEWFIELD

10
WARTIME
WESTERNS

TEAM-UPS AND TECHNICOLOR

World War II shocks the United States into action following the twin outrages in late 1941 of Japan's sneak attack on Pearl Harbor and Nazi Germany's declaration of war. Ramped-up production of weapons and equipment galvanizes domestic industry, creating millions of new jobs and jolting the nation out of its Depression. With disposable income once again plentiful, Americans whose mobility is limited by wartime travel restrictions flock to movie theaters in huge numbers and increased frequency, prompting Westerns to enjoy record-breaking popularity . . .

BELOW: A sequel to 1939's *Jesse James*, Fritz Lang's *The Return of Frank James* continued 20th Century-Fox's whitewashing of the notorious Missouri outlaws. German émigré Fritz Lang proved a surprisingly able director of American-made Westerns, for which he had no cultural affinity.

America's entry into World War II forced immediate cutbacks in most domestic industries, and the motion-picture business was no exception. Raw materials of all kinds were rationed, including celluloid. Decreased gasoline allowances curtailed lengthy excursions to picturesque locations previously visited often by filmmakers, especially those specializing in Westerns. For obvious reasons, supplies of gunpowder (used in blank cartridges) were dramatically reduced, forcing reductions in the length and frequency of shoot-outs.

The federal government, mindful that uninterrupted Hollywood output was critically important to maintaining domestic morale, gave producers a certain amount of leeway and looked the other way when wartime regulations were violated, as long as the infringements weren't too blatant. In response, studios worked closely with federal agencies to supply movies—many of them frankly propagandistic—calculated to stimulate the public's patriotic impulses, especially once war bonds were made available. (It was no accident that movie theaters were authorized to sell bonds to their audiences.)

The government not only rationed material and restricted travel but also imposed strict limits on paper and the dyes used for color inks, thereby affecting poster production. Some studios responded to rationing by cutting down on the quantities of posters they circulated. Others reduced the number of different sizes they offered. Billboard-sized thirty-sheets all but disappeared for the duration, reserved for the most prestigious, major-studio A-movie releases. Those rare exceptions include a notorious Howard Hughes–produced Western,

The Outlaw, and you'll know why when you see the poster art on one of the following pages.

Western-film popularity continued unabated, with both major and minor studios releasing horse operas in prewar quantities, despite the compromises dictated by material shortages. The boom in A Westerns that began in 1939 with *Stagecoach* showed no sign of weakening. Historical figures dominated the big-budget offerings, many of them filmed in Technicolor and produced on a large scale. These included such box-office champs as *Billy the Kid*, *Belle Starr* (both 1941), and *Buffalo Bill* (1944). Whenever possible, producers and screenwriters linked the winning of the West to America's manifest destiny, bringing yet another obvious appeal to the moviegoer's patriotism. A rather different and more complex approach to celebrating American values was taken in *The Ox-Bow Incident* (1943), a somber tale about townspeople who temporarily forget the national commitment to due process of law in their zeal to lynch a band of murdering rustlers. In its own courageous way, *Incident* eschewed escapist entertainment to remind audiences what their loved ones were fighting to preserve.

The B Westerns, meanwhile, went on their merry way. During these years, producers, motivated by the continued success of the Hopalong Cassidy and Three Mesquiteers films, relied heavily on the heroic trio. This concept allowed

ABOVE LEFT: On the basis of the fine job he did with Return of Frank James, Fritz Lang was assigned to direct *Western Union*, another big-budget Technicolor Western from Fox. In this candid photo taken on location in Arizona, he's between male co-stars Robert Young (*left*) and Randolph Scott.

ABOVE RIGHT: *Western Union* was adapted—loosely—from the Zane Grey novel published in 1939. Sadly, Grey did not live to see 20th Century-Fox's lavish film version, having died shortly after the book's publication. Despite its significant differences from the original work, the movie was an enormous hit.

ABOVE: Famous pinup artist Zoë Mozert painted this portrait of Jane Russell, as used in posters and billboards advertising *The Outlaw*, a scandalous 1940s Western produced by Howard Hughes at a cost of nearly three million dollars. The tycoon based his entire promotional campaign around images of the pulchritudinous Russell.

for gambling on minor performers of uncertain box-office appeal, but it also extended the careers of many old-time cowboy stars who had worn out their welcomes as solo attractions.

The first such trio to appear during the forties was Monogram's Range Busters, initially consisting of former Mesquiteers Ray (now "Crash") Corrigan and Max ("Alibi") Terhune, along with one-time Universal serial star John ("Dusty") King. Longtime Western favorites Buck Jones and Tim McCoy joined veteran character actor to play the Rough Riders, potentially the best wartime trio act. Their series was curtailed after just eight entries by Buck's tragic death in the horrific 1942 Boston nightclub fire that took 492 lives altogether.

Ken Maynard, Hoot Gibson, and Bob Steele—all of whom began their starring careers in the silent era, as did Jones and McCoy—teamed up as Monogram's Trail Blazers, a short-lived triumvirate that, ironically, achieved greater popularity on early TV than they did in movie theaters. Other World War II threesomes included PRC's Frontier Marshals and Texas Rangers.

Columbia modified the concept by giving equal billing to star duos, demoting their sidekicks from equal partners to featured players. Wild Bill Elliott shared his series with Tex Ritter, while studio mate Charles Starrett welcomed former Hopalong Cassidy sidekick Russell Hayden. The Elliott-Ritter films had rather dubious comic relief from slapstick vaudevillian Frank Mitchell; Starrett and Hayden fared somewhat better with Cliff "Ukulele Ike" Edwards, whose musical contributions easily surpassed his puerile attempts at humor. Ritter bolted Columbia after one year, signing with Universal to pair with Johnny Mack Brown, whose sidekick Fuzzy Knight retained his position in the series (and, amazingly, received as much fan mail as either of the two stars).

It wasn't just the Bs that experimented with dual leads. Randolph Scott and Robert Young costarred in *Western Union* (1941), Fritz Lang's Technicolored account of pioneering telegraph builders. Scott also teamed with John Wayne in a 1942 remake of Rex Beach's venerable "northern" Western, *The Spoilers*, and with Glenn Ford in *The Desperadoes* (1943), nominally based on a Max Brand story. Ford had previously shared the spotlight with William Holden in *Texas* (1941), a raucous but well-mounted tale with marginally historical overtones.

The aforementioned John Wayne wore stardom well during the war years, steadily building his reputation as an A picture attraction with such profitable and well-received vehicles as *In Old Oklahoma* (a.k.a. *War of the Wildcats*, 1943), *Tall in the Saddle* (1944), and *Dakota* (1945), among others.

Finally achieving leading-man status after two years of supporting roles (including several turns as heavies in Hopalong Cassidy pictures), Robert Mitchum clicked in two modestly produced but quite enjoyable Zane Grey adaptations for RKO: *Nevada* (1944) and *West of the Pecos* (1945). Western fans would see more of him in the postwar years.

The look of Western posters began to change during the war. Exhibitors still received a mix of traditional four-color lithographs with painted images, two-color posters with scene stills laid into their designs, and old-fashioned stone lithographs with renderings of varying quality. But World War II saw a dramatic increase in the use of hand-colored photographs—both portraits and scenes—to save the expense of paintings. Often, the photos were combined with small vignettes lifted from earlier posters. These pieces of artwork had generic Western images such as hard-riding posses or stagecoaches being pursued by bandits, positioned carefully in spaces that otherwise would be blank, imparting dynamic movement to static designs. ✡

ABOVE: Principal photography of *The Outlaw* began in 1940 and dragged into 1941. Producer Howard Hughes clashed with Production Code administrators who refused to give the picture its seal of approval until he made cuts—mostly of shots featuring Jane Russell's bosom. The picture went into limited release in 1943, was pulled, and was then distributed again in 1946, eventually recouping Hughes's $3,000,000 investment.

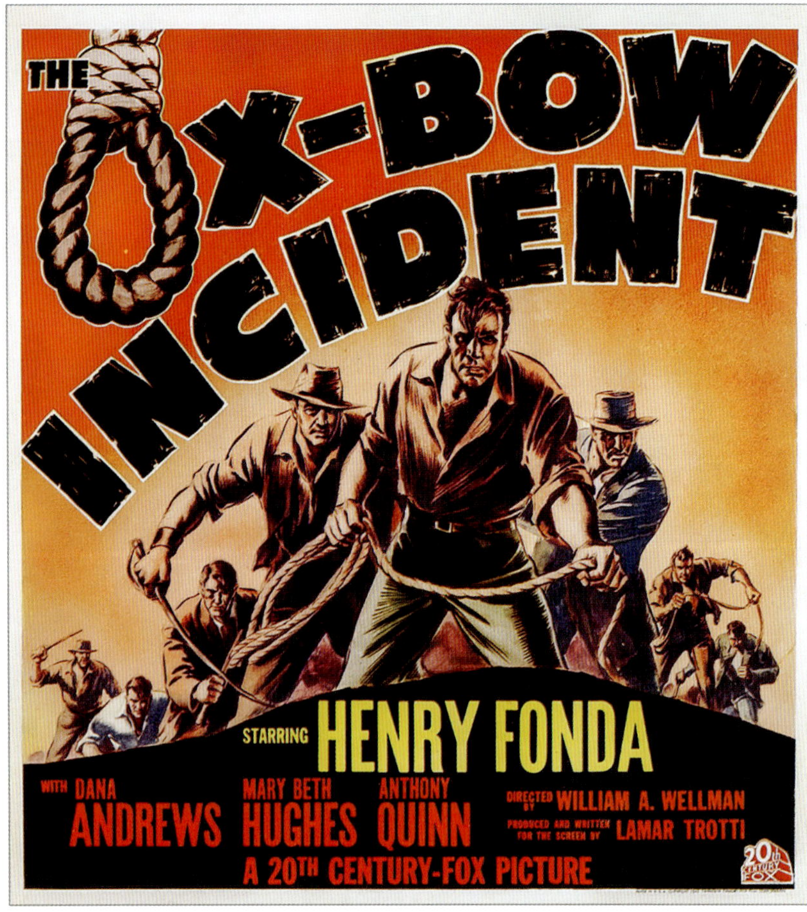

BIG-BUDGET WESTERNS

The epic Western made a dramatic comeback during World War II, largely to satisfy American cravings for escapist entertainment to balance the flood of war-related propaganda films. 20th Century-Fox made a slew of big-budget Westerns, many of them built around historical incidents and real-life characters—and shot in gorgeous Technicolor to boot. However, the company's finest genre offering during this period was a modestly produced black-and-white character study, *The Ox-Bow Incident* (1943). Over at Warner Bros., Errol Flynn played a considerably sanitized General George Armstrong Custer in *They Died with Their Boots On* (1941). Columbia chose an all-star Western, *The Desperadoes* (1943), to be its first film shot in Technicolor—a decision that significantly enhanced box-office performance. And three years later, Paramount dusted off that old favorite, Owen Wister's novel *The Virginian*, for remaking in color. Movie attendance during the war years reached new highs, and Westerns were surpassed in popularity only by musical comedies.

JOEL
McCREA
MAUREEN
O'HARA
LINDA
DARNELL
Buffalo Bill
in
TECHNICOLOR
A 20th CENTURY FOX PICTURE
WITH
Thomas
MITCHELL
Edgar
BUCHANAN
Anthony
QUINN
DIRECTED BY
WILLIAM A. WELLMAN
PRODUCED BY
HARRY A. SHERMAN

ERROL
FLYNN · MIRIAM
HOPKINS
Virginia City
RANDOLPH SCOTT · HUMPHREY BOGART
FRANK McHUGH · ALAN HALE · GUINN WILLIAMS · Directed by Michael Curtiz
Presented by WARNER BROS.

WARNER BROS.
PICTURES INC. PRESENTS
ERROL FLYNN
OLIVIA
DeHAVILLAND
IN
"THEY DIED WITH THEIR BOOTS ON"
ARTHUR KENNEDY · CHARLEY GRAPEWIN · GENE LOCKHART
A WARNER BROS.-FIRST NATIONAL PICTURE
Directed by RAOUL WALSH

in
TECHNICOLOR
THE
DESPERADOES
with
RANDOLPH SCOTT · GLENN FORD · CLAIRE TREVOR
EVELYN KEYES · EDGAR BUCHANAN
Screen play by ROBERT CARSON
Produced by HARRY JOE BROWN · Directed by CHARLES VIDOR
A COLUMBIA PICTURE

JOEL McCREA
BRIAN DONLEVY
SONNY TUFTS
with BARBARA BRITTON
From the World Famous Novel by OWEN WISTER
"The VIRGINIAN"
In TECHNICOLOR
FAY BAINTER
TOM TULLY
HENRY O'NEILL
Produced by PAUL JONES
Directed by STUART GILMORE
A Paramount Picture

WARNERS' ADVENTURE OF THE CENTURY!!!
ERROL FLYNN
ALEXIS SMITH
in Technicolor!
"San Antonio"
S. Z. "CUDDLES" SAKALL • VICTOR FRANCEN • JOHN LITEL
Original Screen Play by Alan LeMay and W. R. Burnett • Music by Max Steiner
DIRECTED BY DAVID BUTLER PRODUCED BY ROBERT BUCKNER
A WARNER BROS. FIRST NATIONAL PICTURE
LITHO. IN U.S.A.

JOHN WAYNE AS AN "A" STAR

With *Stagecoach* (1939), the Duke finally attained A-picture stardom. During the war years, he worked in high-profile films at practically every major studio in Hollywood. With many top male stars serving in the military—Clark Gable, James Stewart, Henry Fonda, and Tyrone Power among them—Wayne had considerably less competition for box-office dollars during this transitional period in his career. Republic Pictures still had some claim on Wayne, and he starred in at least one picture per annum for them. But these weren't ten-day quickies like the Three Mesquiteers films—they were substantial productions aimed at an older clientele. His Republic films post-*Stagecoach* included *The Dark Command* (1940), *In Old California* (1942), *In Old Oklahoma* (1943), and *Dakota* (1945). His best wartime Western by far, though, was RKO's *Tall in the Saddle* (1944), which many aficionados regard as the quintessential Wayne vehicle.

John WAYNE
Ella RAINES
in
TALL IN THE SADDLE
with
WARD BOND
GEORGE "GABBY" HAYES
AUDREY LONG
ELISABETH RISDON
DON DOUGLAS
Produced by
ROBERT FELLOWS
Directed by
EDWIN L. MARIN
SCREEN PLAY BY MICHAEL HOGAN AND PAUL P. FIX
RKO RADIO PICTURES
44/383

POP SHERMAN'S PROGRAMMERS

The Hopalong Cassidy series generally kept producer Harry Sherman busy, but he had ambitions beyond B-grade product and pressed Paramount to let him make slightly more expensive and elaborate Westerns. Such films belonged to a category known as "programmers"—pictures that could play in either the top or bottom half of a double bill or even as a single feature in small-town theaters. While Bs were always booked for flat rates, some programmers—especially those with fairly big stars—could play for a percentage of the box-office receipts, which made more money for producers. Pop Sherman made numerous such Westerns in the forties, generally with Richard Dix in the lead, supported by fine casts that regularly included Preston Foster, Victor Jory, Albert Dekker, Edgar Buchanan, and the like. Probably the best of the group was *Tombstone: The Town Too Tough to Die* (1942), a woefully inaccurate but nonetheless entertaining account of the oft-dramatized Earp-Clanton feud.

RICHARD DIX
KENT TAYLOR
EDGAR BUCHANAN
IN
TOMBSTONE
The Town Too Tough To Die
with FRANCES GIFFORD · DON CASTLE
CLEM BEVANS · VICTOR JORY · REX BELL
Screen Play by Albert Shelby LeVino and Edward E. Paramore
Directed by WILLIAM McGANN · A HARRY SHERMAN Production · A Paramount Picture

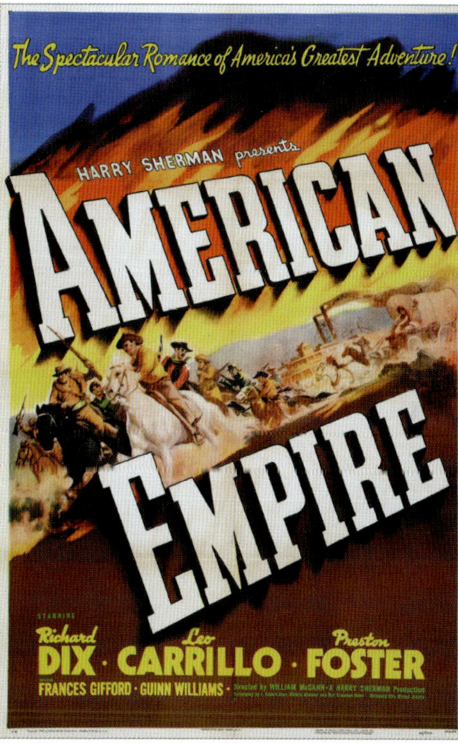

TWO FOR THE PRICE OF ONE

A popular gambit of Western producers looking to increase box-office revenues during the early forties was to pair moderately popular cowboy stars. Columbia started this short-lived trend in 1941 with two series, one featuring Charles Starrett and former Hopalong Cassidy sidekick Russell Hayden, the other teaming Wild Bill Elliott and Tex Ritter, late of Monogram. Scripts often had the costars squabbling for most of the running time, then resolving their difficulties and joining forces to rout bad guys in the last reel. Saturday-matinee audiences ate it up, but the stars—no matter how well they got along offscreen—were unhappy sharing the spotlight. Columbia's experiment ended after one year, but Ritter immediately found himself in the same situation at Universal, where he was linked with Johnny Mack Brown for seven Westerns during 1942–43. That arrangement too lasted just one year, but not before the disgruntled Brown quit Universal for Monogram.

IT'S THE RANGERS' BIGGEST FIGHT
..AS THE ENEMY THREATENS ALASKA!
CHARLES STARRETT
RIDERS OF THE NORTHLAND
with Russell HAYDEN
CLIFF "Ukulele Ike" EDWARDS
SHIRLEY PATTERSON
ORIGINAL SCREEN PLAY BY PAUL FRANKLIN
DIRECTED BY WILLIAM BERKE
A COLUMBIA PICTURE

BILL ELLIOTT AND TEX RITTER
IN
ROARING FRONTIERS
DOUBLE-STARRED BLAST OF THRILLS AND RHYTHM!
with
RUTH FORD
FRANK MITCHELL
Original screen play by ROBERT LEE JOHNSON
Directed by LAMBERT HILLYER
A COLUMBIA Reprint

TWO TOP STARS ROCKING THE SCREEN WITH THRILLS AND SONG......FOR YOU!
BILL ELLIOTT
TEX RITTER
IN
BULLETS FOR BANDITS
with FRANK MITCHELL
ORIGINAL SCREENPLAY BY ROBERT LEE JOHNSON
Directed by WALLACE W. FOX
A COLUMBIA PICTURE

HIT THE HIGH ROAD TO THRILLS WITH TWO TOP STARS!
BILL ELLIOTT
TEX RITTER
IN
THE DEVIL'S TRAIL
with
EILEEN O'HEARN · FRANK MITCHELL
NOAH BEERY, SR.
A COLUMBIA PICTURE
SCREEN PLAY BY ROBERT LEE JOHNSON
Directed by LAMBERT HILLYER

A DOUBLE-STAR COMBINATION TO DOUBLE-UP BANDITS WITH BULLETS!

BILL ELLIOTT and TEX RITTER in THE LONE STAR VIGILANTES

with FRANK MITCHELL

Original screen play by Luci Ward · Directed by WALLACE W. FOX

A COLUMBIA PICTURE

COLUMBIA PICTURES

JOHNNY MACK
BROWN and TEX
RITTER
in
The LONE STAR TRAIL
with
FUZZY KNIGHT
JENNIFER HOLT and THE
JIMMY WAKELY TRIO
UNIVERSAL
Screen Play, Oliver Drake · Original Story, Victor Halperin · Directed by RAY TAYLOR · Associate Producer, OLIVER DRAKE · A UNIVERSAL PICTURE
Country of Origin U.S.A.

MONOGRAM PICTURES CORP.
presents
a GEO. W. WEEKS Production
introducing
RAY "Crash"
CORRIGAN
JOHN "Dusty"
KING
MAX "Alibi"
TERHUNE
IN
The
Range
Busters
with
Le Roy MASON
Luana WALTERS Earle HODGINS
Directed by
ROY LUBY

MONOGRAM PICTURES CORP.
presents A GEO. W. WEEKS
Production
The
Range Busters
RAY "Crash" CORRIGAN
JOHN "Dusty" KING
MAX "Alibi" TERHUNE
IN
"Trailing
Double Trouble"
with
Lita CONWAY · Nancy Louise KING
ROY BARCROFT
Rex FELKER
Directed by S. Roy Luby

TRIGGER TRIOS, PART ONE

After leaving Republic's Three Mesquiteers in 1939, Ray Corrigan and Max Terhune cut a deal with producer George Weeks to trade on their already established personas in another trio series. Securing distribution with Monogram, Weeks cast former Universal contract player John King as the third member of the Range Busters. With occasional cast substitutions, this series lasted three years (1940–43) and racked up twenty-three installments. In 1942, the screen's erstwhile Lone Ranger, Lee Powell, joined forces with Bill Boyd—a singer known as "The Cowboy Rambler," not the Hopalong Cassidy actor—and Art Davis to play the Frontier Marshals in a weak six-picture series. Another vocalist, James Newill, teamed with longtime B-Western utility player Dave O'Brien and lanky comic sidekick Guy Wilkerson to play the Texas Rangers for PRC. A better outfit than the Frontier Marshals (if only by inches), the Texas Rangers lasted for three years, with the hapless Tex Ritter replacing Newell for the 1944–45 season.

"COWBOY COMMANDOS"

with RAY (CRASH) CORRIGAN DENNIS MOORE MAX (ALIBI) TERHUNE

EVELYN FINLEY

Produced by GEORGE W. WEEKS
Directed by S. ROY LUBY
Story Continuity by ELIZABETH BEECHER
Original Story by CLARK PAYLOW
A MONOGRAM PICTURE

MONOGRAM PC PICTURES

MADE IN U.S.A.

Dave (TEX) O'BRIEN ★ Jim NEWILL

as The Texas Rangers in

TRAIL of TERROR

WITH GUY WILKERSON

Produced by ALFRED STERN and ARTHUR ALEXANDER

Directed by OLIVER DRAKE

A P.R.C. PICTURE

MADE IN U.S.A.

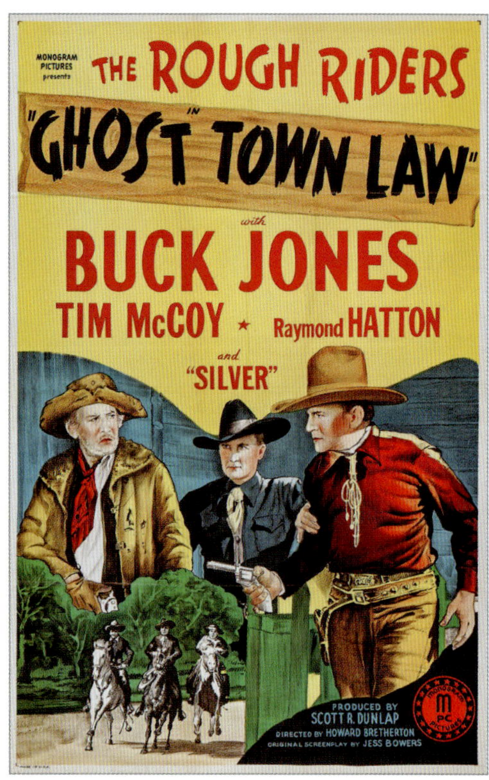

TRIGGER TRIOS, PART TWO

The wartime vogue for Western threesomes temporarily revived the careers of the genre's old guard, even if the starring vehicles were but pale shadows of their earlier, far superior films. Buck Jones and Tim McCoy were paired by Monogram producer Scott Dunlap, who added sidekick Raymond Hatton (late of the Three Mesquiteers) to form the Rough Riders. In eight films released during the 1941–42 season, they delighted a new generation of Saturday-matinee kids who were not even born when Jones and McCoy were in their prime. Ken Maynard, Hoot Gibson, and Bob Steele were dubbed the Trail Blazers for another Monogram series that began in 1943. Even more bloated and cantankerous than in his last group of films several years before, Maynard dropped out after six installments and was replaced by Victor Daniels, a.k.a. Chief Thundercloud. The substitution was not beneficial, however; after completing two more films, the group disbanded. Both series were syndicated to TV stations in the early fifties and entertained yet another generation of kids.

the Trail Blazers
KEN MAYNARD HOOT GIBSON
in
"BLAZING GUNS"
with KAY FORRESTER
Produced and Directed by ROBERT TANSEY
Screenplay by FRANCES KAVANAUGH
A MONOGRAM PICTURE
MADE IN U.S.A.

11
TWILIGHT
OF THE
B WESTERN

FROM BIG SCREENS TO SMALL

As America leads its allies to victory in World War II, bringing down the curtain on history's most momentous armed conflict, soldiers, sailors, pilots, and Marines flood back into the country. Motion-picture attendance swells to historic levels, and Westerns continue to enjoy widespread acceptance. But changing times and tastes dramatically affect the movie industry, accelerating demand for adult Westerns and, eventually, rendering the Saturday-matinee shoot-'em-ups extinct . . .

BELOW: In a role turned down by John Wayne, aging star Gary Cooper played a town marshal left to face three killers by himself, with no help from his deputies or the townspeople who've benefited from his efforts to uphold the law. *High Noon* (1952) was one of the postwar era's very best Westerns aimed at adult audiences.

The Allied forces may have prevailed in World War II, but victory came at a horrendous cost. The United States alone spent $340 billion and lost nearly 420,000 of its citizens. Yet, for all the hardship and suffering, the American economy flourished, and motion-picture attendance surged to levels not seen since before the onset of the Great Depression. The year 1946, which saw US servicemen returning home and eager to resume normal lives, was the most profitable in Hollywood history. Western movies of all budgetary classes continued to proliferate, but the postwar era ushered in changing tastes and altered the genre's trajectory.

First, the big stars of the twenties and early thirties finally vanished from the scene. Tom Mix had died in 1940, Buck Jones in 1942. The wartime boom in trio Westerns provided last hurrahs for Tim McCoy, Hoot Gibson, Ken Maynard, Bob Steele, and Tom Tyler, and henceforth they would be seen, if at all, in supporting roles (Tyler actually built himself a second career as a heavy, inspired by his blood-chilling turn as a ruthless gunman in John Ford's *Stagecoach*).

The B-grade cowboy heroes clinging to prominence in the late 1940s were those who had attained stardom in the mid- and late thirties. Gene Autry, having served with distinction in the Air Transport Command, returned to Republic Pictures in 1946, but he quickly jumped ship to Columbia, where he was given an autonomous production unit and profit participation. Roy Rogers, having been crowned "King of the Cowboys" in Autry's absence, remained at his home studio and enjoyed larger budgets and more generous shooting schedules for his series entries, a number of which were shot using Republic's Trucolor

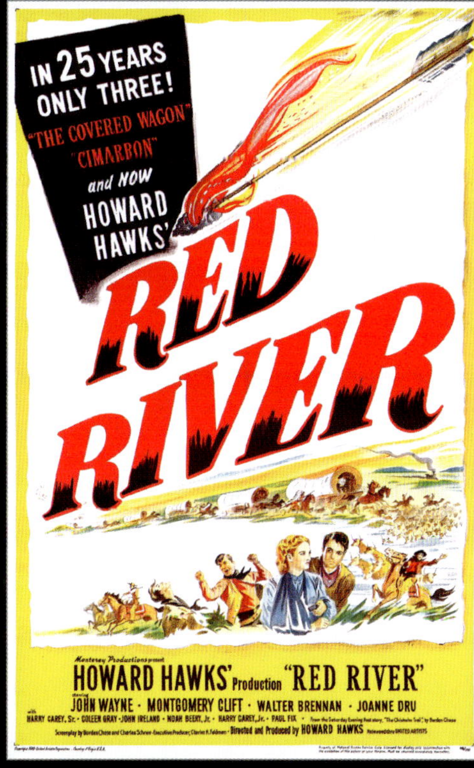

process. William Boyd in 1946 acquired the Hopalong Cassidy property from Harry Sherman and made the films himself, although boosting his own salary at the expense of Paramount-era production values hurt the series.

Columbia's resident star Charles Starrett remained extraordinarily popular, especially in the South and Midwest, although his Durango Kid series steadily degenerated into puerility. Johnny Mack Brown, who like Starrett had established himself as a Western lead in 1935, had gone from Poverty Row's Supreme Pictures to Republic to Universal to Monogram, where the quality of his films slowly deteriorated as the forties gave way to the fifties. Only RKO's Tim Holt, another war hero, returned from service to achieve more popularity

ABOVE LEFT: John Wayne and Joanne Dru consult with director Howard Hawks during the production of *Red River* (1948), which along with John Ford's "Cavalry trilogy" proved once and for all that Duke really *could* act, contrary to the claims of his detractors.

ABOVE RIGHT: Note the blurb on this poster comparing *Red River* to two epic Westerns of the past, *The Covered Wagon* (1923) and *Cimarron* (1931). For once, such a claim wasn't Hollywood hyperbole — *Red River* really *did* have the scope and sweep of those earlier hits.

ABOVE: This gag photo taken during a break in the shooting of *Range Warfare* (1949) purports to show leading man Johnny Mack Brown (holding a mint julep cocktail, no less) being waited on hand and foot by crew members. In reality, Johnny had no ego—he was considered one of the nicest Western stars in Hollywood.

than he had enjoyed prior to leaving Hollywood in late 1942. His postwar films, while still in the B category and aimed primarily at "front-row kids" who populated the Saturday matinees, reflected unusual care in production and strove for novelty in their scripting.

Other cowboy heroes emerged to service the market's low end. Singing cowboy Eddie Dean was not well served by PRC's flaccid scripting and threadbare production values, and his early starring vehicles featured a bullwhip-cracking sidekick billed as "Lash" LaRue, who was spun off to topline his own series. Monogram's Jimmy Wakely, having been elevated to leading man from featured player in Johnny Mack Brown's Universal oaters, unashamedly modeled himself after Gene Autry—not only musically but also in his choice of costume. In some of Wakely's films he was partnered with a Lash LaRue imitator named Whip Wilson, who was also promoted into a series of his own. None of their films could be considered exceptional in any way.

The B Western slowly but inexorably died off. The advent in the late 1940s of commercial television—which played old Western movies incessantly, until major companies began dedicating their resources to original programming—put the last nail in the coffin. Kids weren't willing to pay for the same type of fare they could see on TV for nothing.

Not that the genre itself faced imminent danger of fading away. Major-studio A Westerns during the late forties and early fifties were better than ever. Box-office heavyweights known for their work in other types of films continued to gravitate toward sagebrush sagas, among them Gregory Peck, Spencer Tracy, James Stewart, Dick Powell, Burt Lancaster, Kirk Douglas, and Dana Andrews, while top-billed females who dabbled in horse operas included Barbara Stanwyck, Joan Crawford, and Marlene Dietrich.

Postwar A Westerns were geared to adult audiences and therefore tackled mature themes, saying goodbye to the simple-minded, cut-and-dried morality tales of previous decades. Mood and characterization took precedence over action, with nuanced protagonists replacing the virtuous, white-hatted cowboys of yore. This period in Western filmmaking was an unusually rich one, offering such classics as *My Darling Clementine* (1946), *The Gunfighter* (1950), *High Noon* (1952), and, above all, *Shane* (1953), which gathered together the old archetypes and presented them in an almost mythological framework.

With Autry, Rogers, and Boyd all producing half-hour series for television, the low end of the market was serviced with moderately budgeted pictures starring such marginal personalities as Rory Calhoun, Jock Mahoney, and George Montgomery, to name just a few. Randolph Scott distinguished himself with a group of inexpensive films that allocated their meager resources to careful scripting (mostly by Burt Kennedy) and incisive directing (mostly by Budd Boetticher).

Of course, this period belonged to one man—a man whose identification with Westerns dated back to the dawn of sound. As a result of his stellar output during the late forties and fifties, John Wayne transitioned from popular leading man to cultural icon. Consider the list: *Angel and the Badman* (1947), *Three Godfathers* (1948), *Red River* (1948), *Fort Apache* (1948), *She Wore a Yellow Ribbon* (1949), *Rio Grande* (1950), *Hondo* (1953), and, of course, *The Searchers* (1956).

Westerns had grown up. Whether they would continue to entrance moviegoers as the Atomic Age progressed remained to be seen.

Poster design during this period begins to move away from the imagery that theater patrons had come to expect. The old circus-type posters with their rococo renderings and calligraphy, their riots of color, recede into history. Hand lettering doesn't disappear altogether, but increasingly it's reserved for titles and, occasionally, big-name stars. Less important copy often is typeset. Instead of trying to appeal to theater-front passersby across the street, Western posters gradually seem designed for maximum impact up close, or in a smaller size—such as magazine advertising, which plays a steadily expanding role in movie marketing.★

THE WESTERN GROWS UP

Reflecting the national mood, horse operas matured a great deal after World War II. Protagonists were no longer expected to be impossibly virtuous and self-sacrificing, although even those who operated outside the law generally adhered to a strong moral code. Things weren't always black or white in films such as *Station West* and *Blood on the Moon*. Playing the eponymous role in *The Gunfighter*, Gregory Peck admits to a lifetime of regrets before meeting a tragic end. James Stewart faces the loss of his Indian sweetheart after working tirelessly on behalf of her people in *Broken Arrow*. Even the classic *Shane* portrays multiple facets of its archetypal characters. Western plot conflicts could no longer be neatly resolved with a saloon fistfight or a gun duel in the street; increasingly realistic, mature complications had to be addressed. Even a film such as *Gunfight at the O.K. Corral* showed more psychological complexity than had previous cinematic versions of the notorious Earp-Clanton showdown.

A WOMAN'S BULLET KILLS AS QUICK AS A MAN'S!
ROBERT MITCHUM
BARBARA BEL GEDDES
ROBERT PRESTON
in
BLOOD ON THE MOON
with
Walter BRENNAN · Phyllis THAXTER · Frank FAYLEN · Tom TULLY
EXECUTIVE PRODUCER SID ROGELL · PRODUCED BY THERON WARTH · DIRECTED BY ROBERT WISE · SCREEN PLAY BY LILLIE HAYWARD

UNIVERSAL-INTERNATIONAL presents
James STEWART
Shelley WINTERS
Dan DURYEA
Stephen McNALLY
WINCHESTER '73
with MILLARD MITCHELL · CHARLES DRAKE
JOHN McINTIRE · WILL GEER · JAY C. FLIPPEN
Screenplay by ROBERT L. RICHARDS and BORDEN CHASE · Directed by ANTHONY MANN · Produced by AARON ROSENBERG

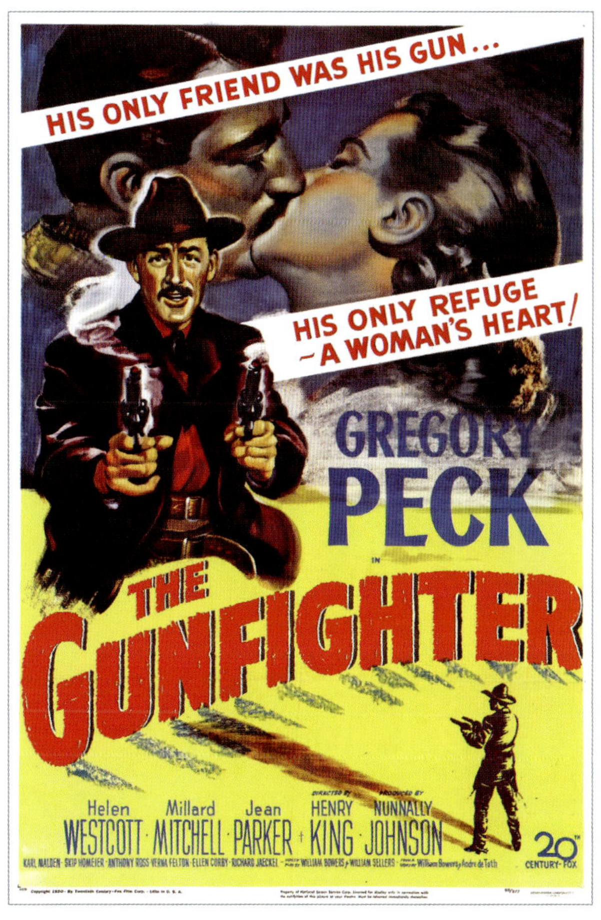
HIS ONLY FRIEND WAS HIS GUN...
HIS ONLY REFUGE –A WOMAN'S HEART!
GREGORY PECK
in
THE GUNFIGHTER
Helen WESTCOTT · Millard MITCHELL · Jean PARKER
DIRECTED BY HENRY KING
PRODUCED BY NUNNALLY JOHNSON
20th CENTURY-FOX

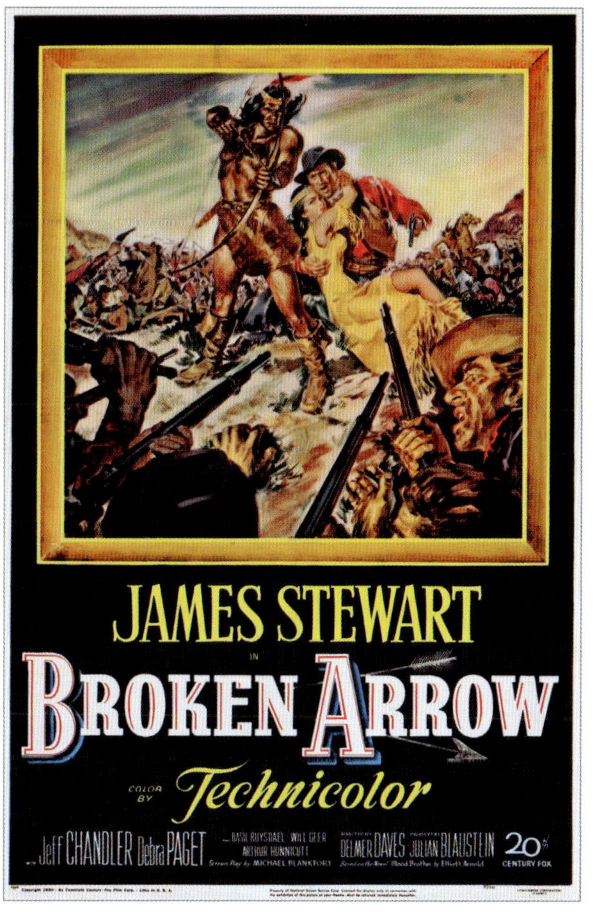
JAMES STEWART
in
BROKEN ARROW
COLOR BY Technicolor
with Jeff CHANDLER Debra PAGET
DELMER DAVES
JULIAN BLAUSTEIN
20th CENTURY-FOX

WHERE ANYTHING GOES
...FOR A PRICE!
MARLENE DIETRICH
ARTHUR KENNEDY
MEL FERRER
in
RANCHO
NOTORIOUS
COLOR BY
TECHNICOLOR
Distributed by
RKO
RADIO
PICTURES
DIRECTED BY FRITZ LANG · PRODUCED BY HOWARD WELSCH · SCREENPLAY BY DANIEL TARADASH

In all your Motion Picture going experience 'SHANE' will remain forever memorable!
PARAMOUNT PRESENTS
ALAN LADD
JEAN ARTHUR
VAN HEFLIN
in GEORGE STEVENS' PRODUCTION OF
SHANE
Color by Technicolor
BRANDON DE WILDE with JACK PALANCE

PACKED WITH TECHNICOLOR THRILLS!
JAMES STEWART · JANET LEIGH
ROBERT RYAN · RALPH MEEKER
MGM's THE NAKED SPUR
with MILLARD MITCHELL
Written by SAM ROLFE and HAROLD JACK BLOOM
Directed by ANTHONY MANN
Produced by WILLIAM H. WRIGHT

PARAMOUNT presents
Burt LANCASTER Kirk DOUGLAS
Co-Starring
RHONDA FLEMING
JO VAN FLEET
JOHN IRELAND
in Hal WALLIS PRODUCTION OF
GUNFIGHT AT THE O.K. CORRAL
VISTAVISION
TECHNICOLOR
Directed by JOHN STURGES
Screenplay by LEON URIS
FOR GENERAL EXHIBITION
a Paramount Picture

JOAN'S GREATEST TRIUMPH
HERBERT J. YATES presents
JOAN CRAWFORD
in "JOHNNY GUITAR"
TRUCOLOR
STERLING HAYDEN · SCOTT BRADY
MERCEDES McCAMBRIDGE
NICHOLAS RAY
A REPUBLIC PICTURE

GARY COOPER
AS THE
MAN OF THE WEST
THE ROLE THAT FITS HIM LIKE A GUN FITS A HOLSTER!
"Take them clothes off girl...real slow like..."
A WALTER M. MIRISCH PRODUCTION
JULIE LONDON · LEE J. COBB
ARTHUR O'CONNELL
JACK LORD
SCREENPLAY BY REGINALD ROSE
Hear JULIE LONDON Sing "Man of the West"!
DIRECTED BY ANTHONY MANN

BURT LANCASTER · KIRK DOUGLAS
HAL WALLIS' PRODUCTION OF
GUNFIGHT AT THE O.K. CORRAL
RHONDA FLEMING · JO VAN FLEET · JOHN IRELAND
TECHNICOLOR
VISTAVISION

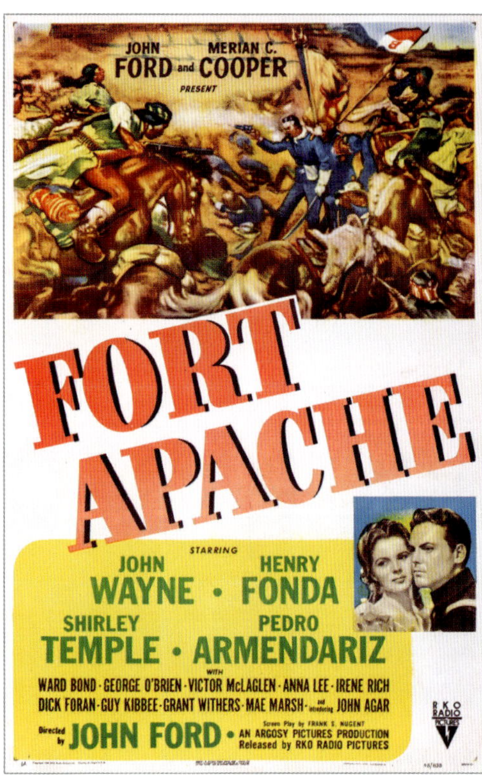

THE DUKE IN HIS PRIME

The John Wayne most fondly remembered by Western fans transitioned from cowboy star to cultural icon as a result of his mature, multilayered characterizations in classic films made in the ten or so years after World War II. This was the loyal, thoughtful, occasionally haunted US Cavalry officer of John Ford's memorable trilogy: *Fort Apache* (1948), *She Wore a Yellow Ribbon* (1949), and *Rio Grande* (1950). *Three Godfathers* (1948), the fourth film version of Peter B. Kyne's venerable novel, showed Duke's gradual metamorphosis from selfish bandit to repentant sinner, while the title role in *Hondo* (1953) helped mythologize his persona of the laconic frontiersman who rises to every challenge. But it was *The Searchers* (1956), of course, that gave him the role of a lifetime and forever altered the perceptions of those who had previously dismissed or underestimated him. The Duke's characterization of solitary, desert-hardened Ethan Edwards was unquestionably the greatest accomplishment of his long career.

he had to find her... he had to find her...
WARNER BROS. PRESENT THE C.V. WHITNEY PICTURE STARRING
JOHN WAYNE IN
THE SEARCHERS
U
VISTAVISION
MOTION PICTURE HIGH-FIDELITY
COLOUR BY TECHNICOLOR
JEFFREY HUNTER · VERA MILES · WARD BOND · NATALIE WOOD
DIRECTED BY JOHN FORD
SCREEN PLAY BY FRANK S NUGENT · EXECUTIVE PRODUCER MERIAN C. COOPER · ASSOCIATE PRODUCER PATRICK FORD
PRESENTED BY WARNER BROS.
WB
ETHAN
Whatever it took – he'd find her!
DEBBIE
Somewhere out there – she was captive!
LAURIE
Her heart wanted to wait – and couldn't!
MARTIN
He started the search as a boy, and ended it a man!
CLAYTON
The Good Book in one hand – and a gun in the other!
PRINTED IN ENGLAND
STAFFORD & CO. LTD., NETHERFIELD, NOTTINGHAM and LONDON

A NEW GENERATION

The earliest Western stars were drawn from the ranks of rodeo riders, Wild West show performers, and even working cowboys. But the genre fixtures of the fifties and sixties were actors trained to ride and fight. Their lack of authenticity was palpable. Rory Calhoun, Dale Robertson, Jim Davis, Jock Mahoney—none of them had the charisma of a Tom Mix or a Buck Jones, but then they didn't need to. Their films were scripted in a way that minimized or camouflaged their shortcomings. The others looked or sounded like sons of the prairie to a greater or lesser degree, but they weren't the real thing, and audiences knew it. This trend in casting reached new heights of absurdity with the appearance onscreen of such actors as Charlton Heston, Victor Mature, Rock Hudson, and Tony Curtis as cowboys and Indians. It heralded the beginning of a long decline for the Western.

ONE RANGER WAS ONE TOO MANY
FOR THE TOUGHEST FIVE IN TEXAS!
Sam Bass
The Knifer
The Lady-Killer
The Sundance Kid
The Duke
Columbia salutes
THE TEXAS RANGERS
THE LONE WOLF WATCHDOGS OF THE LONE STAR STATE
in SUPERcineCOLOR
An EDWARD SMALL Production
starring
GEORGE MONTGOMERY ★ GALE STORM
with JEROME COURTLAND · NOAH BEERY, Jr. · WILLIAM BISHOP
Screen Play by RICHARD SCHAYER · Produced by BERNARD SMALL · Directed by PHIL KARLSON

NOBODY
DRAWS
FASTER
THAN
MASTERSON OF KANSAS
COLOR BY
TECHNICOLOR
starring GEORGE
MONTGOMERY
with NANCY GATES · JAMES GRIFFITH
Story and Screen Play by DOUGLAS HEYES
Produced by SAM KATZMAN · Directed by WILLIAM CASTLE
A COLUMBIA PICTURE

A DAY OF FURY
PRINT BY
TECHNICOLOR
A Universal-International Picture starring
DALE ROBERTSON
MARA CORDAY
JOCK MAHONEY
(TV's sensational "Range Rider" — now in a great new role!)
with CARL BENTON REID · JAN MERLIN
Directed by HARMON JONES · Screenplay by JAMES EDMISTON and OSCAR BRODNEY · Produced by ROBERT ARTHUR

THE WEST'S MOST
STARTLING
STORY!
in Eastman
COLOR
JOE DAKOTA
STARRING
JOCK MAHONEY · LUANA PATTEN
CHARLES McGRAW · BARBARA LAWRENCE
with PAUL BIRCH · ANTHONY CARUSO
DIRECTED BY RICHARD BARTLETT · WRITTEN BY WILLIAM TALMAN AND NORMAN JOLLEY · PRODUCED BY HOWARD CHRISTIE · A UNIVERSAL-INTERNATIONAL PICTURE

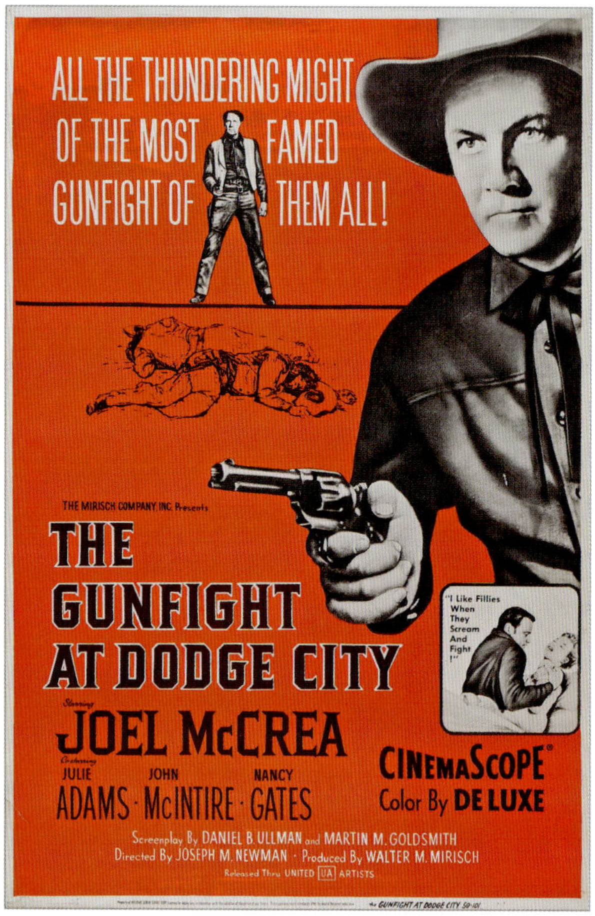

AGING FAVORITES

The fifties *poseurs*—studio contract players groomed to play cowboys, even though they had little aptitude for the job—didn't remotely compare with the middle-aged stars of yore who continued to make Westerns for appreciative fans. Joel McCrea and Randolph Scott had starred in films of all genres—comedies, dramas, mysteries, spy thrillers, and even musicals—yet, both men were best known and most fondly remembered for the horse operas they made as far back as the thirties. And, since the end of World War II, they had starred in little else (only two of McCrea's post-1945 feature films were not Westerns). The quality of their later oaters varied considerably, but both men always performed to the best of their considerable ability and kept their dignity intact. Interestingly, Scott's late-fifties starring vehicles—many scripted by Burt Kennedy and directed by Budd Boetticher—are more highly regarded today than they were upon theatrical release.

IN EASTMAN COLOR AND CINEMASCOPE

THIS IS
THE MAN
CALLED
"BRIGADE"

...silent as
gunsmoke...hot as the revenge
that drove him!

RANDOLPH
SCOTT

Ride
Lonesome

CO-STARRING
KAREN STEELE WITH PERNELL ROBERTS · JAMES BEST · WRITTEN BY BURT KENNEDY

PRODUCED & DIRECTED BY BUDD BOETTICHER · EXECUTIVE PRODUCER HARRY JOE BROWN · A RANOWN PRODUCTION · A COLUMBIA PICTURE

THE OLD GUARD'S LAST GASP

The few remaining cowboy stars who had begun riding the cinematic range during the thirties and early forties found themselves members of an endangered species in the fifties. Both Charles Starrett and Johnny Mack Brown, for example, started making Westerns in 1935. By 1945, Starrett had settled into his new role of the Durango Kid, which he played in sixty-four consecutive feature films before hanging up his mask and spurs in 1952. Brown almost exactly duplicated that record, starring in sixty-five Monogram oaters between 1943 and '52. Tom Holt returned from military service in 1946 and resumed his career at RKO, staying there for six more years. Wild Bill Elliott left Republic in 1950 and spent the next four years making non-series Bs for Monogram and Allied Artists. Allan Lane finished his "Rocky" Lane series for Republic in 1953 after thirty-eight entries. The Saturday-matinee B Western was about to draw its last breath.

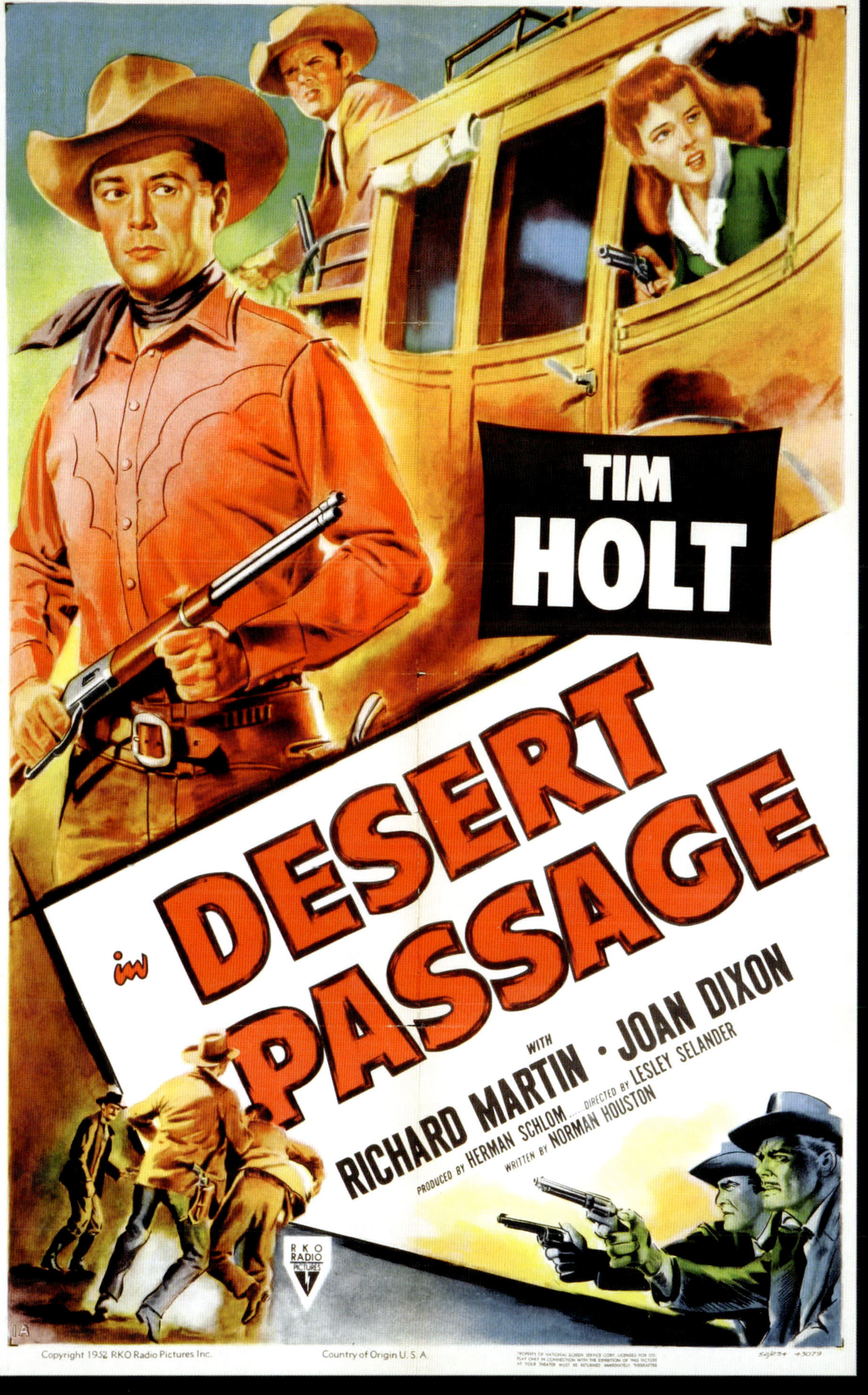
TIM
HOLT
in
DESERT
PASSAGE
WITH
RICHARD MARTIN · JOAN DIXON
PRODUCED BY HERMAN SCHLOM ......DIRECTED BY LESLEY SELANDER
WRITTEN BY NORMAN HOUSTON
RKO RADIO PICTURES
Copyright 1952 RKO Radio Pictures Inc.
Country of Origin U. S. A.

Tim HOLT
in
TRAIL GUIDE
with
RICHARD MARTIN
LINDA DOUGLAS
DIRECTED BY
LESLEY SELANDER
SCREENPLAY BY
ARTHUR E. ORLOFF

ROARIN'!
RIDIN'!
SHOOTIN'!
The GAMBLER
The MARSHAL
The DESPERADO
HELLFIRE
in Trucolor
AN ELLIOTT-McGOWAN PRODUCTION
WILLIAM ELLIOTT
with MARIE WINDSOR · FORREST TUCKER · JIM DAVIS
H. B. WARNER · PAUL FIX · GRANT WITHERS
A REPUBLIC PRODUCTION

MONOGRAM PICTURES presents
JOHNNY
MACK
BROWN
in
Law OF THE Panhandle
Jane ADAMS · Riley HILL · Marshall REED
JERRY THOMAS
Lewis Collins

JOHNNY MACK
BROWN
in
MAN from the Black Hills
co-starring
Jimmy
ELLISON
with FLORENCE LAKE · RAND BROOKS · STANDFORD JOLLEY
Produced by VINCENT M. FENNELLY · Directed by Thomas Carr · Story and Screenplay by Joseph O'Donnell

JOHNNY
MACK
BROWN
in
DEAD MAN'S TRAIL
A MONOGRAM PICTURE
co-starring
JIMMY
ELLISON
with BARBARA ALLEN
STANFORD JOLLEY
PRODUCED BY VINCENT M. FENNELLY · DIRECTED BY Lewis Collins · STORY AND SCREENPLAY BY Joseph Poland

ALLAN
"ROCKY" LANE
AND HIS STALLION
BLACK JACK
Thundering
CARAVANS
with EDDY WALLER
MONA KNOX · ROY BARCROFT
Written by M. Coates Webster · Associate Producer Rudy Ralston
Directed by Harry Keller
A REPUBLIC PICTURE

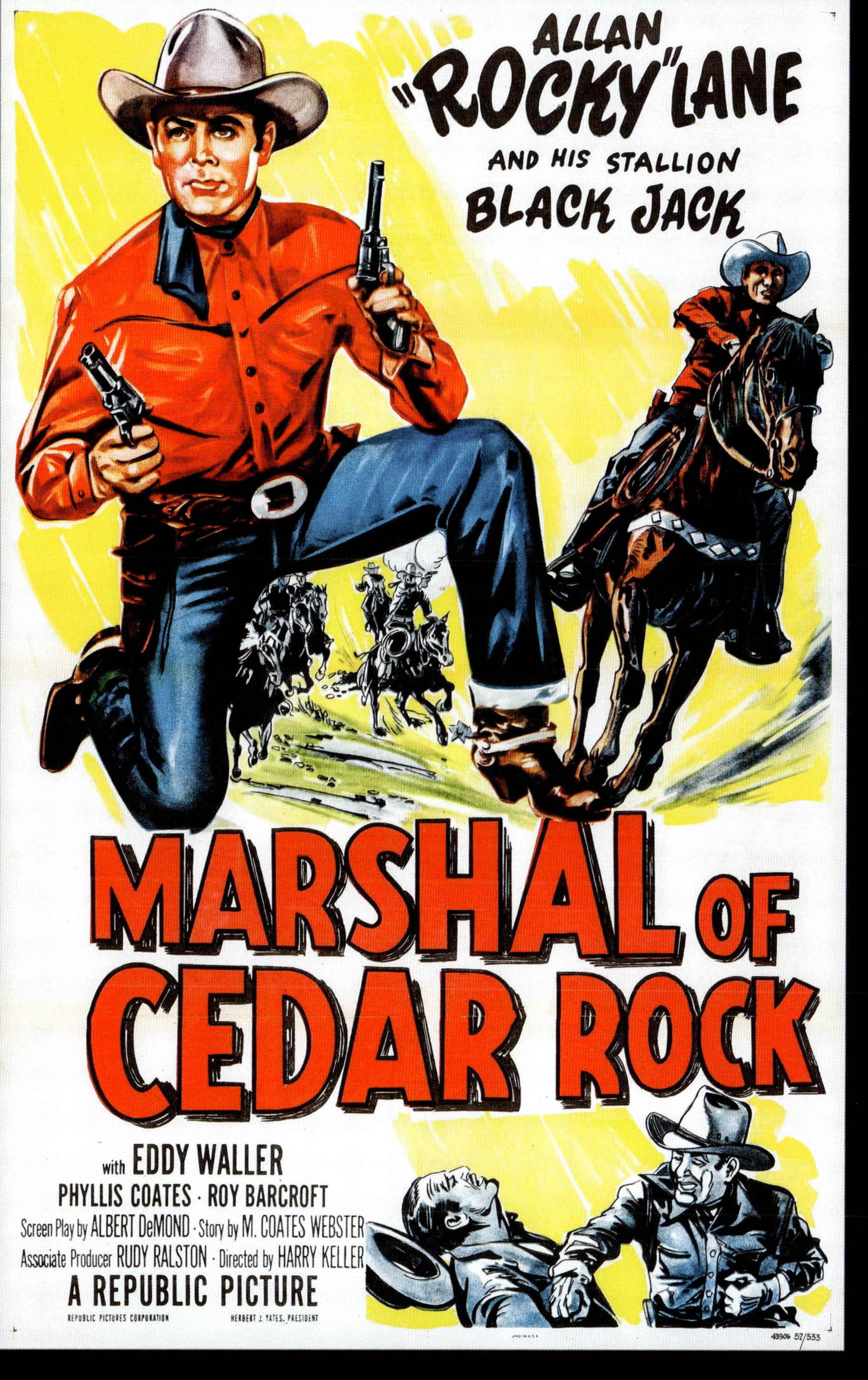
ALLAN
"ROCKY" LANE
AND HIS STALLION
BLACK JACK
MARSHAL OF
CEDAR ROCK
with EDDY WALLER
PHYLLIS COATES · ROY BARCROFT
Screen Play by ALBERT DeMOND · Story by M. COATES WEBSTER
Associate Producer RUDY RALSTON · Directed by HARRY KELLER
A REPUBLIC PICTURE
REPUBLIC PICTURES CORPORATION
HERBERT J. YATES, PRESIDENT
43906 57/533

TWILIGHT OF THE B-SERIES WESTERNS

Minor studios Republic, Monogram, and PRC continued to manufacture Saturday-matinee Westerns for the moppet brigade after the major studios abandoned them. Republic's product maintained solid production values to the end, but the other two companies—lacking any such aspirations or the financial wherewithal to fulfill them—simply ground out product on an assembly-line basis. It didn't help that they had lackluster stars such as bland singing cowboys Eddie Dean and Jimmy Wakely, or bullwhip-wielding Lash LaRue and Whip Wilson. Decades of formulaic, repetitive plotting had finally taken their toll, and now that older, better Westerns were starting to show up on the new medium of commercial television, there seemed little point in continuing to produce theatrical series. Republic's final singing cowboy, Rex Allen, lasted until 1954; then, like his predecessors, he jumped to TV.

NO LAW COULD STOP HIM!! UNTIL HE CAME FACE TO FACE WITH THE...

J. FRANCIS WHITE, Jr. and JOY HOUCK present

KING OF THE BULLWHIP

STARRING "LASH" LaRUE · "FUZZY" St. JOHN

JACK HOLT · TOM NEAL

ANNE GWYNNE

WITH MICHAEL WHALEN · WILLIS HOUCK · MARY LOU WEBB

DENNIS MOORE · JIMMIE MARTIN · CLIFF TAYLOR

Produced and Directed by RON ORMOND · Associate Producer IRA WEBB

Story and Screenplay by JACK LEWIS and IRA WEBB

A WESTERN ADVENTURE PRODUCTION

Whip
WILSON
Lawless
Cowboys
with Fuzzy
Knight
Jim Bannon · Pamela Duncan
A MONOGRAM PICTURE
Produced by VINCENT M. FENNELLY
Directed by Lewis Collins · Screenplay by Maurice Tombragel

Whip Wilson
"MONTANA
INCIDENT"
with
RAND BROOKS
NOEL NEIL · BRUCE EDWARDS
PRODUCED BY
VINCENT M. FENNELLY
DIRECTED BY
Lewis Collins
WRITTEN BY
Dan Ullman
A SILVERMINE PRODUCTION

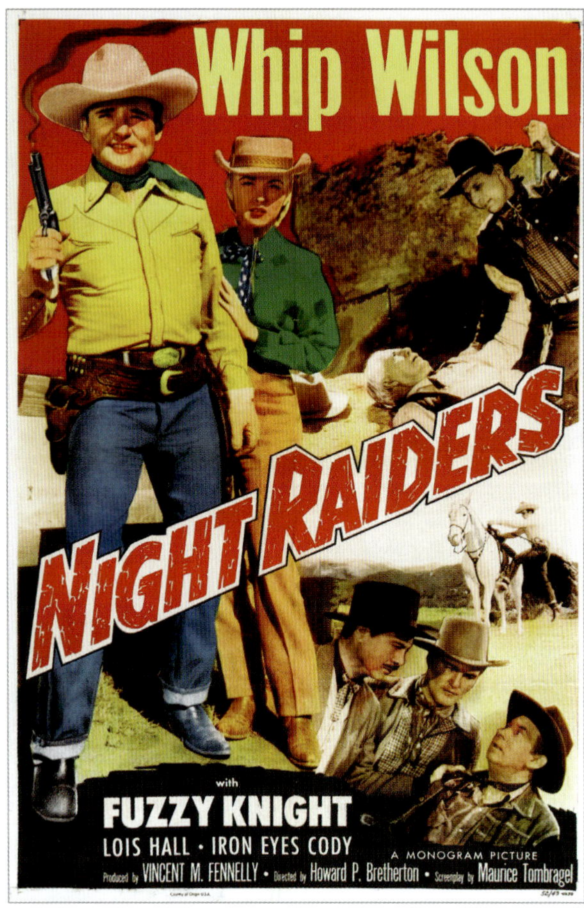
Whip Wilson
NIGHT RAIDERS
with
FUZZY KNIGHT
LOIS HALL · IRON EYES CODY
A MONOGRAM PICTURE
Produced by VINCENT M. FENNELLY · Directed by Howard P. Bretherton · Screenplay by Maurice Tombragel

MONOGRAM PICTURES PRESENTS
JIMMY
WAKELY
SILVER
TRAILS
with
"CANNONBALL" TAYLOR
Produced by LOUIS GRAY · Directed by Christy Cabanne
Original Screenplay by J. Benton Cheney

MONOGRAM PICTURES presents

JIMMY WAKELY

in

"Oklahoma Blues"

with

"CANNONBALL" TAYLOR

VIRGINIA BELMONT

Hear Jimmy sing his Latest Tune Sensation:
"OKLAHOMA BLUES" – and Other Hits!

Produced by LOUIS GRAY • Directed by Lambert Hillyer • Screenplay by Bennett Cohen

Country of Origin U. S. A.

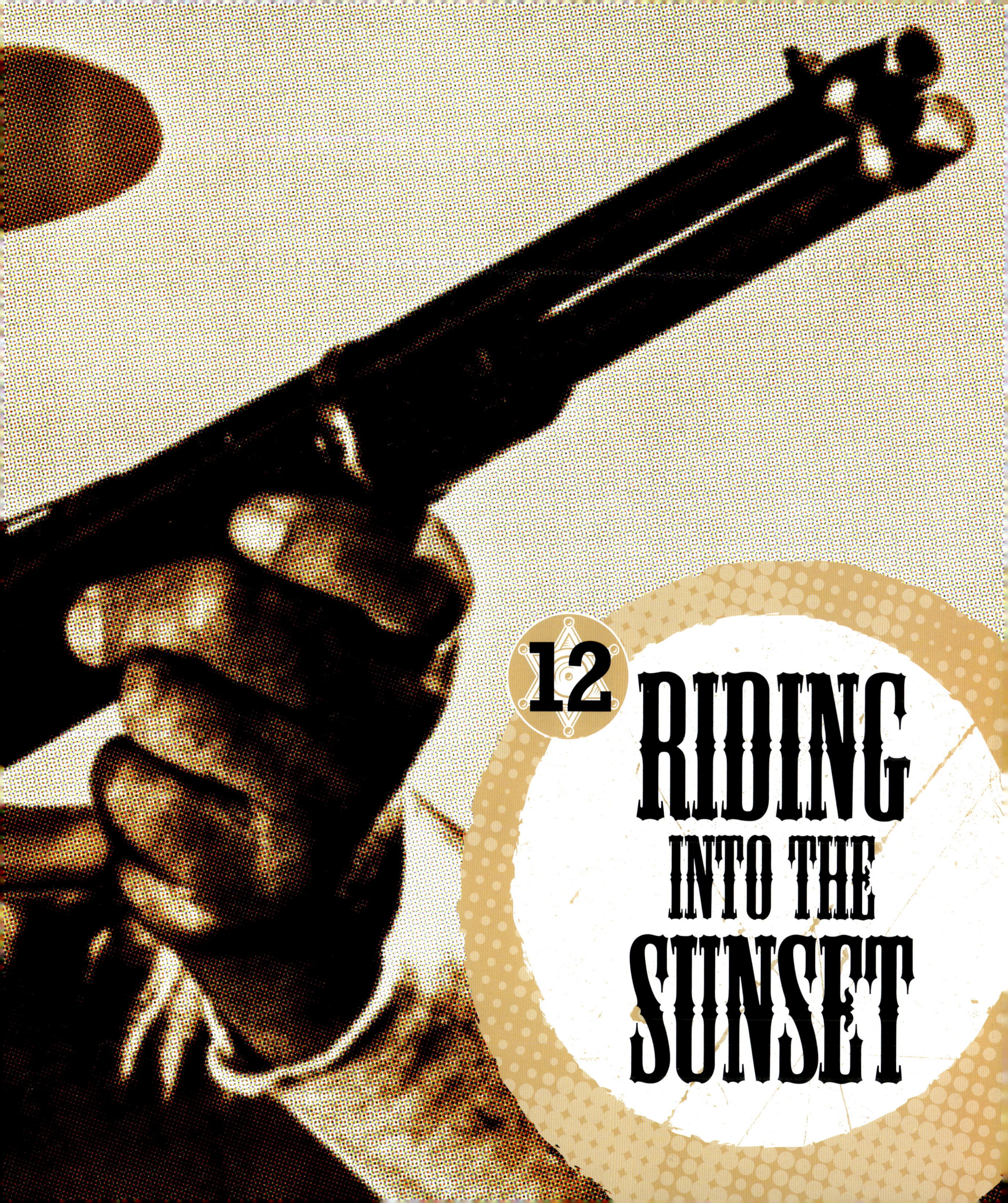
12
RIDING
INTO THE
SUNSET

THE WESTERN'S WANING DAYS

During the sixties and seventies, changing times, tastes, and attitudes take their toll on the Western's popularity, and increasingly the horse opera is regarded as a quaint relic of a bygone era, subject to unflattering reinterpretations. Societal upheaval promotes widespread distrust in and contempt for long-standing institutions. This dissatisfaction extends to pop-culture forms espousing traditional values, and old-school horse operas almost completely vanish from view in just a few years . . .

BELOW: John Wayne spent more than ten years and most of his personal fortune bringing *The Alamo* to the screen, encountering countless obstacles along the way. Despite all the time and expense, the three-hour epic was deeply flawed and, while not a total flop, failed to recoup the Duke's money.

Television played a major role in satisfying the American consumer's appetite for Westerns. As previously noted, old B-grade horse operas from the thirties and forties composed much of the early programming for the three major networks as well as independent stations scattered across the country. By 1953 Gene Autry, Roy Rogers, and William Boyd had already transitioned from big screen to small, and within another few years they would be joined by former Western stars whose moribund careers had flickered back to life as a new generation of youthful fans discovered their old work on the tube.

The mid-fifties saw a veritable explosion of newly produced Western series in both half-hour and one-hour lengths. *Gunsmoke*, *Cheyenne*, *Maverick*, *The Life and Legend of Wyatt Earp*, and others were tailored for adult viewers, joining a long list of kiddie-oriented skeins such as *The Lone Ranger*, *Wild Bill Hickok*, and *The Cisco Kid*. They provided steady employment for such aging stars as Henry Fonda and Joel McCrea, then experiencing a diminution in their box-office potency. Audie Murphy, the boyish-looking World War II hero and star of NBC's *Whispering Smith* (1961), continued to turn out theatrical Westerns well into the sixties, but with one major exception he was the last of the big-screen cowboy heroes to do so.

Unfortunately, in those days, most TV series aired thirty-nine episodes per season, and the sheer volume of shows being filmed exhausted the genre's story variations. Although a few top favorites maintained their favored-nation status with viewers—*Gunsmoke* and *Bonanza* leading the pack—TV Westerns in general eventually wore out their welcome by virtue of similarity and repetition.

TOGETHER FOR THE FIRST TIME

JAMES STEWART

JOHN WAYNE

in the masterpiece of four-time Academy Award winner

JOHN FORD

The Man Who Shot Liberty Valance

VERA MILES · LEE MARVIN · EDMOND O'BRIEN · ANDY DEVINE · KEN MURRAY

ABOVE LEFT: James Stewart and John Wayne flank director John Ford in this publicity photo taken on location during the filming of *The Man Who Shot Liberty Valance* (1962). The film was a valedictory of sorts for Ford, enabling him to gather together many of the actors who had worked with him over the previous thirty years.

ABOVE RIGHT: *Liberty Valance* contains a line of dialogue that has attained cinematic immortality: "When the legend becomes fact, print the legend." Ironically, that statement has come to apply to chronicling the history of motion pictures, whose participants behind and in front of the camera often have vested interests in leaving movie mythology undisturbed.

Audiences increasingly turned to other types of weekly entertainment: sitcoms, cop shows, medical dramas, and the like.

Moviegoers continued to patronize theaters that ran Westerns, but they weren't getting old-school oaters with traditional values. During the 1960s, American society was roiled by countercultural influences, which inevitably seeped into the popular culture. Revisionist Westerns reflected such contemporaneous phenomena as the rise of the antihero in all forms of storytelling, and shifting values affected the portrayal of historical figures as well as fictional protagonists.

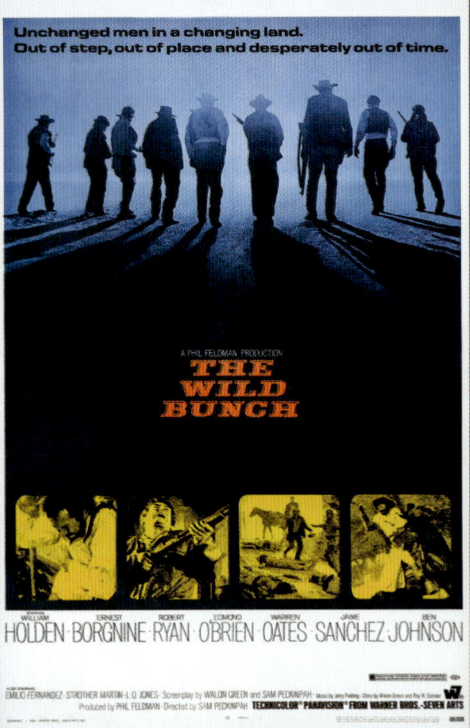

Butch Cassidy and the Sundance Kid (1969) romanticized two of the West's most notorious outlaws, turning them into a contemporary version of the characters played by Bob Hope and Bing Crosby in the famous "Road" movies. *Hour of the Gun* (1967) upended the legend of frontier lawman Wyatt Earp, turning him into a deeply flawed and troubled person. *Little Big Man* (1970) was one of several quasi-historical Westerns that portrayed General George Armstrong Custer as a raging lunatic.

This trend continued into the seventies with such antiheroic oaters as *Doc* (1971) and *Pat Garrett and Billy the Kid* (1973). The former treated gambler and killer Doc Holliday sympathetically while depicting Wyatt Earp as dangerously unhinged. The latter characterized vicious William Bonney as, well, misunderstood. It was directed by Sam Peckinpah, whose career had kicked into high gear with the elegiac *Ride the High Country* (1962). That film acknowledged changing attitudes in Westerns by pitting aging lawman Joel McCrea against former compatriot Randolph Scott. Peckinpah's subsequent Westerns, including *Major Dundee* (1965) and *The Wild Bunch* (1969), trafficked in cynicism, disillusionment, and unnecessarily brutal violence, as though the

ABOVE LEFT: *The Wild Bunch* (1969) is acknowledged by most cineastes to be one of modern cinema's classics, but Sam Peckinpah's revisionist Western alienated many horse-opera devotees by pointedly ignoring or actively undermining genre traditions that had endured for many decades.

ABOVE RIGHT: Top-billed William Holden stands next to camera operator Thomas Laughridge as he lines up a shot for *The Wild Bunch*. Director Sam Peckinpah (*wearing sunglasses*) is at lower left, observing. Highly regarded today, the film was a huge box-office flop upon its original release.

director had made it his life's work to undermine confidence in genre entries with traditional values.

The subversive quality of Peckinpah's films—which, it should be noted, were dramatically sound, vividly acted, and technically excellent—carried over to another sixties innovation: the so-called spaghetti Western, produced in Italy but brought to the US by director Sergio Leone with *A Fistful of Dollars* (1964), the first of three moody, eccentric pictures starring second-rate American actor Clint Eastwood, late of TV's *Rawhide*. As a poncho-wearing, cigarillo-chewing, signally amoral gunman called the Man with No Name, Eastwood became an international star as a result of his participation in Leone's trilogy and other Westerns trading on the persona he established it. Leone gleefully obliterated horse-opera conventions and imbued his oaters with an anticapitalist, antiestablishment tone then fashionable in European circles.

Spaghetti-Western production spread throughout the continent, with German and Spanish filmmakers joining in the fun. Dozens of such films—which starred not only European actors but also Hollywood thespians including James Garner, Lee Van Cleef, and even Henry Fonda—flickered on big screens worldwide until the subgenre flamed out in the late 1970s.

During these tumultuous decades for the motion-picture Western, one star and one alone kept faith with the genre that had made him a worldwide box-office sensation. John Wayne started the sixties with his dream project, *The Alamo*, which dramatized on an epic scale the famous early battle for Texas independence. In addition to starring as Davy Crockett, Wayne directed the film and helped shape its screenplay. He insisted that the story be told with an emphasis on traditional heroics, emphasizing the mythic stature of the historic personages involved. Duke spent years and most of his personal fortune on the film, but upon initial release *The Alamo* failed to recoup its costs. At the time, some critics declared it out of date—a victim of changing attitudes toward old-fashioned historical Westerns.

Wayne soldiered on, notching a superb performance in *The Man Who Shot Liberty Valance*, directed by his old mentor, John Ford. And he singlehandedly bucked the trend for antiheroic, revisionist Westerns. He continued to star in traditional horse operas calculated to exploit the persona he had taken decades to establish. The notable exceptions were *True Grit* (1969), which won Duke a "Best Actor" Oscar for his self-parodying portrayal of drunken old marshal Rooster Cogburn, and his final film, *The Shootist* (1976), a career valedictory in which he stars as a cancer-stricken gunfighter who realizes he has outlived the Old West.

By the late 1970s, Westerns had fallen out of favor, supplanted by gangster films such as *The Godfather*, science-fiction movies such as *Star Wars*, and slasher films such as *Halloween*. There have been occasional resurgences of interest in the genre, and great Westerns continue to appear on big screens and small, though not in the mass quantities of the twentieth century's early decades. ✸

ABOVE: Director Sergio Leone and star Clint Eastwood survey the Western town set while the crew gets ready for the filming of *For a Few Dollars More*, the second of Eastwood's three "Man with No Name" spaghetti Westerns—the films that made him an international superstar.

THE GREAT DIRECTORS

The movie Western's waning days saw such legendary Hollywood directors as John Ford, Howard Hawks, and John Huston continuing to work in the genre, albeit with diminished capacity. Ford's steadily deteriorating health affected his work and was the chief reason for the unevenness of his latter-day output. *Two Rode Together* (1961), *Cheyenne Autumn* (1964), and *7 Women* (1971) all suffered because he lacked the energy to direct them properly. Hawks, meanwhile, increasingly viewed his film projects as opportunities to socialize with old friends and coworkers. *El Dorado* (1967) and *Rio Lobo* (1971) were essentially uncredited remakes of *Rio Bravo* (1959), but they enabled Hawks to work again with his pal John Wayne. As the old-timers gradually faded away, Sam Peckinpah became the genre's chief exponent. His elegiac *Ride the High Country* (1962) demonstrated a rare facility for Western filmmaking, and while his later oaters were firmly in the "revisionist" camp, they were fine showcases for his creativity.

THE WEST'S MOST VIOLENT STORY...
THE WEST'S MOST VALIANT HOUR!
COLUMBIA PICTURES presents
A JOHN FORD PRODUCTION
JAMES STEWART
RICHARD WIDMARK
SHIRLEY JONES
"TWO RODE TOGETHER"
Eastman COLOR
co-starring
LINDA CRISTAL · ANDY DEVINE · JOHN McINTIRE
Screenplay by FRANK NUGENT · Produced by STAN SHPETNER · Directed by JOHN FORD

SHOWDOWN IN THE HIGH SIERRA!
METRO-GOLDWYN-MAYER presents
RANDOLPH SCOTT
RIDE THE HIGH COUNTRY
JOEL McCREA
WITH
MARIETTE HARTLEY
WRITTEN BY N. B. STONE, JR. · DIRECTED BY SAM PECKINPAH · PRODUCED BY RICHARD E. LYONS
in CinemaScope and METROCOLOR

COLUMBIA PICTURES presents A JERRY BRESLER Production
Major Dundee
starring
CHARLTON HESTON · RICHARD HARRIS · JIM HUTTON · JAMES COBURN · and MICHAEL ANDERSON, JR.
co-starring MARIO ADORF · BROCK PETERS · and SENTA BERGER
Screenplay by HARRY JULIAN FINK, OSCAR SAUL and SAM PECKINPAH · Story by HARRY JULIAN FINK
Produced by JERRY BRESLER · Directed by SAM PECKINPAH
FILMED IN PANAVISION · COLOR

Sam Peckinpah's
PAT GARRETT AND BILLY THE KID
Best of enemies.
Deadliest of friends.
MGM Presents
"PAT GARRETT AND BILLY THE KID"
Starring
JAMES COBURN · KRIS KRISTOFFERSON · BOB DYLAN
And Also Starring JASON ROBARDS · Music by BOB DYLAN
Written by RUDOLPH WURLITZER · Produced by GORDON CARROLL
Directed by SAM PECKINPAH · METROCOLOR · PANAVISION

THE THROWBACK: A. C. LYLES

Until the day he died in 2013 at the age of ninety-five, Andrew Craddock Lyles was known as "the man with the shortest resume in Hollywood." As a grade-school boy, he worked as an usher in the local Paramount-owned theater; a chance meeting with studio president Adolph Zukor enabled him to get a job in Paramount's mailroom, and he eventually graduated to a job as a publicist. Lyles worked his way up to producer, although he never made an important picture. Instead, he concentrated on moderately budgeted Westerns, all made during the sixties. As a lifelong movie fan and lover of anything and anybody smacking of Old Hollywood, he delighted in casting his pictures with former stars, some of whom had worked in the silent era. Many of them were personal friends who came out of retirement temporarily, just to work in his Westerns. Lyles later worked in TV; one of his last jobs was as a "consulting producer" on the Paramount-owned HBO series *Deadwood*.

THIS WAS THE TOWN WHERE HE MUST KILL...OR BE KILLED!
Paramount Pictures presents
DANA ANDREWS
as
the
TOWN TAMER
an A.C.LYLES production
TECHNICOLOR®
TECHNISCOPE®
CO-STARRING
TERRY MOORE · PAT O'BRIEN · LON CHANEY · BRUCE CABOT
LYLE BETTGER · RICHARD ARLEN · BARTON MacLANE · RICHARD JAECKEL · PHILIP CAREY · SONNY TUFTS AND COLEEN GRAY ·
DIRECTED BY LESLEY SELANDER
SCREENPLAY BY FRANK GRUBER
FROM HIS NOVEL "TOWN TAMER"

HIS CAUSE —VENGEANCE!
HIS CREED —VIOLENCE!
HIS WOMEN —SULTRY!
He came to steal a town and take a woman.
WACO
an A.C. LYLES production
TECHNICOLOR®
STARRING HOWARD KEEL · JANE RUSSELL · BRIAN DONLEVY · WENDELL COREY · JOHN SMITH and TERRY MOORE
Directed by R.G. SPRINGSTEEN · Screenplay by STEVE FISHER · TECHNISCOPE®

PARAMOUNT PICTURES PRESENTS
DANA ANDREWS
JANE RUSSELL
GUNS BLAZING ON THE PLAINS...
FISTS FLYING IN THE CASINO...
WHEREVER THERE'S ACTION THERE'S...
JOHNNY RENO
The hard-fisted Texan with the easy-loving way!
AN A.C.LYLES PRODUCTION
CO-STARRING
LON CHANEY · JOHN AGAR · LYLE BETTGER · TOM DRAKE · RICHARD ARLEN
TECHNISCOPE® Screenplay by STEVE FISHER · Directed by R.G. SPRINGSTEEN
TECHNICOLOR®

He fought on the most dangerous trail a man ever dared to ride!
PARAMOUNT PICTURES presents
HOSTILE GUNS
AN A.C.LYLES PRODUCTION
TECHNICOLOR®
STARRING GEORGE MONTGOMERY · YVONNE De CARLO · TAB HUNTER · BRIAN DONLEVY
Screenplay by STEVE FISHER and SLOAN NIBLEY · Directed by R.G. SPRINGSTEEN · TECHNISCOPE®
Copyright © 1967 by Paramount Pictures Corporation and A. C. Lyles Productions, Inc.

AUDIE MURPHY

Enlisting in the US Army in 1942, at the age of seventeen, Texas native Audie Leon Murphy became the nation's most decorated combat soldier of World War II, winning thirty-three awards, including the Congressional Medal of Honor. After mustering out of the army, he went to Hollywood as a would-be actor. Following several tough years of struggling to make the grade, Murphy in 1950 wangled a contract with Universal Pictures. Just twenty-five years old—but looking even younger—the shy, slight, soft-spoken Texan was cast as Billy the Kid in a Technicolor starring vehicle, *The Kid from Texas.* He clicked with audiences, and shortly thereafter he played a young Jesse James in *Kansas Raiders.* A mediocre actor at first, Murphy gradually improved. He played himself in the autobiographical *To Hell and Back* (1955) and starred in three dozen Western features, the last of which was released in 1969. Murphy, who suffered from what we now know as PTSD, died in a plane crash in 1971.

When in Southern California visit Universal City Studios
The Story Of A Town With A Gun In Its Back!
AUDIE MURPHY
GUNPOINT
Technicolor
CO-STARRING
JOAN STALEY · WARREN STEVENS
WITH EDGAR BUCHANAN · DENVER PYLE
DAVID MACKLIN · ROBERT PINE
WRITTEN BY MARY and WILLARD WILLINGHAM · DIRECTED BY EARL BELLAMY · PRODUCED BY GORDON KAY
A UNIVERSAL PICTURE

AUDIE MURPHY · DAN DURYEA
JOAN O'BRIEN
"6 BLACK HORSES"
in Eastman COLOR
Written by BURT KENNEDY · Directed by HARRY KELLER · Produced by GORDON KAY
A Universal-International Picture

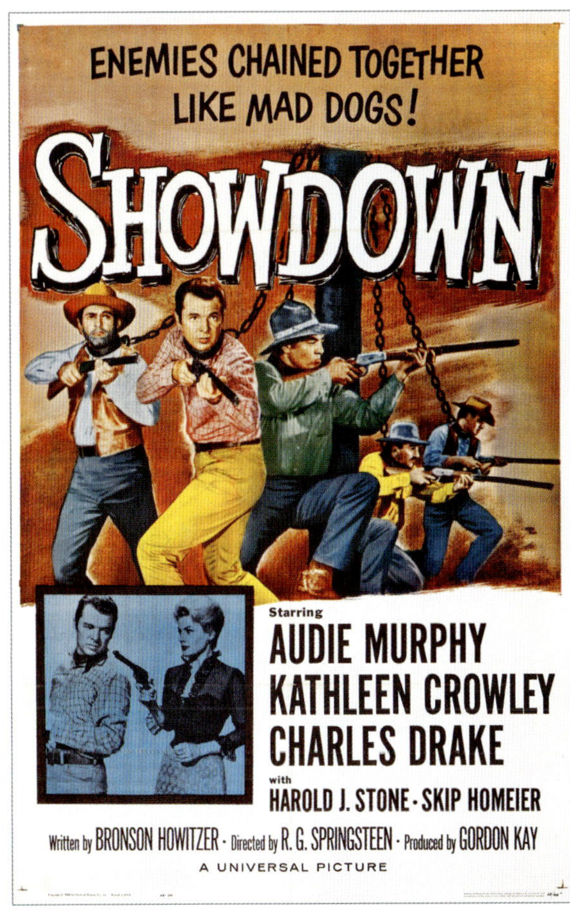
ENEMIES CHAINED TOGETHER LIKE MAD DOGS!
SHOWDOWN
Starring
AUDIE MURPHY
KATHLEEN CROWLEY
CHARLES DRAKE
with
HAROLD J. STONE · SKIP HOMEIER
Written by BRONSON HOWITZER · Directed by R. G. SPRINGSTEEN · Produced by GORDON KAY
A UNIVERSAL PICTURE

"HERE IS ALL THE RAW RAMPAGING FURY OF THE WEST!"
COLUMBIA PICTURES presents
AUDIE MURPHY
THE QUICK GUN
FILMED IN TECHNISCOPE
COLOR BY TECHNICOLOR
Co-Starring MERRY ANDERS
Screenplay by ROBERT E. KENT · Based on a story by STEVE FISHER · Directed by SIDNEY SALKOW
Produced by GRANT WHYTOCK · AN ADMIRAL PICTURES PRODUCTION

JOHN WAYNE, LIVING LEGEND

Having lost millions of dollars on his dream project, *The Alamo*, Wayne worked harder than ever just to rebuild his fortune. Fortunately, during the sixties and seventies, he remained the one veteran cowboy star who still was a marketable commodity. True, his audiences tended to be older, but the movie business was only just beginning its obsession with the youth market, and Duke was virtually alone in making unabashedly old-fashioned Westerns. Top directors such as Howard Hawks and Henry Hathaway happily worked with him, and he sought out younger costars who appealed to a different demographic than the typical John Wayne fan—hence the appearance in his pictures of such performers as James Caan, Ann-Margret, and Glen Campbell. Naturally, he saved parts for old drinking buddies Paul Fix and Bruce Cabot, old cronies from the thirties. Inevitably, his starring vehicles became caricatures, playing on an image regularly and mercilessly lampooned by hipsters, but his Oscar-winning turn in *True Grit* (1969) inspired new respect, and his farewell performance in *The Shootist* (1976) was a fitting valedictory.

When in Southern California visit Universal City Studios

THE WAR WAGON ROLLS AND THE SCREEN EXPLODES!

JOHN WAYNE

KIRK DOUGLAS

"THE WAR WAGON"

CO-STARRING

HOWARD KEEL · ROBERT WALKER

KEENAN WYNN · BRUCE CABOT · JOANNA BARNES

TECHNICOLOR®/PANAVISION®

Music by DIMITRI TIOMKIN · Screenplay by CLAIR HUFFAKER Based on his book "Badman" · Directed by BURT KENNEDY · Produced by MARVIN SCHWARTZ · A BATJAC PRESENTATION · A MARVIN SCHWARTZ PRODUCTION

A Universal Picture

Property of NATIONAL SCREEN SERVICE CORP. licensed for display only in connection with the exhibition of this picture at your theatre. Please pack and return immediately after the close of the current weeks show.

"THE WAR WAGON" – 67/152

PARAMOUNT PICTURES Presents
JOHN WAYNE · GLEN CAMPBELL · KIM DARBY
IN HAL WALLIS' PRODUCTION
TRUE GRIT
The strangest trio ever to track a killer.
A fearless, one-eyed U.S. marshal who never knew a dry day in his life...
a Texas ranger thirsty for bounty money...
and a girl still wet behind the ears who didn't care what they were or who they were as long as they had true grit.
THE YEAR'S BEST SELLER ABOUT THE TRUE WEST!
"TRUE GRIT is lively, uproarious high adventure!"
—Saturday Review
TRUE GRIT A NOVEL BY CHARLES PORTIS
A BRAND NEW BRAND OF AMERICAN FRONTIER STORY
CO-STARRING JEREMY SLATE · ROBERT DUVALL · STROTHER MARTIN · DIRECTED BY HENRY HATHAWAY · SCREENPLAY BY MARGUERITE ROBERTS
FROM THE NOVEL BY CHARLES PORTIS · Title Song Sung by GLEN CAMPBELL Music Scored by ELMER BERNSTEIN · TECHNICOLOR® A PARAMOUNT PICTURE
MUSIC FROM THE SCORE AVAILABLE ON CAPITOL RECORDS.
Paramount A Gulf + Western Company

THE LEGEND
Warner Bros. presents A Batjac Production
John Wayne is "Chisum"
Forrest Tucker · Christopher George · Ben Johnson · Bruce Cabot
Glenn Corbett · Patric Knowles · Andrew Prine · Richard Jaeckel
Lynda Day · And Introducing Geoffrey Deuel & Pamela McMyler
Executive Producer Michael Wayne · Written and Produced by Andrew J. Fenady
Directed by Andrew V. McLaglen · Panavision® Technicolor®

Cursed gold, a vanished train and a thief's widow. He'd do better walking into hell!
JOHN WAYNE · ANN-MARGRET
ROD TAYLOR
THE TRAIN ROBBERS
A BATJAC PRODUCTION · BEN JOHNSON · CHRISTOPHER GEORGE · BOBBY VINTON · JERRY GATLIN and RICARDO MONTALBAN
Produced by MICHAEL WAYNE · Written and Directed by BURT KENNEDY · PANAVISION® · TECHNICOLOR®
Celebrating Warner Bros. 50th Anniversary · A Warner Communications Company

GIVE 'EM HELL, JOHN.
John Wayne in
A Howard Hawks Production
"Rio Lobo"
A Cinema Center Films Presentation
Co-starring Jorge Rivero · Jennifer O'Neil · Jack Elam · Victor French · Susana Dosamantes
Screenplay by Burton Wohl and Leigh Brackett · Story by Burton Wohl · Music by Jerry Goldsmith
Directed by Howard Hawks · Technicolor® A National General Picture Release
71/5

Big Jake...A legend of a man.
A man who fought his way through hell
to save a grandson he had never seen!
John Wayne - Richard Boone
"Big Jake"
A CINEMA CENTER FILMS PRESENTATION
co-starring Patrick Wayne · Christopher Mitchum
Bobby Vinton · Bruce Cabot · Glenn Corbett · John Doucette
and Maureen O'Hara as MARTHA
Written by HARRY JULIAN FINK and R. M. FINK Produced by MICHAEL WAYNE Directed by GEORGE SHERMAN Music by ELMER BERNSTEIN
TECHNICOLOR® PANAVISION® A BATJAC PRODUCTION A NATIONAL GENERAL PICTURES RELEASE
STYLE B
71/154

JOHN WAYNE & THE COWBOYS
A MARK RYDELL FILM
All they wanted was their chance to be men...and he gave it to them.
JOHN WAYNE in A Mark Rydell Film "THE COWBOYS" Co-Starring ROSCOE LEE BROWNE · BRUCE DERN · COLLEEN DEWHURST as Kate · Music by John Williams
Screenplay by Irving Ravetch & Harriet Frank, Jr. and William Dale Jennings · Produced and Directed by Mark Rydell · Panavision® Technicolor®
From Warner Bros. A Kinney Company
GP

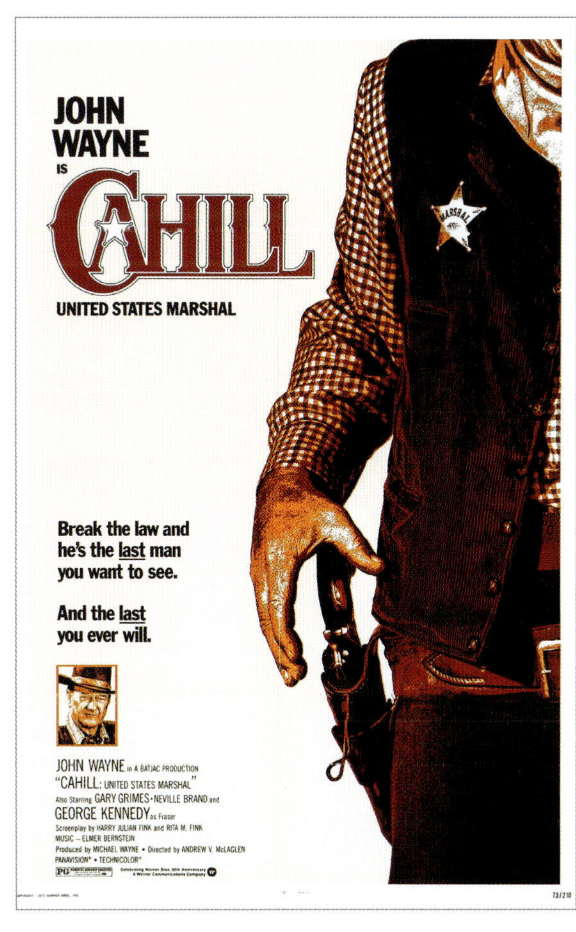
JOHN WAYNE
IS
CAHILL
UNITED STATES MARSHAL
Break the law and he's the last man you want to see.
And the last you ever will.
JOHN WAYNE in A BATJAC PRODUCTION
"CAHILL: UNITED STATES MARSHAL"
Also Starring GARY GRIMES · NEVILLE BRAND and
GEORGE KENNEDY as Fraser
Screenplay by HARRY JULIAN FINK and RITA M. FINK
MUSIC – ELMER BERNSTEIN
Produced by MICHAEL WAYNE • Directed by ANDREW V. McLAGLEN
PANAVISION® • TECHNICOLOR®
PG
Celebrating Warner Bros. 50th Anniversary
A Warner Communications Company
73/218

SPAGHETTI WESTERNS

Reportedly coined by Spanish journalist Alfonso Sanchez, the term "spaghetti Western" initially described the internationally famous collaborations between actor Clint Eastwood and Italian director Sergio Leone. Most imitators of the "Man with No Name" films were indeed Leone's countrymen, but spaghetti Western characteristics could be found in most genre offerings produced in Europe. In fact, entries in the subgenre were often international coproductions involving investors and filmmakers from Spain, France, Germany, Portugal, and Greece. But they all had certain thematic and stylistic similarities that recalled Leone's *A Fistful of Dollars* (1964) and its two sequels: the European obsessions with zoom shots, for example, and an overreliance on tight facial close-ups. The conventions of American Westerns were deliberately ignored, satirized, or ridiculed. Different cultural backgrounds accounted for part of this strategy, but Leone and his mostly socialist acolytes also used spaghetti Westerns as vehicles to criticize capitalism. The subgenre lasted roughly fifteen years but descended into self-parody long before the last entries were made.

For Three Men The Civil War Wasn't Hell. It Was Practice!

CLINT EASTWOOD in

"THE GOOD, THE BAD AND THE UGLY"

co-starring
LEE VAN CLEEF ALDO GIUFFRE | and with MARIO BREGA

also starring
ELI WALLACH
in the role of Tuco

Screenplay by AGE-SCARPELLI, LUCIANO VINCENZONI and SERGIO LEONE Directed by SERGIO LEONE Music by ENNIO MORRICONE

Produced by ALBERTO GRIMALDI for P. E. A.–Produzioni Europee Associate, Rome

TECHNISCOPE® TECHNICOLOR®

68/...

They call him PRETTY FACE!"
...and his credo is simple and short and sweet!
"GOD FORGIVES --I DON'T"!
STARRING
TERENCE HILL · FRANK WOLFF · BUD SPENCER IN COLOR BY BERKEY-PATHÉ
STORY AND SCREENPLAY BY GIUSEPPE COLIZZI · DIRECTED BY GIUSEPPE COLIZZI · AN AMERICAN INTERNATIONAL RELEASE

Mr. Ugly comes to town!...
big action and big excitement!
COLUMBIA PICTURES presents
LEE VAN CLEEF
TOMAS MILIAN
WALTER BARNES
"THE BIG GUNDOWN"
Directed by SERGIO SOLLIMA Produced by ALBERTO GRIMALDI
TECHNICOLOR TECHNISCOPE

sabata-
THE MAN WITH GUNSIGHT EYES COMES TO KILL!
An ALBERTO GRIMALDI Production
LEE VAN CLEEF "sabata" WILLIAM BERGER
with PEDRO SANCHEZ · NICK JORDAN · LINDA VERAS · FRANCO RESSELL · ANTHONY GRADWELL
with ROBERT HUNDAR and with GIANNI RIZZO · Story and Screenplay by RENATO IZZO and GIANFRANCO PAROLINI · Directed by FRANK KRAMER
TECHNICOLOR TECHNISCOPE
United Artists

HE'S JUDGE...JURY... EXECUTIONER!
THE MAN WITH THE GUNSIGHT EYES IS BACK!
An ALBERTO GRIMALDI Production
LEE VAN CLEEF
in
"RETURN of SABATA"
with REINER SCHONE
and ANNABELLA INCONTRERA GIANPIERO ALBERTINI JACQUELINE ALEXANDRE PEDRO SANCHEZ NICK JORDAN VASSILLI KARIS
and with GIANNI RIZZO Story and Screenplay by RENATO IZZO and GIANFRANCO PAROLINI A Film by FRANK KRAMER
A COPRODUCTION PEA/ROME-LES PRODUCTIONS ARTISTES ASSOCIES/PARIS-ARTEMIS FILM/BERLIN
TECHNICOLOR TECHNISCOPE United Artists

An ALBERTO GRIMALDI Production

YUL BRYNNER

in

"ADIÓS, SABATA"

SABATA AIMS TO KILL ...and his gun does the rest!

with

DEAN REED

PEDRO SANCHEZ

JOSEPH PERSAUD

SUSAN SCOTT and with GIANNI RIZZO

Story and Screenplay by RENATO IZZO and GIANFRANCO PAROLINI

Produced by ALBERTO GRIMALDI · A Film by FRANK KRAMER COLOR

GP ALL AGES ADMITTED Parental Guidance Suggested

United Artists Entertainment from Transamerica Corporation

COPYRIGHT ©1971 UNITED ARTISTS CORPORATION

71/120

REVISIONIST WESTERNS

In a misguided attempt to keep the Western genre commercially viable, filmmakers in the sixties and seventies made pictures that deliberately upended horse-opera traditions and grafted contemporaneous cultural preoccupations onto stories taking place in the nineteenth century. Historical figures previously thought of as heroes became villains, while real-life villains became heroes (or, at worst, antiheroes) whose immorality was part of their dubious charm. Some of these recastings were innocuous and appealing, as in *Butch Cassidy and the Sundance Kid* (1969) and *Blazing Saddles* (1974), but others were subversive, such as the manipulative and dishonest *Little Big Man* (1970), *Doc* (1971), and *The Life and Times of Judge Roy Bean* (1972). A third group, typified by such films as Clint Eastwood's *Hang 'Em High* (1968) and *The Outlaw Josey Wales* (1976), justified the depredations of their antiheroes without celebrating them. In the end, it mattered little: once the likes of *Jaws*, *Star Wars*, and *The Godfather* came along, Westerns were dead.

Monte Walsh
is what the West was all about.
LEE MARVIN
"MONTE WALSH"
A Real Western
JEANNE MOREAU · JACK PALANCE
A CINEMA CENTER FILMS PRESENTATION

The fight was against the raiders... but the feud was between themselves!
COLUMBIA PICTURES Presents
SIDNEY POITIER · HARRY BELAFONTE
BUCK and The PREACHER
with
RUBY DEE · CAMERON MITCHELL
Screenplay by ERNEST KINOY · Story by ERNEST KINOY and DRAKE WALKER · Music by BENNY CARTER
Produced by JOEL GLICKMAN · Directed by SIDNEY POITIER · An E & R/BEI PRODUCTION

MARLON BRANDO
JACK NICHOLSON
"THE MISSOURI BREAKS"
ELLIOTT KASTNER presents
MARLON BRANDO and JACK NICHOLSON
in An ARTHUR PENN Film
"THE MISSOURI BREAKS"
Directed by ARTHUR PENN
Produced by ELLIOTT KASTNER and ROBERT M. SHERMAN
Written by THOMAS McGUANE
Music by JOHN WILLIAMS
A ROBERT M. SHERMAN Production
United Artists

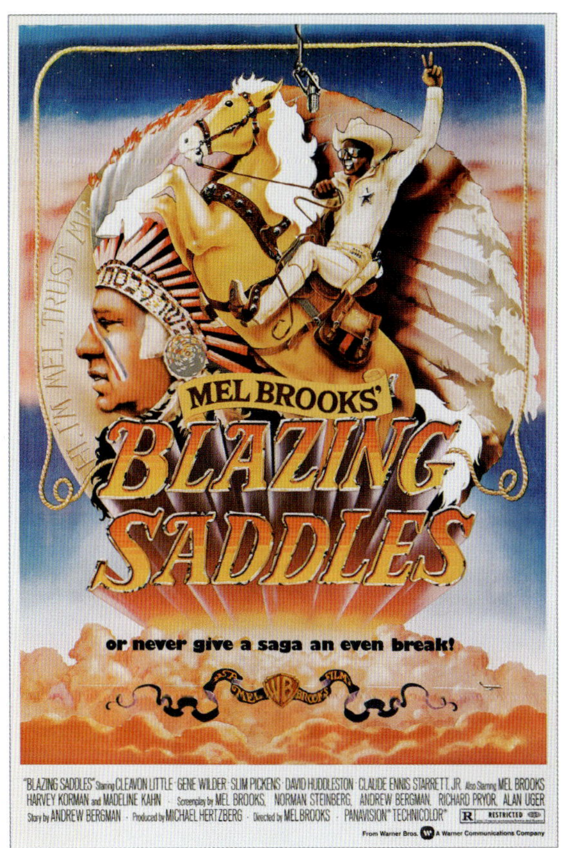
MEL BROOKS'
BLAZING SADDLES
or never give a saga an even break!
"BLAZING SADDLES" Starring CLEAVON LITTLE · GENE WILDER · SLIM PICKENS · DAVID HUDDLESTON · CLAUDE ENNIS STARRETT, JR. Also Starring MEL BROOKS
HARVEY KORMAN and MADELINE KAHN · Screenplay by MEL BROOKS, NORMAN STEINBERG, ANDREW BERGMAN, RICHARD PRYOR, ALAN UGER
Story by ANDREW BERGMAN · Produced by MICHAEL HERTZBERG · Directed by MEL BROOKS · PANAVISION® TECHNICOLOR®
R RESTRICTED
From Warner Bros. A Warner Communications Company

The hanging was the best show in town.
But they made two mistakes.
They hung the wrong man and they didn't finish the job.

CLINT EASTWOOD
IN
"HANG 'EM HIGH"

A LEONARD FREEMAN PRODUCTION co-starring
INGER STEVENS · ED BEGLEY · PAT HINGLE as Judge Fenton

Written by LEONARD FREEMAN and MEL GOLDBERG · Directed by TED POST · Produced by LEONARD FREEMAN · MUSIC—DOMINIC FRONTIERE · A CO-PRODUCTION OF LEONARD FREEMAN PRODUCTIONS AND THE MALPASO COMPANY

Suggested For Mature Audiences

COLOR by DeLuxe

ORIGINAL MOTION PICTURE SCORE AVAILABLE ON UNITED ARTISTS RECORDS

HANG 'EM HIGH 68/108

CLINT EASTWOOD
THE
OUTLAW JOSEY WALES
...an army of one.
CLINT EASTWOOD "THE OUTLAW JOSEY WALES" A MALPASO COMPANY FILM CHIEF DAN GEORGE · SONDRA LOCKE · BILL McKINNEY
and JOHN VERNON as Fletcher · Screenplay by PHIL KAUFMAN and SONIA CHERNUS · Produced by ROBERT DALEY · Directed by CLINT EASTWOOD
Music by JERRY FIELDING · Panavision® Color by De Luxe® Distributed by Warner Bros. A Warner Communications Company
PG
PARENTAL GUIDANCE SUGGESTED
COPYRIGHT © 1976 WARNER BROS., INC.
76/152

AFTERWORD

ABOVE: Despite its formidable cast, sprawling storyline, and impressive production values, Michael Cimino's *Heaven's Gate* (1980) flopped badly, pleasing neither fans of traditional Westerns nor younger, hipper audiences. Its failure was a setback for the entire genre.

By the 1970s, Americans had tired of Westerns: Western fiction, Western movies, and Western TV shows. There were exceptions, of course, and some of them were exceptionally fine. In the main, though, the genre seemed exhausted, played out.

It wasn't just the endless repetition of clichés that soured readers and movie audiences. Cultural shifts accounted for much of the dissatisfaction with horse operas. A new generation, cognizant of the degree to which American pioneers had displaced and persecuted Indians during their procession westward, looked upon the white frontiersmen as oppressors carrying on a genocidal campaign against the continent's Indigenous people. The big cattle ranchers who fed people in the East for decades with the beef they raised and drove to market were seen as rapacious monsters. Revisionist histories of the West characterized lawmen such as Wyatt Earp and Wild Bill Hickok as being little better than the outlaws they pursued.

Of course, there was some truth in all these accusations, although they were exaggerated by scholars and activists having axes to grind. American society was beginning its lengthy flirtation with the politics of grievance, which persists to this day. The Western fell out of favor because it celebrated a way of life that had become anathema to young people raised in and influenced by urban culture.

Still, the genre didn't entirely disappear. Former pulp fictioneer Louis L'Amour continued to write Westerns, and in the 1970s he was hitting lists of mainstream bestsellers. That same decade, enterprising publishers introduced "adult" Westerns, which generally were like the regular kind except for the addition of sexy scenes. These gave raise to multiple series of paperback originals that were still narrowly targeted at a niche market. New exploits of Slocum, Longarm, the Trailsman, and the Gunsmith found loyal readers who collect these books with the same fervor as those Depression-era kids who scraped up pennies and nickels to buy pulp magazines such as *Wild West Weekly* and *Western Story Magazine*.

Losing as iconic a figure as John Wayne would have stopped any film genre in its well-worn tracks, but the Duke's passing in 1979 served as a prelude to a bigger catastrophe. Michael Cimino's epic Western *Heaven's Gate*, released in November 1980, is now considered a modern classic, but at the time it was a momentous flop, eliciting scathing reviews and recouping a mere $3.5 million of its $44 million cost. Hardly a traditional genre offering, it also had the disadvantage of an admittedly talented cast almost completely lacking in Western-movie cred. Top-billed country singer Kris Kristofferson had previously appeared in a revisionist Western for Sam Peckinpah, *Pat Garrett and Billy the Kid* (1973), but fellow players Christopher Walken, John Hurt, Sat Waterston, Brad Dourif, and Isabelle Huppert were plainly out of their element, and their discomfort was obvious. The film's failure stopped Cimino's career in its tracks and prompted Hollywood wags to declare the movie Western dead.

The *Heaven's Gate* debacle reflected poorly on other big-screen Westerns already in production. Later that same year, the traditional Western *Wild Times* failed to find a receptive audience despite having a cast filled with genre heavyweights, among them Sam Elliott, Ben Johnson, Harry Carey Jr., Buck Taylor, Gene Evans, Leif Erickson, and L. Q. Jones.

The 1980 flops spooked the major producers, and for the rest of the decade it was extremely difficult to arrange financing for horse operas. Even 1981's *The Legend of the Lone Ranger*—a reboot of one of the most profitable Western properties in *any* medium—went down in flames, losing a reported $10 million.

Other Western films of the eighties met with indifference at the nation's box offices. An exception was *Silverado* (1985), produced, directed, and cowritten by Lawrence Kasdan, who had also coscripted *Raiders of the Lost Ark*, *The Empire Strikes Back*, and *Return of the Jedi*. The all-star cast featured a number of players without genre standing—although one of them, Kevin Costner, would go on to great success in other Westerns.

Oddly, it was easier during the Reagan era to finance made-for-TV Western movies. Country singer Kenny Rogers did a number of them, playing a character called the Gambler. A 1980 production titled *More Wild Wild West* revived the mid-sixties series starring Robert Conrad and Ross Martin, while *The Shadow Riders* (1982), based on a novel by L'Amour, stars Tom Selleck and Sam Elliott as brothers who fought on opposite sides during the Civil War but reunite to rescue other family members kidnapped by guerrilla raiders.

The decade's standout TV Western was, of course, *Lonesome Dove*, a four-part miniseries adapted from Larry McMurtry's Pulitzer Prize–winning 1985 novel. It stars Robert Duvall and Tommy Lee Jones as former Texas Rangers who decide to leave their dusty border town, relocate to the pristine Montana frontier, and establish themselves as cattle ranchers. Lavishly produced on a budget of $20 million, *Lonesome Dove* aired in February 1989 and was a ratings powerhouse. It was nominated for eighteen Emmy Awards, won seven, and spawned several sequels. More than any TV production of the decade, it sparked a resurgence of interest in Westerns.

The following year, Kevin Costner gave another boost to the genre by directing and starring in *Dances with Wolves*, a three-hour epic shot on location in South

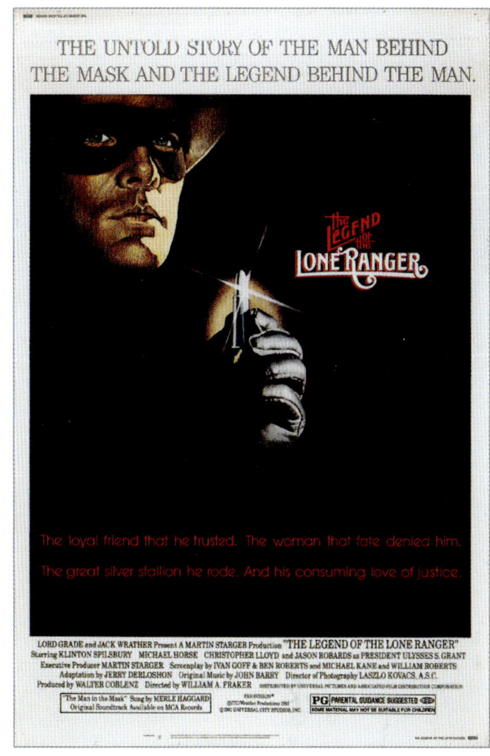

ABOVE: An extravagant updating of one of the Western's most venerable properties met with ridicule from 1981 audiences, although it wasn't anywhere near the turkey its detractors claimed. *The Legend of the Lone Ranger* is more fondly regarded today, especially in the wake of the disastrous 2013 reboot starring Johnny Depp and Armie Hammer.

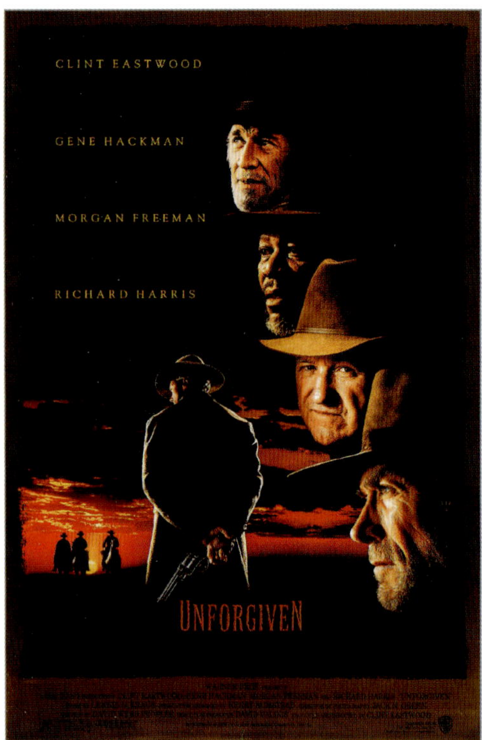

Dakota and Wyoming for approximately $20 million. Costner plays a Union Cavalry officer wounded in the Civil War who, upon recovering, is reassigned to the Western frontier. There he establishes a rapport with Sioux Indians and eventually marries a squaw, only to have his newfound happiness shattered and his adopted people driven from their own land into exile.

Dances with Wolves stakes out the same territory as previous revisionist Westerns, but it struck the right chord with audiences and won seven Academy Awards, including for "Best Picture." The last Western to achieve that feat had been 1931's *Cimarron*. (To date, there has been only one subsequent Western named "Best Picture," 1992's *Unforgiven* with Clint Eastwood.)

Actually, to the extent that the cinematic Western has enjoyed a renaissance in recent decades, it's Costner that genre fans have to thank. Four years after *Dances with Wolves*, he coproduced and starred in *Wyatt Earp*, a serious biopic of the famous lawman that occasionally skirts the facts but treats its subject soberly, and with dignity. Sadly, Costner's picture had the bad luck to follow a more entertaining take on Wyatt, *Tombstone*, which opened seven months previously. Many critics thought *Wyatt Earp* the better picture, but it failed to recoup its enormous cost.

Undeterred, Costner never lost his passion for Westerns. While he spent the next nine years making films in a variety of genres, he carefully laid plans for a character-driven homage to traditional horse operas. He produced, directed, starred in, and reportedly contributed to the script for *Open Range* (2003), in which he and costar Robert Duvall play poor but honest "free rangers," forced to take on a corrupt cattle baron and the sheriff who works for him. A critical

ABOVE LEFT: Clint Eastwood's elegiac *Unforgiven* (1992) was the antithesis of the traditional Western, featuring a flawed protagonist and well-rounded supporting characters interacting believably in a more realistic interpretation of life on the frontier as civilization encroaches.

ABOUT RIGHT: *Silverado* (1985) pulled off the neat trick of paying homage to traditional Westerns while good-naturedly spoofing them. Curiously, the picture's Reagan-era excess and exuberance dates it badly, and the powerhouse cast seems glaringly out of place today.

and commercial success, *Open Range* celebrates the values of old-fashioned Westerns while providing its dual protagonists interesting backstories that are revealed at key moments during the film.

More recently, Costner has starred in the Paramount TV show *Yellowstone*, a modern-day Western in which he plays a rancher trying to prevent Native American tribes and ruthless land developers alike from carving up the property his family has owned for generations. This show, too, is rich in characterization, but it doesn't stint on action—even if it is considerably more brutal than anything kids used to see in their Saturday-matinee oaters.

Thus, the Western hero endures. He might not be as simon-pure as the characters played by the likes of Tom Mix and Buck Jones, but he still follows a personalized moral code. He still believes in rough justice, even if the local sheriff is venal and corrupt. He still cherishes liberty and laments the gradual loss of autonomy as civilization encroaches upon the inexorably dwindling frontier. He and his rapidly dwindling band of brothers are an endangered species—yet, they endure. And that, dear readers, is the essence of Western storytelling: enduring against all odds in a hostile country. ✶

ABOVE: Now just a crumbling relic of a bygone era, the Mount Vernon Theatre in Washington, DC—seen here in a photo from 1969—was another nickelodeon that transitioned to neighborhood house and for many years reverberated on Saturday afternoons with the whoops and hollers of young Western fans who fired their cap pistols at the screen to help their favorite movie cowboys.

INDEX

CONTRIBUTORS

ED HULSE is a journalist and pop-culture historian who covered the home-video and motion-picture industries for more than thirty years. His work has appeared in *Premiere*, *Variety*, *Playboy*, *Entertainment Weekly*, the *New Yorker*, the *New York Times*, and numerous trade publications. Between 1986 and 1990, he edited *Video Review's Previews*, a monthly magazine spotlighting new video releases. In the late eighties, his articles and movie reviews were syndicated to newspapers by the Washington Post Writers Group. In 1993, he coedited with Packy Smith a greatly expanded version of *Don Miller's Hollywood Corral: A Comprehensive B-Western Roundup*, considered by most aficionados to be the definitive work on the genre. Since 2002, Hulse has edited and published the award-winning journal *Blood 'n' Thunder*, which covers vintage pulp fiction and related pop-culture media. His books include *The Blood 'n' Thunder Guide to Pulp Fiction*, *The Wild West of Fiction and Film*, *Filming the West of Zane Grey*, *Distressed Damsels and Masked Marauders*, and most recently *Wage Slaves in the Dream Factory*. In 2017, he coedited *The Art of the Pulps* with Doug Ellis and the late Robert Weinberg. Four years later, he edited *The Art of Pulp Fiction: An Illustrated History of Vintage Paperbacks*. Under his Murania Press imprint, Hulse has published forty books and monographs covering various aspects of American pop culture from the late nineteenth and early twentieth centuries. His website is muraniapress.com.

JAY DEE WITNEY was born in Los Angeles, the only child of director William Witney and actress Maxine Doyle. His film and television work ranged from bit parts to minor stunts and background acting in shows such as *Room 222*, *The Lucy Show*, *Gomer Pyle USMC*, *Mission: Impossible*, and *The Fugitive*. After leaving show business, he worked in emergency services and for private businesses, but in recent years he has dipped his toes back into the motion-picture business with screenwriting, photography, videography editing, and production. A current and continuing SAG–AFTRA card member since 1965, he is also the proprietor of Old Clapperboard Productions and @Pixeladog. Additionally, Jay Dee manages the website williamwitney.com, devoted to celebrating the work of his father.

ACKNOWLEDGMENTS

This book is the product of a fascination with Western movies that has endured for more than a half-century. During that time, I've studied them exhaustively, gleaning information not only from contemporaneous source materials (such as industry trade journals) but also from interviews with actors, writers, producers, directors, and stuntmen. Those movie professionals who have particularly aided in my research include Bob Allen, Gene Autry, Don "Red" Barry, Yakima Canutt, Ray "Crash" Corrigan, Buster Crabbe, Eddie Dean, Alex Gordon, Russell Hayden, Jennifer Holt, Lash LaRue, A. C. Lyles, Richard Martin, Iris Meredith, Robert Mitchum, Clayton Moore, George O'Brien, Roy Rogers, David Sharpe, George Sherman, Barry Shipman, Charles Starrett, Peggy Stewart, Linda Stirling, and William Witney. Among the film historians to whom I am indebted are several whose books I've cherished nearly as much as their friendship, including Richard W. Bann, Alan G. Barbour, Robert S. Birchard, John Cocchi, William K. Everson, and Francis M. Nevins. Most of all, I remain forever indebted to my late collaborator and business partner, M. P. "Packy" Smith, the best friend and biggest booster the movie Western ever had.